MEDIEVAL DEVON AND CORNWALL

Medieval Devon and Cornwall

Shaping an Ancient Countryside

Edited by Sam Turner

WINDgather
PRESS

Medieval Devon and Cornwall: Shaping an Ancient Countryside

Published by: Windgather Press Ltd, 29 Bishop Road, Bollington, Macclesfield, Cheshire SK10 5NX

Distributed by: Central Books Ltd, 99 Wallis Road, London E9 5LN

British Library Cataloguing in Publication Data

A catalogue record for this book is available from the British Library

ISBN 10 1-905119-07-0
ISBN 13 978-1-905119-07-3

Designed, typeset and originated by Carnegie Publishing Ltd, Chatsworth Road, Lancaster

Printed and bound by Cambridge University Press

Contents

Acknowledgements

....

Many people have helped in the production of this book. The editor is grateful to Oscar Aldred, Peter Child, Anne Dick, Harold Fox, Martin Gillard, Faye Glover, Frances Griffith, Debbie Griffiths, Peter Herring, Bill Horner, Anne Richards and Steve Rippon for many insights and discussions on the medieval landscape of south-west England. Sincere thanks are also due to the referees who read and commented on all the papers prior to publication. The editor owes most to the authors of each of the chapters, who all replied to queries and suggestions with great speed and good humour.

List of Illustrations

For Maggsie and Mondo
– a souvenir

Foreword

....

Harold Fox

It gives me great pleasure to welcome this book because it reports on so many recent advances in interpretations of the landscape history of Devon and Cornwall. I began research into this subject in an intellectual tradition which had been laid down in a few formative years between 1952 and 1954. It is worthwhile to look back upon that advance, to ask how well the ideas which it contained have fared and to mention a little of the new work undertaken since the 1950s, culminating in this book.

In 1954 W. G. V. Balchin published his *Cornwall: An Illustrated Essay on the History of the Landscape*, part of a series edited by W. G. Hoskins. Balchin acknowledged that between the fifth century and the eleventh some developments took place in the Cornish landscape, 'in the darkness of this period', but considered that they had only a small impact. Then comes the remarkable statement that, in 1086, 'Cornwall ... had fewer than 20,000 people all told – fewer than either Penzance or St Austell today'. It followed from this that much in the landscape was thought to be later: 'between the twelfth and fourteenth centuries a remarkable number of new farms came into existence, as in Devon' (Balchin 1954, 34–40). Two years earlier Hoskins had published his long, magisterial essay on 'The making of the agrarian landscape' of Devon, arguing that approximately 12,500 new farms were created between 1086 and around 1350, and that the twelfth and thirteenth centuries were 'the most formative years in the making of the rural landscape' (Hoskins 1952, 316–21). He thus minimised the pre-Saxon contribution (though later he wisely changed his mind, as in Hoskins 1968, 6) and stressed a relatively brief episode after the Norman Conquest. When I began my research, the only available overviews were those of Hoskins and Balchin but I did not then have the competence to query them. They are still treasures of mine which I turn to frequently, and the period when I first read them is one to which I look back now with unclouded affection.

Hoskins wrote at a time when nucleated villages were regarded as 'early' and the dispersed settlement so characteristic of the South West as 'late'. His thought was probably influenced by the great French historian Marc Bloch who had called the twelfth and thirteenth centuries 'the age of large-scale colonization' (Bloch 1931, 5–17). Moreover, he could trace his family back to an isolated farm in the moorland parish of Chagford and, always an independent spirit, he no doubt took pride in a descent from pioneering stock. His views on the importance of the thirteenth century in the making of the landscape have been repeated in general works: Postan, for example, in an influential chapter in the *Cambridge Economic History of Europe*, wrote that 'most of Devonshire's combes and valleys and much of Cornwall's interior were not fully occupied until the thirteenth century' (Postan 1966, 550). But, away from the high moorlands and a few other localities, there has been little work on new settlement in the centuries immediately following the Norman Conquest – and that is because so little of it in fact took place.

Hoskins's figure of 12,500 new farms colonised in Devon between 1086 and 1350 was the difference between the number of settlements named in Domesday Book, plus a few others, a total of 2,500 in all; and the number of farming families represented by the poll tax of 1377, namely 15,000 (Hoskins 1952, 316–17). The comparison was a brave one – but surely invalid, because in all probability free tenants, a numerous class on some manors in Devon and Cornwall, are generally omitted from Domesday Book's folios on those counties. Hoskins believed that the farms of free tenants were first created in the twelfth and thirteenth centuries (Hoskins 1952, 321–2). This cannot have been so, because many of them have place-names incorporating Old English personal names (Ecgmund, Cynemann, Eadgar, Tetti and the like, to use some Hartland examples) and the change in naming habits in favour of French ones (William, Richard, Robert, Geoffrey, again from Hartland) was well established by 1150 and was probably adopted all the more rapidly among fashion-conscious freemen. Hoskins wrote of the huge manor of Hartland as one where 'the majority of … farms began their existence in the thirteenth or early fourteenth century as limited clearings in the woods or moorland' (Hoskins 1952, 326). Unfortunately for this argument, many of the manor's very numerous free tenants (named in a rental of 1301) lived in farms or hamlets with place-names incorporating Old English personal names and it is very unlikely – virtually impossible – that the establishment of all these was crammed into the years between 1086 and 1150, when names of this type were fast going out of fashion. Balchin's amazement at finding apparently so few people in Cornwall in 1086 may also be explained by under-recording in Domesday Book of existing free tenants; these are very common in later sources (e.g. Hull 1971; Fox and Padel 2000). In any case, as Sam Turner explains in this volume, by the time of the Norman Conquest the Cornish landscape was dotted by a respectable number of churches, crosses and monasteries which one would not expect in an under-developed, moribund society.

A continuity of settlement from well before the Norman Conquest should be our theme, rather than a series of episodes such as the supposed boom of the thirteenth century. And if we explore that theme further, remarkable discoveries can sometimes be made. For example, on the manor of Ashwater in Devon, Domesday Book gives 40 villeins and 12 bordars, with 6 slaves attached to the demesne. A survey of 1346 gives 38 privileged unfree tenures and 13 serfs, with 6 cottages at the churchtown, near the demesne. The probability that this coincidence is by chance is very low indeed. There was very little change in numbers of occupiers of tenements between 1086 and 1346, and, therefore, very little change in the settlement pattern: the many moory acres between the settlements here were left uncolonised in the thirteenth century, though not unused. Even more remarkable are figures from the later unified manor of South Brent, with land stretching up to the southern flanks of Dartmoor (in Domesday two manors of Brent plus Charford). The occupiers of land in Domesday Book number 56 – and 56 unfree tenures are described in detail in a survey of the late sixteenth century. It clearly looks as if the whole landscape of settlement on the manor has roots which we can confidently project back to the late Saxon period at the latest. The many free tenures of South Brent, some at sites with Old English personal names in their place-names, are absent from Domesday Book but were almost certainly present in 1086. Everything seems very ancient. Many examples may also be found of manors where the number of farms increased after 1086, though this did not necessarily affect the settlement pattern very greatly.

There were, of course, many very important changes in rural landscapes in the South West between the Norman Conquest and the present day, some of which are now more fully understood than in the days of Hoskins and Balchin. We now know much more about the colonisation of the flanks of the high moorlands in the twelfth and thirteenth centuries, localities for which Hoskins was absolutely correct in his periodisation (Beresford 1979 with Austin and Walker 1985; Herring this volume; see also Hoskins 1952a, a brilliant vignette of the foundation of the Dartmoor-border farm of Cholwich, omitting only the relevance of the name, which probably harks back to an antecedent phase of transhumance). We now largely understand the elaboration and enclosure of strip-field systems (Fox 1972 and 1975 following Hoskins 1954, 72–3; Fox and Padel 2000, lxxvii–xciii; Herring this volume); we now have studies of castles in the landscape (the work of Bob Higham, and the novel interpretation by Creighton and Freeman in this volume); and of processes of desertion in the context of dispersed settlement patterns (Fox 1991, 163–72). When Hoskins (1954, 130–59) wrote about tin extraction in Devon, it was as an economic historian and the word 'landscape' did not come into his mind (although he did, later, write a pioneering paper on industrial archaeology: Hoskins 1966), but now the very important legacy of the industry has been studied in great detail (e.g. Austin and others 1989; Newman this volume). There are still gaps in our knowledge, especially about woodland history; about the development of parks (following Herring 2003); the evolution of field patterns in the post-medieval period (following Hoskins 1952, 325–33, a vivid picture of the reclamation of moorland in Devon between 1550 and the end of the nineteenth century; also Turner 2004); about desertion of farmsteads in the nineteenth century (discussed in Hoskins 1940); and about landscapes associated with transhumance (Herring 1996 and Fox forthcoming).

Despite these gaps in our understanding of the later evolution of the rural landscape, it still seems to me that it is study of the history of settlement in the period before 1066 which offers the greatest opportunities and challenges. More palaeoenvironmental work away from the high moorlands needs to be done, following Fyfe (in this volume, and his other papers there cited). Albeit for a limited area, he has at a stroke dispelled a myth which, in part, led Hoskins (1954, 46–7) to minimise the importance of pre-Saxon settlement, namely the view that, because of emigration to Armorica, 'no considerable native population remained to complicate the life of the new [West Saxon] settlers' in the seventh and eighth centuries (Gover and others 1931–32, xx). Fyfe's work makes it quite clear that there were no major changes in land use in Devon between the fifth and seventh centuries, certainly none which support the idea of a massive evacuation to Armorica, leaving the land abandoned. In any case, the well-recorded stout resistance of the people of Devon and Cornwall to the West Saxons, occurring after a migration of some kind to Armorica (not necessarily a flight; a blood-letting perhaps?) argues against the old view of abandonment.

The materials which touch on settlement before 1066 are now nearly all in place, although the archaeological work is patchy indeed. Remarkable advances, especially in works of reference, have been made over the last fifteen years or so, giving us access to materials which Hoskins and Balchin lacked. We now have, in one place, a complete corpus of all terms relating to landscape and settlement used in Anglo-Saxon charters for the South West (Hooke 1994). Cornish place-names have been tackled, in a complete glossary of elements and in a dictionary of major names (Padel 1985 and 1988). The inscribed stones have been re-examined from two viewpoints (Okasha 1993; Simms-Williams 2003). Great advances have been made in the study of the religious sites which in various ways served early settlements. We now have a complete survey of the evidence for early Cornish monasteries (Olson 1989) and a discussion of those further east (Pearce 2004, 168–81). Churchyard shapes have been surveyed (Preston-Jones 1992; Pearce 2004, 152–9); there is a complete inventory of all medieval chapels in Devon (James 1997) and a discussion of all of those, in both counties, associated with Cornish saints (Orme 2000). Finally, a corpus of church dedications has been completed (Orme 1996), some securely dated to the Middle Ages, others (like the evidence of folklore discussed by Franklin, this volume) with unknown, but possibly early, horizons. Certain gaps remain: the pioneering work of Hoskins on village morphology, done when that research method was virtually unknown anywhere in England (Hoskins 1952, 290–3, 308–10), needs to be followed up, particularly his suggestion that, in Devon, villages were instruments of royal plantation (in eastern Cornwall too, I wonder). There is also still a need for re-examination of the enormous body of material in *The Place-Names of Devon* (Gover and others 1931–32), particularly habitative names, those associated with land use and those with Celtic elements which the book's authors minimised in their introduction (hence their statement quoted above).

All of the above work needs to be synthesised, and there will be time for this in the future. Meanwhile, each chapter in this book makes a significant contribution towards our understanding of this complex, rich and beautiful landscape of Devon and Cornwall in the Middle Ages.

References

Austin, D., Gerrard, G. A. M. and Greeves, T. A. P. (1989) 'Tin and agriculture in the Middle Ages and beyond: landscape archaeology in St Neot parish, Cornwall', *Cornish Archaeology* **28**, 7–251.

Austin, D. and Walker, M. J. C. (1985) 'A new landscape context for Hound Tor', *Medieval Archaeology* **29**, 147–32.

Balchin, W. G. V. (1954) *Cornwall: An Illustrated Essay on the History of the Landscape*, Hodder and Stoughton, London.

Beresford, G. (1979) 'Three deserted medieval settlements on Dartmoor: a report on the late E. Marie Minter's excavations', *Medieval Archaeology* **23**, 98–158.

Bloch, M. (1931) *Les Charactères Originaux de l'Histoire Rurale Francaise*, Aschehoug, Oslo.

Fox, H. S. A. (1972) 'Field systems of East and South Devon. Part I: East Devon' *Transactions of the Devonshire Association* **104**, 81–135.

Fox, H. S. A. (1975) 'The chronology of enclosure and economic development in medieval Devon', *Economic History Review* **28**, 181–202.

Fox, H. S. A. (1991) 'The occupation of the land: Devon and Cornwall' in *The Agrarian History of England and Wales* Vol. 3, 1348–1350, ed. E. Miller, Cambridge University Press, Cambridge, 152–74.

Fox, H. S. A. (forthcoming) *Alluring Uplands: Transhumance and Pastoral Management on Dartmoor, 950–1550*.

Fox, H. S. A. and Padel, O. J. (2000) *The Cornish Lands of the Arundells of Lanherne, Fourteenth to Sixteenth Centuries*, Devon and Cornwall Record Society, Exeter.

Gover, J. E. B., Mawer, A. and Stenton, F. M. (1931–32) *The Place-Names of Devon*, Cambridge University Press, Cambridge.

Herring, P. (1996) 'Transhumance in medieval Cornwall' in *Seasonal Settlement*, ed. H. S. A. Fox, University of Leicester Department of Adult Education, Leicester, 35–44.

Herring, P. (2003) 'Cornish medieval deer parks' in *The Lie of the Land*, ed. R. Wilson-North, Mint Press, Exeter, 34–50.

Hooke, D. (1994) *Pre-Conquest Charter Boundaries of Devon and Cornwall*, Boydell, Woodbridge.

Hoskins, W. G. (1940) 'The occupation of land in Devonshire', *Devon and Cornwall Notes and Queries* **21**, 2–12.

Hoskins, W. G. (1952) 'The making of the agrarian landscape' in *Devonshire Studies*, W. G. Hoskins and H. P. R. Finberg, Cape, London, 289–333.

Hoskins, W. G. (1952a) 'Cholwich' in W. G. Hoskins and H. P. R. Finberg, *Devonshire Studies*, Cape, London, 78–94.

Hoskins, W. G. (1954) *Devon*, Collins, London.

Hoskins, W. G. (1966) 'Industrial archaeology in Devon' in his *Old Devon*, David and Charles, Newton Abbot, 28–40 (reprinted from an article published earlier in *The Western Morning News*).

Hoskins, W. G. (1968) *The Human Geography of the South West* (a printing of the George Johnstone Lecture delivered at Seale-Hayne Agricultural College), South Western Electricity Board, no place.

Hull, P. (1971) *The Caption of Seisin of the Duchy of Cornwall (1337)*, Devon and Cornwall Record Society, Torquay.

James, J. (1997) *Medieval chapels in Devon*, unpublished MPhil thesis, University of Exeter.

Okasha, E. (1993) *Corpus of Early Christian Inscribed Stones of South-west Britain*, Leicester University Press, London.

Olson, L. (1989) *Early Monasteries in Cornwall*, Boydell and Brewer, Woodbridge.

Orme, N. (1996) *English Church Dedications with a Survey of Cornwall and Devon*, University of Exeter Press, Exeter.

Orme, N. (2000) *The Saints of Cornwall*, Oxford University Press, Oxford.

Padel, O. (1985) *Cornish Place-Name Elements*, English Place-Name Society, Nottingham.

Padel, O.J. (1988) *A Popular Dictionary of Cornish Place-Names*, Alison Hodge, Penzance.

Pearce, S. (2004) *South-western Britain in the Early Middle Ages*, Leicester University Press, London.

Postan, M.M. (1966) 'Medieval agrarian society in its prime: England' in *The Cambridge Economic History of Europe* Vol.1, *The Agrarian Life of the Middle Ages*, ed. M.M.Postan, Cambridge University Press, Cambridge, 548–632.

Preston-Jones, A. (1992) 'Decoding Cornish churchyards' in *The Early Church in Wales and the West*, eds N.Edwards and A.Lane, Oxbow Books, Oxford, 105–24.

Simms-Williams, P. (2003) *The Celtic Inscriptions of Britain: Phonology and Chronology, c. 400–1200*, Philological Society, Oxford.

Turner, S. (2004) 'The changing ancient landscape: south-west England *c.*1700–1900', *Landscapes* 5.1, 18–34.

CHAPTER I

The Medieval Landscape
of Devon and Cornwall

Sam Turner

The countryside of Devon and Cornwall preserves an unusually rich legacy from its medieval past. The sites of farms and other settlements, the ruins and grassed-over earthworks of fortifications, miners' abandoned pits and tinworks, churches, chapels and crosses: all can have their origins in the Middle Ages. Perhaps even more significant is the very fabric of the ancient countryside, which stretches out across the landscape like an intricately-worked counter-pane of hedgebanks and winding lanes. Most of these boundaries date to the sixteenth century and before, but some are considerably older: early medieval and prehistoric boundaries lie beneath many of them to this day. Each of the chapters in this book examines different aspects of this historic landscape.

We have learned to think of the Middle Ages as the time between the Roman period and the Reformation. It might be argued that characteristically medieval forms of landscape organisation were not much changed in the South West until rather later than this conventional end-point, and some of the chapters in this book discuss developments up to *c.* 1700. During this long period there were massive economic, political and cultural changes; many can be linked to revolutions in the structure of the rural landscape. Good examples include the reorganisation of the countryside into open strip fields, the conversion to Christianity, later medieval enclosure, or post-Conquest castle-building (see the chapters in this book by Peter Herring, Sam Turner, and Oliver Creighton and John Freeman). Changes like these provide land-scape historians with waymarkers for their narratives, but it is crucial to remember that in the South West earlier elements of the landscape were often retained through periods of transformation. The region's historic countryside provides unusually rich opportunities for understanding how and why some things changed whilst others remained. The aim of this introductory chapter is to provide some contexts for what follows and to outline just a few of the themes that are developed later in the book.

During the Roman period, the two modern counties of Devon and Cornwall formed most of the region known as the *Civitas Dumnoniorum*. The area was not affected as much by 'Romanisation' as other parts of Britain, and though archaeological sites the length of the peninsula have produced limited quantities of typically Roman material culture, the social fabric seems not to have undergone revolutionary change in the first or second centuries AD (Todd 1987; Pearce 2004). Despite this, the apparent geographical unity of the region was not necessarily reflected in cultural or political unity in the Roman period, and the *Civitas* was probably a loose association of different groups rather than a well-defined polity. Even so, the administrative structure imposed by the Romans appears to have gained some degree of permanence. When early medieval kingdoms began to be established in Britain in the later fifth and sixth centuries (Charles-Edwards 2003), earlier boundaries were probably perpetuated with the emergence of the Kingdom of Dumnonia.

We know of the kingdom's existence from documentary sources including Gildas in the sixth century and Aldhelm in the seventh or early eighth (Winterbottom 1978; Lapidge and Herren 1979). Its early eastern boundaries are uncertain, but they were probably somewhere in east Devon and west Somerset, perhaps between the valleys of the Axe and Parrett; they certainly moved westwards under pressure from an expanding Wessex. The kings of Wessex (and later England) incorporated the South West peninsula into their kingdom between the seventh and tenth centuries, when an independent Dumnonia probably ceased to exist. The dates at which different regions fell under their control are hard to establish, but English kings were able to grant land in west Devon to the monastery at Glastonbury (Somerset) in the early eighth century and in east Cornwall to Sherborne (Dorset) in the early ninth (Edwards 1988). This suggests that these areas were by then securely under their control. The dates that different parts of Cornwall and Devon were incorporated into Wessex seems to lie at the root of some important contrasts between the two counties, not least of which is the pattern of English and Cornish place-names. In Devon there are very few place-names with Brittonic origins, whereas in Cornwall (apart from a few areas in the east) the great majority of those first recorded before 1550 are Cornish in origin (Padel 1999). Likewise, differences in the distribution of certain types of monuments may owe their origins to different political and economic structures in the early Middle Ages. The use of medieval stone crosses, which were much more common in Cornwall than Devon, is discussed by Sam Turner in Chapter 3 on the medieval religious landscape.

The apparent coherence of the South West peninsula is distinguished on closer examination by a range of interesting internal similarities and contrasts, not only between the two counties, but also between regions within them. The pattern of medieval agriculture and its relationship to the underlying geology of the region makes an interesting example (for a recent discussion of another region, see Williamson 2003).

The geology of the Cornubian peninsula west of the Blackdown Hills is distinctively different to that found in Wessex proper (i.e. in most of Somerset, Dorset, Wiltshire and Hampshire). Much of inland Cornwall and southern Devon is dominated by rolling hills and deeply-incised valleys. These are cut through Devonian rocks including complex areas of sedimentary slates,

FIGURE 1
Bodmin Moor
(Cornwall) in snow,
looking south-east
across the fields of
Tresellern towards
Trewortha Tor.
SAM TURNER

2

siltstones, gritstones, sandstones and limestones (Edmonds *et al.* 1975, 21–33; Todd 1987, 3–6). The valley bottoms are normally narrow, and lack the broad floodplains so common in central parts of southern England. The valley sides are mostly convex in section, so that valley bottoms cannot normally be seen from hilltops, and vice-versa. The brown soils of this zone provide farmland that is fairly easily worked (Caseldine 1999).

In some areas variations in the local geology mean less steeply incised plateaux and broader, shallower valleys occur, for example in north Cornwall around St Kew and above cliffs on the north coast around Newquay. The 'Culm Measures' of north Devon and north-east Cornwall lie between Exmoor and the granite moors. This area of Carboniferous rocks is fairly gentle country topographically, but has smaller areas of easily-worked soils than the south of Devon and Cornwall.

High granite masses are roughly aligned along the spine of the peninsula in a row leading westwards from the eastern edge of Dartmoor (Edmonds *et al.* 1975, 43–51). The same geological processes that led to the igneous intrusion of Dartmoor also gave rise to the granite of Bodmin Moor (Figure 1), Hensbarrow, Carnmenellis, Penwith and the Scilly Isles. Associated metamorphic activity created rich mineral deposits which were exploited in many areas during the Middle Ages (as discussed below by Phil Newman). The granite and the podzolic soils of the uplands have helped to create landscapes with a highly distinctive character in all these areas.

Despite the peninsula's varying geology, Bronze Age, late-medieval, and post-medieval fields on the high moors and heaths show that almost all areas can be farmed with sufficient effort. With the exception of some coastal sand dunes, virtually none of Devon or Cornwall's soils have escaped significant alteration by human action. Even the acidic podsols of the uplands are anthropogenic: they first began to form around 8,000 years ago as a result of mesolithic tree-clearance, and replaced earlier brown soils that are sometimes found preserved beneath prehistoric monuments (Caseldine 1999, 29). C.J. Caseldine has suggested that the relatively minor climatic variations of the last 5,000 years would not necessarily have had an effect on the ability of people to support themselves from the land in any part of the peninsula (Caseldine 1999, 32; see also Caseldine and Hatton 1994, 44–5).

How did this varying geology affect the character of the peninsula's medieval landscapes? New techniques and ongoing research are helping to answer questions such as these. Historic Landscape Characterisations (HLCs) have now been completed for both Devon and Cornwall, and they give some insights into the differences and similarities between regions (DCC 2005; Herring 1998). Perhaps most significantly for understanding medieval farming, the HLCs have shown that despite the differences in soil type and geology, strip-field farming was ubiquitous in the south-western landscape (Figure 2), a point made persuasively by Peter Herring in his two contributions to this book on medieval Cornwall. The most significant discrepancies were probably not to be found in the basic form of the fields, but in the overall structure of the medieval landscape.

In almost every part of the peninsula the contrasts between the steep valleys and the rolling hilltops and plateaux are accentuated by the different land uses to which they have been put. A fundamental characteristic of the south-western landscape is the close juxtaposition of these different elements. Woods, meadows, pasture, gardens, rough grazing and arable land are all found side-by-side 'interdigitated' in complex patterns (Williamson 2002, 118). Most commonly it is woodland, meadow and pasture that occur on the steeper, lower valley slopes, with arable land on gentler hillslopes above. Rough pasture is characteristic of the moors, ridges and sea-clifftops (Herring 1998; Figure 3).

In some areas, however, there were much more extensive patches of rough grazing ground or woodland between the settlements than in others. This was not only the case on and around the high uplands, but also in areas like the Culm Measures. Different regional landscapes also carried different combinations of land use. In west Cornwall, for example, woodland was virtually absent (Fox and Padel 2000), whereas it was plentiful in some of the steep river valleys of east Cornwall and Devon. Likewise orchards were probably common in some late-medieval landscapes (e.g. the Tamar valley), but much rarer in others (Fox and Padel 2000, lxxvi). The relative frequencies of meadowland, pasture and arable can be traced through the patterns they have left in the post-medieval and later countryside using HLC or other types of landscape analysis (Herring 1998; DCC 2005).

Other variations between different parts of the peninsula relate to the size of the settlements associated with the fields (whether small villages, hamlets, or individual farmsteads), or even the methods of cultivation (whether strips were dug by hand or turned with the plough). Such discrepancies cannot necessarily be attributed to geology. Neighbouring parishes on similar soils apparently had quite different landscape structures, like Bigbury and Aveton Gifford in south Devon (the former with a small nucleated village, the latter with many scattered farmsteads). As well as the natural environment, divergent customs and landholding practices strongly affected the medieval landscape, a theme that is brought out in several of the following chapters. As Lucy Franklin shows in her discussion, the sensitive application of new techniques and the integration of new types of information can provide a valuable way to gain insights into these questions.

In some ways, then, the medieval countryside of Devon and Cornwall was broadly united, but in others it was divided into sub-regions by a range of environmental factors and distinctive local customs. It was certainly different to much of England, in particular the 'Central Province' of open fields and nucleated villages that stretches north-east from Dorset up to Northumberland (Roberts and Wrathmell 2000). For many people this sense of difference is to be linked with the 'Celtic' people who lived there, the 'original' inhabitants of the peninsula before the coming of the English. Issues of Celtic identity and its relationship to the landscape are touched on by several of the contributors to this volume (particularly Peter Herring), but it is worth noting here that the physical and cultural landscape of the South West has much in common with other traditionally 'Celtic' areas, not only in Wales and Ireland, but also Brittany and north-west Spain. When thinking about the medieval landscape, a crucial question that remains to be answered relates to the reasons for these similarities: how much do they owe to similar environments, and how much to shared cultures?

The sea and sea-borne communications have certainly played a vital role in the cultural, political and economic history of Devon and Cornwall. In the post-medieval period fishing villages were established on narrow patches of land between the fields and the sea, and in the Middle Ages fishing was an important activity that supplemented the incomes and diets of many farmers in seaside parishes (Fox 2001). Evidence shows that there had been communication and contact along the western seaways long before that, and interest in these questions amongst scholars has grown in recent years. This work has been prompted largely by the research of archaeologists like Professors Richard Bradley and Barry Cunliffe, who have examined the cultural links between the peoples of the Atlantic façade both in prehistory and more recent times, and highlighted the important role of the ocean in facilitating contacts (Bradley 1997; Cunliffe 2001). In the medieval period there were many kinds of links between the Atlantic regions, and records of them survive in historical and literary texts, place-names and archaeology. Saints' *Lives* provide evidence for the movements of specific people, and from them

FIGURE 2
Coombe, Lifton
(Devon), looking
south-east. Unusual
surviving earthworks
of outfield strip
cultivation are visible
on Tinhay Down
(centre left).
SAM TURNER

we learn of men like Samson and Paul Aurelian who travelled extensively between Ireland, Wales, the South West and Brittany (Olson 1989). Shorter texts are preserved on the monuments known as 'inscribed stones', memorials to the dead that are found not only in parts of Scotland, Ireland, Wales, and south-west England, but also in Brittany (CISP 2001). Their presence in all these regions probably reflects the movement of people and ideas between them. The fact that people spoke similar languages in Wales, Cornwall and Brittany during the early Middle Ages is reflected not only by the names and languages inscribed onto the stones, but also in the Brittonic place-names these regions share.

A further aspect of this medieval contact across the Atlantic seaways was the trade and exchange of imported goods. Pottery and other material from the Mediterranean and western Gaul reached British shores in the fifth to seventh centuries, and there was an extensive later medieval trade between the ports of western France and those of south-west England (Allan 1984; Allan and Langman 2003). In addition, historians interested in the South West have begun to explore the links between individuals and families across Ireland, Britain and Wales (Burls 2003).

Such contacts were clearly frequent and widespread, but little work has been carried out into their significance for our understanding of the medieval landscape. Pioneering historical work on medieval enclosure was undertaken in the earlier part of the twentieth century by Pierre Flatrès (1949; 1957), but since then there have been relatively few studies of the relationships between the medieval landscapes of the Atlantic regions. There are marked similarities between the dispersed settlement patterns and heavily enclosed countryside of south-west England, Wales, Brittany and parts of Ireland and northern Spain, but it is unclear why these have arisen. Virtually all the chapters in this book make reference to these international links and cite examples from other parts of the Atlantic seaboard. They will have relevance either as foundations for future research or as comparative studies to scholars interested in many of the other regions.

A good example is the consensus that emerges from several of the chapters on the date a distinctively medieval type of landscape organisation developed in the South West. A range of sources including pollen evidence (see the chapter by Ralph Fyfe), landscape survey (the chapters by Peter Herring) and early Christian archaeology are beginning to suggest that the key period for the creation of the medieval landscape lay between the seventh and ninth centuries. In much of western Britain it is increasingly apparent that the end of the Roman period did not necessarily herald a complete break-down in the social fabric or in the organisation of the countryside. Instead, during the late fourth to sixth centuries the region seems to have been a distinctive but integral part of the 'late Antique' culture of Atlantic Europe (Handley 2003; Turner 2004). We are beginning to suspect that the crucial transformations that led to the creation of the medieval landscape probably occurred slightly

FIGURE 3
Rough grazing on the north Cornish coast. Looking north-east from Tintagel Island across Barras Nose.
SAM TURNER

later, and that their legacies are found in the patterns of settlements and fields that still dominate the South West's ancient countryside (Turner 2003).

This book's aims are to outline our current knowledge of Devon and Cornwall's medieval landscape, to consider how recent research has begun to change our perceptions, and to highlight topics or approaches that might be fruitful for future research. It will be clear that a great deal remains to be done, and it is to be hoped that the work described in the following chapters will engage both the many people who are already interested in the South West's landscape and those who are coming to this fascinating subject from fresh perspectives. It is a rich, beautiful and ancient countryside that will generously repay the efforts of our research.

References

Allan, J. (1984) *Medieval and Post-Medieval Finds from Exeter, 1971–1980*, Exeter City Council and University of Exeter, Exeter.

Allan, J. and Langman, G. (2003) 'Appendix 1: the Dung Quay pottery' in 'Excavation of the medieval and later waterfront at Dung Quay, Plymouth' P. Stead, *Devon Archaeological Society Proceedings* **61**, 47–63.

Bradley, R. (1997) *Rock Art and the Prehistory of Atlantic Europe*, Routledge, London.

Burls, R. (2003) 'Medieval 'Severnside': Devon and its overseas neighbours before *c.* 1360' *Transactions of the Devonshire Association* **135**, 71–98.

Caseldine, C. (1999) 'Environmental setting' in *Historical Atlas of South-West England*, eds R. Kain and W. Ravenhill, University of Exeter Press, Exeter, 25–34.

Caseldine, C. and Hatton, J. (1994) 'Into the mists? Thoughts on the prehistoric and historic environmental history of Dartmoor', *Devon Archaeological Society Proceedings* **52**, 35–47.

Charles-Edwards, T. (2003) 'Introduction' in *After Rome*, ed. T. Charles-Edwards, Oxford University Press, Oxford, 1–20.

CISP (2001) *Celtic Inscribed Stones: Language Location and Environment*, available http://www.ucl.ac.uk/archaeology/cisp/database/ (consulted 13 September 2006).

Cunliffe, B. (2001) *Facing the Ocean: the Atlantic and its Peoples*, Oxford University Press, Oxford.

D.C.C. (2005) 'Devon Historic Landscape Characterisation: Methods, Classification and Preliminary Analysis', unpublished report, Devon County Council/English Heritage, Exeter.

Edmonds, E., McKeown, M. and Williams, M. (1975) *British Regional Geology: South-West England*, HMSO, London.

Edwards, H. (1988) *The Charters of the Early West Saxon Kingdom*, British Archaeological Reports (British Series) 198, Oxford.

Flatrès, P. (1949) 'La structure agraire ancienne du Devon et du Cornwall et les enclôtures des XIIIe et XIVe siècles', *Annales de Bretagne* **56**, 130–4.

Flatres, P. (1957) *Géographie Rurale de Quatre Contrées Celtiques: Irlande, Galles, Cornwall et Man*, J. Plihon, Rennes.

Fox, H. (2001) *The Evolution of the Fishing Village*, Leopard's Head Press, Oxford.

Fox, H. and Padel, O. (2000) *Cornish Lands of the Arundells of Lanherne*, Devon and Cornwall Record Society new series 41, Exeter.

Handley, M. (2003) *Inscriptions and Epitaphs in Gaul and Spain, AD 300–750*, BAR International Series 1135, Oxford.

Herring, P. (1998) *Cornwall's Historic Landscape: Presenting a Method of Historic Landscape Character Assessment*, Cornwall Archaeological Unit, Truro.

Lapidge, M. and Herren, M. (1979) *Aldhelm: The Prose Works*, Brewer, Cambridge.

Padel, O. (1999) 'Place-names' in *Historical Atlas of South-West England*, eds R. Kain and W. Ravenhill, University of Exeter Press, Exeter, 88–94.

Pearce, S. (2004) *South-western Britain in the Early Middle Ages*, Continuum, London.

Roberts, B. and Wrathmell, S. (2000) *An Atlas of Rural Settlement in England*, English Heritage, London.

Thomas, C. (1958) *Gwithian: Ten Years' Work*, West Cornwall Field Club, Camborne.

Todd, M. (1987) *The South West to AD 1000*, Longman, London.

Turner, S. (2003) 'Making a Christian landscape: early medieval Cornwall' in *The Cross Goes North: Processes of Conversion in Northern Europe, AD 300–1300,* ed. M. Carver, Boydell and Brewer, Woodbridge, 171–94.

Turner, S. (2004) 'Coast and countryside in 'Late Antique' south-west England, AD *c.* 400–600' in *Debating Late Antiquity in Britain, AD 300–700*, eds J. Gerrard and R. Collins, BAR British Series 365, Oxford, 25–32.

Williamson, T. (2002) *The Transformation of Rural England: Farming and the Landscape, 1700–1870*, University of Exeter Press, Exeter.

Williamson, T. (2003) *Shaping Medieval Landscapes*, Windgather Press, Macclesfield.

Winterbottom, M. (1978) *Gildas: The Ruin of Britain and Other Documents*, Phillimore, Chichester.

CHAPTER 2

Palaeoenvironmental Perspectives on Medieval Landscape Development

Ralph Fyfe

Introduction

The South West, from a line running between the Blackdown and Quantock Hills, has long been recognised as a distinct historic landscape within Britain. This regional difference appears to be long-lived: the Blackdown–Quantocks line marked the western limit of the Durotriges during the Iron Age, as reflected in their pottery, coins, and massively defended hillforts (Cunliffe 1991). The same line marks the western limit of extensive Romanisation, with few villas and no small towns beyond (Jones and Mattingley 1990). This divide similarly represents the western limit for evidence of early Anglo-Saxon settlement, acculturation, and exchange networks as reflected in diagnostic structures (e.g. sunken feature buildings), burials and artefacts (Arnold 1988). In the medieval period these hills also mark the western-most limit of parishes with a predominantly nucleated settlement pattern and associated regularly arranged open fields (Rippon 2004; in press).

This chapter focuses on understanding the development of this distinctive medieval south-western landscape. It is one characterised by dispersed settlement and sprawling hamlets, with a mixture of open and enclosed field systems. These features of the landscape are clearly in existence by the tenth and eleventh centuries, when they are described in charter boundary clauses (Hooke 1994) and the Domesday survey (Darby 1967), but their origins are unclear. Furthermore, a regionally distinct form of agriculture known as convertible husbandry is known from manorial records by the thirteenth century (Fox 1991), although the dating of its emergence is also unclear. This was a rotational cropping system within which the majority of fields (closes or parcels of open fields) were subject to alternating grain and grass crops, often with a short period of cultivation (two to three years) followed by a long grass ley (six to eight years), producing a rotation of around ten years (Fox 1991).

Given the apparent lack of Romanisation within the South West, it might be thought that the later medieval landscapes of this region were inherited from late prehistoric patterns. Perhaps convertible husbandry also had its roots in a prehistoric agrarian system? Survey and excavation in Devon has shown that the late prehistoric and Romano-British landscape was characterised by small enclosed settlements containing one or more roundhouses, quite unlike the sprawling unenclosed hamlets and isolated farmsteads with rectangular longhouses that characterised the medieval countryside (Fitzpatrick *et al.* 1999; Griffith 1994; Riley and Wilson-North 2001). Furthermore, where the late prehistoric and Romano-British settlements are associated with field systems, these show little resemblance to the historic landscape (e.g. Rose and Preston-Jones 1995). It is therefore unlikely that the medieval landscape represents continuity from early periods; there must have been a period of change between the end of the Romano-British period and the later medieval.

The intervening period (the early medieval) is a difficult one to study due to the lack of pottery from all but the highest-status fifth- and sixth-century sites. The increasing use of radiocarbon dating is starting to reveal features of the wider landscape including lower-status settlement, and significantly this appears to represent a continuation of the late prehistoric/Romano-British tradition of enclosed settlements into the sixth century (Turner 2004). There remains, though, a break in evidence between this time and the emergence of the documentary sources, crucial in the light of the changes that appear to have taken place between the end of the Romano-British period and the documented later Middle Ages. This 'dark' period raises three tantalising questions:

Firstly, does a lack of archaeological evidence for settlement indicate a period of population contraction, resulting in landscape abandonment? Secondly, when does the transition to the landscape documented in the later medieval period occur, and is it a gradual process or a rapid one? And finally, is the process of change the same across the South West as a whole?

A palaeoenvironmental approach

Palaeoenvironmental research has been routinely applied in research projects with a prehistoric focus, to elucidate patterns of land use, landscape character and significant periods of landscape change caused by human agency, and there are several excellent examples within the region (see for example the Shaugh Moor Project on Dartmoor: Smith *et al.* 1981, or the Somerset Levels Project: Beckett and Hibbert 1979; Coles 1989). However, they have rarely been applied to medieval landscapes either in the South West or beyond (Dark 2000).

In explaining the poor integration of palaeoenvironmental data into medieval landscape research, it is important to first review the nature of the evidence. Palaeoenvironmental research can be divided into two main areas: on-site and off-site work. On-site research focuses on recovering the remains of plants, animals and insects from excavations to determine the nature of the economic activities associated with the site. In the case of settlement excavation, analysis of plant remains provides information on the types of crops around the site, evidence for crop processing, and storage. Animal bones, where present, can be very informative regarding the way in which animal husbandry was undertaken, and insects can provide a range of information from seasonality of settlement to local landscape conditions.

Off-site research tends to focus on the microscopic remains of plants (pollen and spores) that reflect the nature of the broader landscape of settlement sites. Of the pollen and spores dispersed from host plants, a majority are deposited on the ground, a proportion of which fall onto wetlands (fens, small bogs or lakes), and are preserved in anoxic conditions as a record of the landscape as the wetland continues to develop (Figure 4). If suitable wetlands can be identified within the landscape, and these were developing and accumulating pollen over the last 2,000 years, then pollen can be extracted from sediment sequences that will offer a continuous record of the changing landscape over this time period. Sometimes this record is also spatially precise enough to describe the *extent* of agricultural activities as well as their character.

These two broad categories of environmental evidence pose several different problems. As already mentioned, settlements which date to this difficult post-Roman/early medieval period are virtually unknown in the South West: the potential of on-site environmental data is therefore low in the region. On the face of it off-site research should offer high potential. However, compared to the prehistoric period there has been disappointingly little work on sequences that cover the Romano-British and medieval periods in Britain (Dark 2000). Most of the work that has been undertaken has focused on blanket peat from the high uplands: these are areas that lay beyond the core medieval settlement areas or areas demonstrably settled during the high medieval period, and so offer imprecise and often inaccurate impressions of the wider agrarian landscape. This has led to a significant upland bias in the palaeoenvironmental record, with little or no evidence for the nature of the lowland landscape. As a result the landscapes of the lowlands can only be inferred by extrapolation

FIGURE 4
The incorporation of pollen into peatland systems. The pollen deposited on the site is a combination of several different sources: Cr is a rain component, Cc a canopy component, Ct a trunk space component, Cl a local component and Cw local transport possibly from eroding soils (after Tauber, 1965).

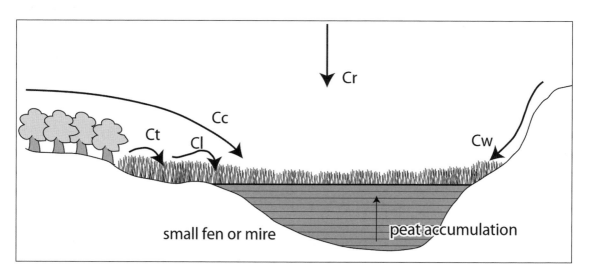

FIGURE 5
The location of pollen sites within mid-Devon and Exmoor, demonstrating the lowland-upland transect, and spatial patterning of sites. Details for individual sites can be found in (1) Merryfield and Moore (1974), (2) Francis and Slater (1990), (3) Francis and Slater (1992), (4) Fyfe (2000), (5–8) Fyfe et al. (2004), (9–11) Fyfe et al. (2003a) and (12–13) Rippon et al. (in press).

between (and from) the uplands – a very unsatisfactory situation. On a pragmatic level, work has had to focus on the uplands because of a number of factors, primarily concerning survival of suitable deposits. The types of sites that are commonly used for off-site palaeoenvironmental work – blanket peat, ombrotrophic mires and lakes – are clearly not present in the lowlands of Devon and Cornwall. The medieval and later agrarian systems are considered to have been very intensive, particularly in the lowlands, and peat was commonly extracted for fuel. The lowlands have also been well-drained by modern agriculture. It might, therefore, be thought that lowland landscapes simply do not contain or preserve suitable wetlands and peatland for this type of study. But is this in fact the case?

Extensive fieldwork by the author has located a number of very small, discrete peatlands across a transect from the lowlands of mid-Devon to the high upland (Figure 5), whose sedimentary records all cover at least the last 2,000 years (Fyfe *et al.* 2003a; Fyfe *et al.* 2004). These include small fens at the headwaters of streams, and mires associated with spring and seepage lines. Their fortuitous survival appears to owe much to their size: they are commonly less than 30 m across and have therefore avoided being drained or cut for peat. Some of these newly-discovered sites are firmly embedded within the

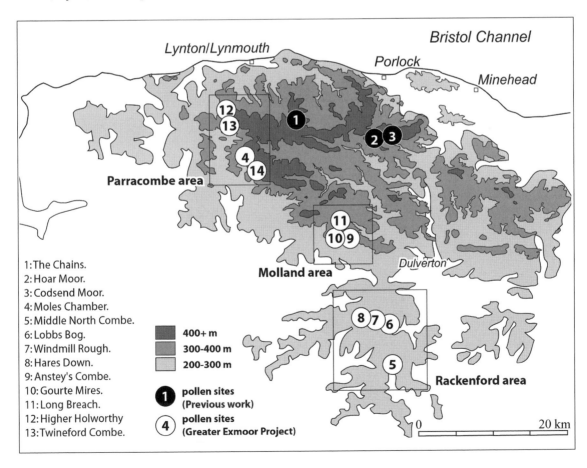

1: The Chains.
2: Hoar Moor.
3: Codsend Moor.
4: Moles Chamber.
5: Middle North Combe.
6: Lobbs Bog.
7: Windmill Rough.
8: Hares Down.
9: Anstey's Combe.
10: Gourte Mires.
11: Long Breach.
12: Higher Holworthy.
13: Twineford Combe.

400+ m
300–400 m
200–300 m

pollen sites (Previous work)
pollen sites (Greater Exmoor Project)

0   20 km

historic landscape, and offer very high potential for elucidating changes in the landscape during the medieval period. Locating sites along a lowland–upland transect allows us to address the nature of the entire South West landscape, rather than imparting a lowland or upland bias to the analysis. Furthermore, a conscious effort to locate several pollen sites within small geographic spaces (a series of defined study areas within the transect) allows us to analyse spatial aspects of the landscape (Figure 5). The pollen records from these small peat systems, along with previously published palaeoenvironmental research from the region, allow us to chart landscape development over time.

The pre-medieval development of the South West cultural landscape

In order to understand the changes that occur during the medieval period, it is necessary to step back in time to the pre-medieval landscape. The medieval landscape was one which reflected processes that began millennia before. The high open moorland on Dartmoor was created during the later Mesolithic period through controlled use of fire, and woodland has never fully developed on the upland since that period (Caseldine and Hatton 1993). By the end of the Neolithic substantial landscape clearance had taken place, both on the high uplands for a grazing economy (Caseldine 1999; Gearey *et al.* 2000) and in the lowlands for both grazing and crop growing (Fyfe *et al.* 2003b).

It is clear that by the middle Bronze Age substantial subdivision of land was taking place across North West Europe, the most extensive example being the reave systems established on Dartmoor (Fleming 1988). Recent excavation has also extended this co-axial land division into lowland South West contexts (e.g. Fitzpatrick *et al.* 1999), all of which points towards a well-organised, substantial agricultural society. By the Late Iron Age further substantial woodland clearance had taken place across the South West both in the lowlands and the uplands, probably leaving the landscape as open as it has ever been since the development of woodland after the end of the last glacial period (Fyfe *et al.* 2003b). What was left of the woodland was probably managed in some way for a variety of domestic and agricultural purposes (Ralston 1999).

Coming closer to the medieval period, Fyfe and Rippon (2004) have argued that the impact of Romanisation on the character of the South West was probably very marginal, and the end of the Romano-British period equally unremarkable in terms of its impact on the agricultural landscape. On reflection, this is perhaps unsurprising. The importance of the well-established Blackdown–Quantocks divide on the settlement character of the region appears to be reflected as well in the landscape history. What is interesting to draw from the palaeoecological evidence is that the data suggest continuity of land use from late prehistory until around the eighth century AD, whereupon a series of significant changes are recorded. The landscape up to this point in time was one in which the lowlands were the main settlement zone, showing local arable cultivation, probably at a small scale, and high quality pasture land. Although there is no direct evidence to show it, the mid-Devon area was most likely dominated by animal husbandry. The valleys leading onto the higher uplands appear to have retained woodland areas: Fyfe *et al.* (2003a) demonstrated a significant difference between the lower upland fringes and the valleys draining them by obtaining pollen sequences from both contexts. The valleys were dominated by oak and hazel. They tend to be steep-sided and less suited to clearance for agriculture; however, they would have offered important resources, such as pannage, fuel for domestic fires, timber for structures, and charcoal production for industrial activities (Ralston 1999), and were no doubt managed for such, through coppicing and pollarding. The high uplands were utilised for seasonal grazing: pollen evidence from the upland fringes and central Exmoor suggests a maintained pastoral system (Merryfield and Moore 1974; Francis and Slater 1990; 1992), although the intensity of this pressure probably declined with distance from the upland edge.

The development of the medieval lowland landscape

This places the landscape of pre-medieval Devon and Cornwall in its context, but what of the changes alluded to around the eighth century? The palaeoenvironmental evidence throws valuable light into this archaeological 'dark age': a major shift in the character of land exploitation occurred at this time. Several key features are evident from the pollen assemblages from the lowlands (i.e. those sites below 300 m OD) which post-date this transition (Figure 6): there are significant increases in the pollen of cereals; heathland appears to become better represented within the lowlands; pastoral indicators continue to suggest good quality grazing in the area; and woodland representation continues at similar levels: there is no woodland clearance.

FIGURE 6
Selected summary pollen diagrams from the mid-Devon lowland to Exmoor upland transect (redrawn from Fyfe and Rippon 2004). In A, the Horizontal axis on each graph represent the proportion of each vegetation group at the site. B represents the altitude of the pollen sites detailed above in A.

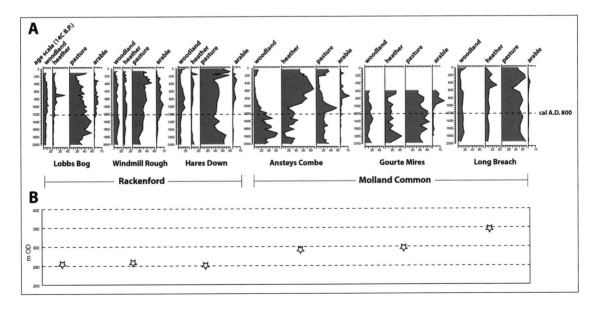

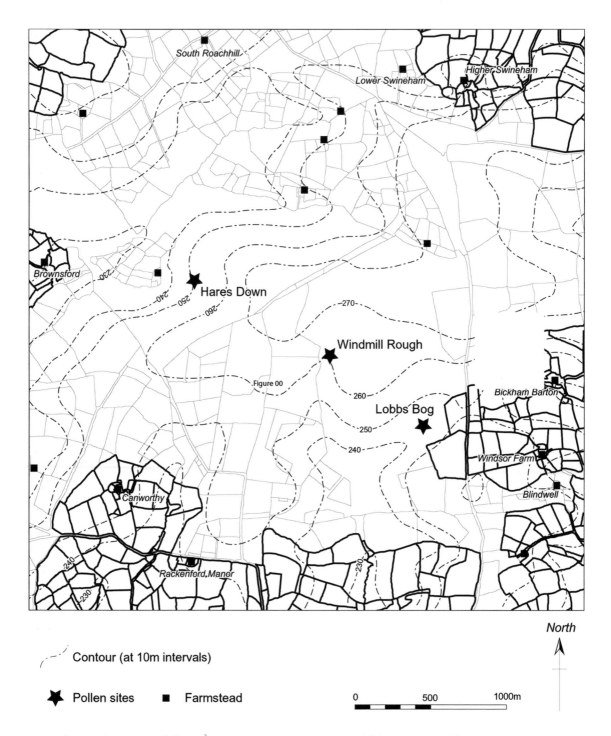

South Roachhill

Lower Swineham

Higher Swineham

Brownsford

Hares Down

Figure 00

Windmill Rough

260

Lobbs Bog

250

240

270

Bickham Barton

Windsor Farm

Blindwell

Canworthy

Rackenford Manor

230

240

230

250

260

North

Contour (at 10m intervals)

★ Pollen sites   ■ Farmstead

0   500   1000m

At first sight some of these features may seem irreconcilable. How could heathland have developed at the same time as the area under cereal cultivation was apparently expanding? And how could good quality grazing have continued at the same time? Surely there must have been a squeeze within the landscape, reflected perhaps in a loss of woodland. It is at this point that the spatial dimension of the pollen record becomes very useful. The sites do not all reflect these changes with the same intensity, although they all bear the same overall signal.

The value of studying pollen records from a range of locations is shown by the four sites in the area around Rackenford (Figure 7). The full details of the pollen records are given in Fyfe *et al.* (2004), and the following discussion represents a summary of these records. Middle North Combe is located well within the enclosed medieval landscape – the pattern of farms and fields characteristic of this particular historic landscape. Lobbs Bog and Windmill Rough are positioned at its edge, and Hares Down is more remote from what are considered to be medieval enclosures. Generally, the enclosed fieldscape around Rackenford lies in topographically lower areas, with the unenclosed ground restricted to the higher parts of the lowland landscape.

The indications of cereal cultivation are strongest at the site within the historic fieldscape (Middle North Combe), and the sites at the margins (Windmill Rough and Lobbs Bog) also show clear indications of the increase in cereal cultivation. Cereal pollen is notorious for its poor dispersal (Vourela 1970), and the levels recorded suggest significant cultivation adjacent to and in the vicinity of the sites. The development of heathland is most strongly associated with the sites at the margins or beyond the historic fieldscape (Hares Down, Windmill Rough, Lobbs Bog), while all sites maintain good pastoral indicators. Woodland also shows spatial patterning, with very low levels within the historic fieldscape, and higher levels at the margins.

These changes suggest a more formalised division of the landscape into separate compartments, and may, in fact, chart the emergence of the historic fieldscape. Within this historic fieldscape cereal cultivation began, alongside continued high quality grazing land. At the edges of the fieldscape, possibly in the steeper, less 'useful' agricultural land, woodland resources were maintained and managed for a variety of purposes. Beyond the edge of the historic fieldscape the heathland probably reflects the development, or formalisation, of areas of common rough grazing, beyond the 'infield' improved pasturage. The persistence of a cereal record from this 'outfield' suggests that areas of it may have been periodically ploughed, although this is unlikely to have occurred on a regular basis. The temporal resolution of pollen analysis should be borne in mind: the nature of pollen sampling means that a pollen level will represent an average of several years pollen deposition (on a raised mire, for example, one centimetre of peat may represent ten years of peat growth). If a parcel of land on the upland margin is ploughed every five years, it may appear as a continuous, rather than discontinuous, record within the pollen sequence.

FIGURE 7
The relationship
between the pollen
sites in mid-Devon
around Rackenford
and the historic
landscape. Field
boundaries shown
in bolder strokes are
those believed to
relate to the earliest
('ancient') enclosure of
the landscape. Middle
North Combe is not
shown, the site is
located 5 km to the
south-west embedded
within the 'ancient'
landscape.

The medieval upland margins and beyond

Although the changes visible in the lowland pollen sequences are clear around the eighth century, it is not until the eleventh century that this pattern can be recognised on the uplands. At this time the pollen sequences recovered from sites at elevations around 350 m, on the southern flanks of Exmoor, begin to record a similar, if somewhat more subtle, pattern of changes (Fyfe *et al.* 2003a). It is likely that these later changes reflect increasing population pressure on land and resources, possibly resulting from settlement expansion and the inclusion of what was seasonal pastoral land into the mixed agrarian system. There is abundant field evidence across the upland margins on Exmoor of field systems covering now-open areas such as Molland Common (Figure 8), and evidence of a greater density of settlement than that which remains today; the now-shrunken Danes' Brook 'hamlet' is an example. It is unlikely, however, that the upland margins were ploughed on an annual basis and these field systems are more likely to represent formal enclosure of pastoral land. The pollen record does, however, demonstrate that these were areas which were periodically under arable cultivation, since there is near continuous, albeit low, level of cereals recorded around the sites.

The high uplands remote from lowland settlement also need to be considered. The evidence from this zone does not show any of the changes that are recorded in the lowlands or the upland margins (Merryfield and Moore 1974; Francis and Slater 1990; 1992). There had been evidence of a possible retreat from the highest uplands during the fifth and sixth centuries, but as this was not recorded from the upland margins the extent of this retreat must have been local. Throughout the medieval period the uplands remained an open landscape used for seasonal grazing.

The nature of the agricultural landscape

A picture therefore emerges of the medieval landscape which developed in mid-Devon around the eighth century. More formalised division of the landscape appears to have taken place; in the lowlands an intensive agrarian system developed that had elements of extensive arable cultivation and high quality pasture, alongside open commons with rough grazing. The upland fringes and beyond remained as seasonal grazing areas until the eleventh century, when intensification of land use extended into the upland margins. This pattern of land use continued throughout the medieval period.

This lack of change in the pollen signature from the eighth century now allows us to consider the nature of the agrarian regime. It is known from documentary sources that a regionally distinct agrarian system was in place in the South West by the thirteenth century. As we have seen, this appears in the pollen record to be identical to the system that developed around five centuries earlier. The early medieval transition identified in the pollen record probably reflects the beginnings of 'convertible husbandry', and we need to

FIGURE 8
The later medieval field system and settlement pattern on Molland Common, southern Exmoor. Dashed lines represent the relict fieldscape recorded across the open commons on southern Exmoor. Lyshwell and Cloggs are the only remaining settlements in The Danes' Brook 'hamlet'.

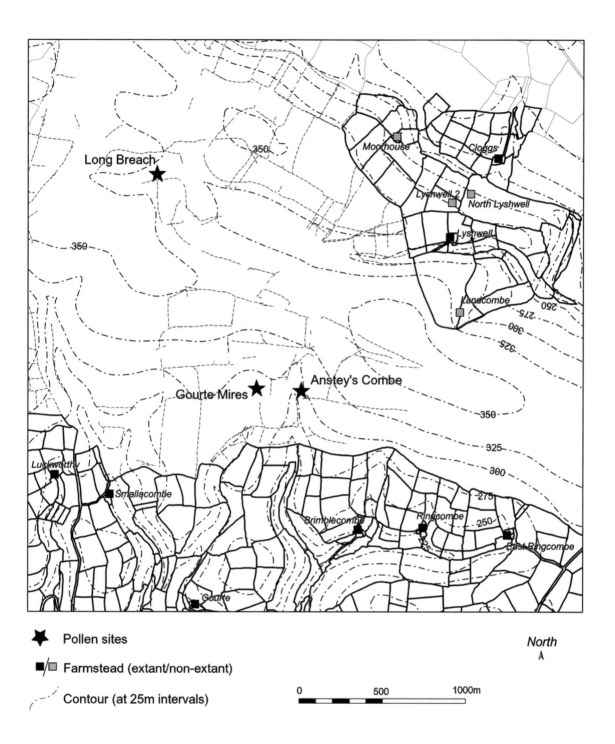

★ Pollen sites

■/□ Farmstead (extant/non-extant)

╱╴╯ Contour (at 25m intervals)

North
∧

```
0          500         1000m
▰▰▱▱▰▰▱▱▰▰
```

ask what kind of system this was. The pollen evidence suggests that it involved both arable and pastoral elements, and may have included subdivision of the landscape, though the data is too crude to allow us to do any more than speculate. However, documentary evidence allows us to examine the mechanics of the system in the later medieval period. Hatcher (1988) confirms that there were intensive farming practices in place in the twelfth century in the South West which included enclosed fields with rough grazing beyond them. Fox (1991) describes convertible husbandry as recorded in the thirteenth century documents: the majority of fields were subject to alternating grain and grass crops, often with a long grass ley. Little land would have been permanent grassland, though it is unlikely that meadows or woodland would ever have been ploughed. Outfield pasturing, combined with folding animals into the infields to introduce nutrients from the outfield, would have enhanced soil fertility, along with practices such as burn beating (the burning of the tuft before ploughing). The system allowed yields to be managed flexibly, since only a part of the land available for arable was under crops at any one time. During periods of economic pressure or increasing population, yields could be increased by shortening ley periods and occasional ploughing of the rough pasture beyond the enclosed land (Fox 1991). Conversely, during periods of lower land pressure, lengthened ley periods would have prevented excess production, and allowed more time for ley parcels to recover. This flexibility in the system is what would have made it so successful, and the unchanging nature of the pollen signature between the eighth and fifteenth centuries suggests that convertible husbandry continued well into the later medieval period, and probably until at least the fifteenth century. It can be argued that the 'revolution' that occurred around the eighth century was the key transition that marked the development of the historic landscape of the South West.

Conclusions

We can now return to the three questions outlined at the start of this chapter. First, does a lack of archaeological evidence for settlement indicate a period of population contraction, resulting in landscape abandonment? The environmental evidence suggests not. With the exception of possible contraction from the highest upland areas on Exmoor, there is no evidence from the historic landscape, or from the margins of this landscape, of a reduction in pressure in land use at the end of the Romano-British period. In the face of reduced pressure on resources, one might expect to see indications of scrub regeneration and woodland development, particularly at the margins. Although there is scrub development on the high uplands (Merryfield and Moore 1974) it may be possible to see this as a vegetation response to a drier/warmer national climate at this time (as damp peatlands dry out scrub invasion may take place). In the absence of good palaeoclimatic data from the region this must remain conjecture, and is reliant on analogy with work from northern Britain (e.g. Barber *et al.* 2003). In respect of settlement history, recent work has begun to demonstrate continuity of settlement and occupation in Cornwall and west Devon into the fifth and sixth centuries (see Turner 2004). Again, this shows that people remained in the area, and does not support a model based on population decline.

Second, when does the transition from the Romano-British settlement pattern to the landscape documented in the later medieval period occur, and is it a gradual process or a rapid one? It appears from the environmental evidence to have occurred by the eighth century, although it is clear that the landscape does not change overnight. The lag in time for the 'development' of the upland margins may reflect a gradual increase in population pressure; once certain thresholds had been reached the system may have had to expand to take in more land. The whole process of change is likely to have taken decades, if not longer. As new innovations came about the process of diffusion will have taken time. More work is needed in this field, though, and the process of innovation cannot be explained solely through the interpretation of palaeoenvironmental data. Furthermore, the precise organisation of the landscape will only be explicable through survey and excavation, a challenge if the boundaries or divisions were characterised by earthen banks which have now been ploughed out, or which remain fossilised in the modern landscape. The nature of crop regimes may be deduced from documentary sources, but can only be confirmed through on-site palaeoenvironmental evidence, a source reliant on the discovery and excavation of well-dated settlement related to the period.

Finally, our last question addresses the geographic relevance of the transition discussed here. Did the same thing happen across the entire South West? All the data presented and assimilated concerns a lowland to upland transect from mid-Devon to Exmoor (Figure 5). The topography and geology of Devon and Cornwall is tremendously varied, and it is possible, indeed likely, that there is sub-regional variation in land use practices even within Devon and Cornwall. This may also be reflected in the varied nature of settlement from the Romano-British period on. The hinterland of Exeter and the lower Exe valley, for example, is atypical, characterised by sub-rectilinear enclosures (recorded from aerial survey), on what is today high-grade agricultural land (Griffith 1994). Although these are for the most part undated, they reflect a sub-regional difference that may have affected subsequent trajectories of landscape development. What is encouraging is that across the wider region there is evidence for discontinuity between Romano-British period field systems and medieval field systems (see Turner 2004). We may therefore anticipate there having been a period of reorganisation of the landscape across the region, which the evidence here suggests may have taken place by the eighth century.

On a final note, the overwhelming upland bias in the environmental record for Devon and Cornwall is beginning to be addressed by work such as that presented here from Devon. The very clear difference between the history from the high uplands and that now derived from the lowlands and upland margin cannot be stressed enough, and underlines the physical differences between the two landscapes. However, further palaeoenvironmental research is needed over a wider geographic area (particularly in west Devon and Cornwall), in order to ensure that the upland bias that had prevailed in the environmental history of the South West is not simply replaced by a mid-Devon bias!

Acknowledgements

The Greater Exmoor Project was funded by a research grant from the Leverhulme Trust [grant number F/00144/D] to Stephen Rippon and Tony Brown, who are thanked for giving the author the opportunity to engage in this work. The ideas presented here are the author's own, but would not have emerged without discussions with Stephen Rippon, Tony Brown, Harold Fox and Rob Wilson-North. Much of this chapter was written whilst the author was a guest of the Department of Forest Vegetation Ecology in the Swedish University of Agricultural Sciences (SLU), Umeå, and the Department is thanked for their hospitality.

References

Arnold, C. (1988) *An Archaeology of the Early Anglo-Saxon Kingdoms*, Routledge, London.

Barber, K.E., Chamber, F.M. and Maddy, D. (2003) 'Holocene palaeoclimates from peat stratigraphy: macrofossil proxy climate records from three oceanic raised bogs in England and Ireland', *Quaternary Science Reviews* **22**, 521–39.

Beckett, S.C. and Hibbert, F.A. (1979) 'Vegetational change and the influence of prehistoric man in the Somerset Levels', *New Phytologist* **83**, 577–600.

Caseldine, C.J. (1999) 'Archaeological and environmental change on Prehistoric Dartmoor – current understandings and future directions', *Journal of Quaternary Science* **14**, 575–83.

Caseldine, C.J. and Hatton, J. (1993) 'The development of high moorland on Dartmoor: fire and the influence of Mesolithic activity on vegetation change' in *Climate Change and Human Impact on the Landscape*, ed. F.M.Chambers, Chapman and Hall, London, 119–32.

Coles, J.M. (1989) 'The Somerset Levels Project 1973–1989', *Somerset Levels Papers* **15**, 5–14.

Cunliffe, B. (1991) *Iron Age Communities in Britain*, Routledge, London.

Darby, H.C. (1967) 'The south-western counties' in *The Domesday Geography of South-West England*, eds H.C.Darby and R.Welldon-Finn, Cambridge University Press, Cambridge.

Dark, P. (2000) *The Environment of Britain in the First Millennium AD*, Duckworth, London.

Fitzpatrick, A.P., Butterworth, C.A. and Grove, J. (1999) *Prehistoric and Roman Sites in East Devon: the A30 Honiton to Exeter DBFO scheme, 1996–99*, The Trust for Wessex Archaeology, Salisbury.

Fleming, A. (1988) *The Dartmoor Reaves*, Batsford, London.

Fox, H.S.A. (1991) 'Farming practice and techniques, Devon and Cornwall' in *The Agrarian History of England and Wales, vol 3, 1348–1500*, ed. E.Miller, Cambridge University Press, Cambridge, 303–23.

Francis, P.D. and Slater, D.S. (1990) 'A record of vegetation and land use change from upland peat deposits on Exmoor. Part 2: Hoar Moor', *Somerset Archaeology and Natural History Society Proceedings* **134**, 1–25.

Francis, P.D. and Slater, D.S. (1992) 'A record of vegetation and land use change from upland peat deposits on Exmoor. Part 3: Codsend Moor', *Somerset Archaeology and Natural History Society Proceedings* **136**, 9–28.

Fyfe, R.M. (2000) 'Palaeochannels of the Exe catchment: their age and an assessment of their archaeological and palaoeecological potential', unpublished PhD Thesis, University of Exeter.

Fyfe, R.M., Brown, A.G. and Coles, B.J. (2003b) 'Mesolithic to Bronze Age vegetation change and human activity in the Exe Valley, Devon, UK', *Proceedings of the Prehistoric Society* **69**, 161–81.

Fyfe, R.M., Brown, A.G. and Rippon, S.J. (2003a) 'Mid- to late-Holocene vegetation history of Greater Exmoor, UK: estimating the spatial extent of human-induced vegetation change', *Vegetation History and Archaeobotany* **12**, 215–32.

Fyfe, R.M., Brown, A.G. and Rippon, S.J. (2004) 'Characterising the late prehistoric, "Romano-British" and medieval landscape, and dating the emergence of a regionally distinct agricultural system in South West Britain', *Journal of Archaeological Science* **31**, 1699–1714.

Fyfe, R.M. and Rippon, S.J. (2004) 'A landscape in transition? Palaeoenvironmental evidence for the end of the 'Romano-British' period in southwest England' in *Debating Late Antiquity in Britain AD 300–700*, eds R.Collins and J.Gerrard, BAR British Series **365**, 33–42.

Gearey B.R, Charman, D.J. and Kent, M. (2000) 'Palaeoecological Evidence for the Prehistoric Settlement of Bodmin Moor, Cornwall, Southwest England. Part I: The Status of Woodland and Early Human Impacts', *Journal of Archaeological Science* **27**, 423–38.

Griffith, F.M. (1994) 'Changing perceptions of the context of prehistoric Dartmoor', *Proceedings of the Devon Archaeological Society* **52**, 85–99.

Hatcher, J. (1988) 'New Settlement: south west England' in *The Agrarian History of England and Wales, vol 2, 1042–1350*, ed. H.E.Hallam, Cambridge University Press, Cambridge, 234–44.

Hooke, D. (1994) *The Pre-Conquest Charter-Bounds of Devon and Cornwall*, Boydell Press, Woodbridge.

Jones, B. and Mattingly, D. (1990) *An Atlas of Roman Britain*, Blackwell, Oxford.

Merryfield, D.L. and Moore, P.D. (1974) 'Prehistoric human activity and blanket peat initition on Exmoor', *Nature* **250**, 439–41.

Ralston, I. (1999) 'The Iron Age: aspects of the human communities and their environments', *Quaternary Proceedings* **7**, 501–12.

Riley, H. and Wilson-North, R. (2001) *The Field Archaeology of Exmoor*, English Heritage, Swindon.

Rippon, S. (2004) *Historic Landscape Analysis: Deciphering the Countryside*, Council for British Archaeology, York.

Rippon, S. (in press) 'Landscapes of pre-medieval occupation' in *England's Landscapes, Volume 3: Landscapes of South-West England*, ed. R.Kain, English Heritage, London.

Rippon, S., Fyfe, R.M. and Brown, A.G. (in press) 'Beyond villages and open fields: the origins and development of a historic landscape characterised by dispersed settlement in South West England' *Medieval Archaeology.*

Rose, P. and Preston-Jones, A. (1995) 'Changes in the Cornish countryside, AD 400–1100' in *Landscape and Settlement in Britain AD 400–1066*, eds D.Hooke and S.Burnell, University of Exeter Press, Exeter, 51–68.

Smith, K., Coppen, J., Wainwright, G.J. and Beckett, S. (1981) 'The Shaugh Moor project: third report, settlement and environmental investigations', *Proceedings of the Prehistoric Society* **47**, 205–73.

Tauber, H. (1965) 'Differential pollen dispersal and the interpretation of pollen diagrams', *Danmarks Geologiske Undersøgelse Årbog* **89**, 1–69.

Turner, S. (2004) 'Coast and countryside in 'Late Antique' south-west England, *c.* AD 400–600' in *Debating Late Antiquity in Britain AD 300–700*, eds R.Collins and J.Gerrard, BAR British Series 365, 25–32.

Vourela, I. (1970) 'The indication of farming in pollen diagrams from Southern Finland', *Acta Botanica Fennica* **87**, 1–40.

CHAPTER 3

The Christian Landscape: Churches, Chapels and Crosses

Sam Turner

Introduction

This chapter discusses the appearance and development of Christian monuments in the landscape of the former kingdom of Dumnonia (Todd 1987, 236–66; Pearce 2004, 25). In common with other chapters in this book (see for example Herring and Fyfe), it argues that the medieval pattern seems most likely to have emerged between the seventh and ninth centuries, after the end of the period that archaeologists of western Britain have begun to call 'Late Antiquity' (Gerrard and Collins 2004). Over the course of three or four centuries after *c.* AD 550, a basic 'vocabulary' of Christian sites was established that continued to provide a framework until the Reformation. By the fourteenth and fifteenth centuries many churches, chapels, and holy wells were far more elaborate than the simple sites of the early Middle Ages, but they nevertheless formed part of a continuum whose beginnings lay 900 years earlier. The first part of the chapter considers what kinds of sites were established during the early medieval period, and the second part looks at some uses of one particular type of monument, crosses in stone.

The religious landscape of the early Middle Ages

The South West has no great historical narrative to tell us the origins of its earliest churches. For the North and East of England, the writings of Bede record the names of many churches dating to the early eighth century and before, but of south-western establishments he mentions only Malmesbury in Wiltshire (Farmer 1990, 298); not even Glastonbury or Sherborne find their way into his pages.

Despite the lack of written histories, there are good reasons for thinking there were some churches and monasteries in Devon and Cornwall during the fifth and sixth centuries. Gildas' sixth-century text *On the Destruction of Britain* is richly seamed with biblical learning and its composition implies the existence of a widespread Christian culture in western Britain. Gildas was probably describing events that had taken place in a south-western monastic church when he reported a double murder supposedly perpetrated by King Constantine of Dumnonia before 'a holy altar' (*sacrosancta alteria*): Constantine's victims were meant to have been *sub sancti abbatis amphibalo*, 'under the protection of the holy abbot' (Winterbottom 1978, 99–100). Where in Dumnonia this monastery might have been we cannot tell, but perhaps a royal centre like Tintagel is most likely (see below).

Early beginnings for the church in the South West are also hinted at by conservative practices first recorded in the eighth century. The so-called 'Easter Controversy' provides an example (Stevens 1999). The western church in Europe had changed the way it calculated the date of Easter several times during the sixth century, but the churches of Atlantic Britain and Ireland had retained their earlier methods (Sharpe 1995, 36–9). In the seventh century, much of England and southern Ireland chose a system thought to be the one followed in Rome. However, in common with Wales and northern parts of Ireland we know that the church in south-west Britain was still using old ways of calculating the date of Easter around the year 700, because Aldhelm (abbot of Malmesbury and bishop of Sherborne) wrote to the Dumnonian king Gereint urging him to instruct his churchmen to mend their ways (Lapidge and Herren 1979, 155–60). The 'Easter Controversy' could be a political tool used by powerful statesmen to assert the superiority of their own ideological positions; a mid-ninth-century profession of obedience by the Cornish bishop Kenstec to the archbishop of Canterbury suggests Cornish practice had by then become one with that of England (Olson 1989, 51–6). This religious unity is at least in part a reflection of the political dominance Wessex held over Cornwall by this time.

The most commonly asked questions about early Christianity in the far South West are also the ones with the most elusive answers: who were the first churchmen, where did they come from, and where are their churches? Historians have identified several possible sources of influence – from Roman Britain (Handley 2001), from Wales and Ireland, and from continental Europe and the Mediterranean. Some urge us that early Christian Wales must have been most important, and that communications with Europe were only of limited significance (Thomas 1988; 1998); others have suggested much stronger links – perhaps even political dependence – on the Mediterranean world of late Antiquity (Harris 2003). The debate is not without importance today, particularly for those who seek to construct strong ancient foundations for modern 'Celtic' identity: framed in these terms, the coherence of the 'Celtic' Irish Sea world as an ancient unified region might be at stake.

The problem turns partly on how we think of 'influence.' If we understand it to describe an unequal relationship where a 'weak' culture passively absorbs some characteristics of a 'stronger' and more powerful one, then it is easy to see why those seeking to justify a 'Celtic' identity might feel threatened by European or Byzantine interference. It must be more accurate, though, to think of 'influence' not as a passive process of absorption, but as the manifestation of active and creative choices (Dodds 1990, 3). The rulers of early medieval kingdoms did not drift into new religions, but chose (for any number of reasons) what elements to accept and what symbols to adopt (Carver 2003). Realising this, it becomes easier to appreciate that many influences could have been present in the earliest Christianity of Devon, Cornwall and Atlantic Britain. It might also put us less at the mercy of the '… essentially romantically constructed individualistic Celt …' and his ready-made cultural preferences and roles (see Chapter 5).

Throughout the 1990s Charles Thomas explored the cultural associations of the monuments known as inscribed stones (e.g. Thomas 1994; 1998). These are found across the Irish Sea world, with the majority distributed in Wales and Ireland. In the South West there are around 50 surviving monuments, the majority in Cornwall (Figure 9). They are usually quite rough stone pillars bearing short inscriptions in Latin. Some have additional texts in the Irish ogam alphabet, and some bear crosses or other simple symbols. As a group they carry a variety of personal names in the Irish, British and Latin languages. There is no question that they reflect the presence of social groups with strong connections to Ireland and Wales across Atlantic Britain. However, there are also a few inscriptions in Dumnonia with longer Latin texts. Mark Handley has highlighted the similarities between funerary inscriptions across the late Antique world (Handley 2003, 8–22), and also pointed out that the inscriptions of Britain may owe more than is usually recognised to the late Roman

FIGURE 9
The inscribed stone at St Samson's, South Hill (Cornwall). The inscription on the stone reads CUMREGNI FILI MAUCI ('[the stone] of Cumregnus, son of Maucus'; Okasha 1993, 264–7), and is surmounted by a chi-rho monogram.
SAM TURNER

FIGURE 10
Tintagel Island, viewed
from Glebe Cliff below
St Matheriana's church
(Cornwall).
SAM TURNER

Christianity of Britain (Handley 2001). Formulae like *hic iacit* ('here lies') and *memoria* ('memorial of') occur on memorials not only elsewhere in Britain but also in Gaul, Spain, and further afield – Italy, north Africa and the Balkans. In south-west Britain the two traditions were clearly not mutually exclusive: two stones with 'extended Latinate' inscriptions at Lewannick in Cornwall (*ingenui memoria* and [hi]*c iacit ulcagni*) both also have ogam texts (Okasha 1993, 146–53). These inscribed stones were among the first Christian monuments in the Dumnonian landscape. They were memorials to the dead, and some undoubtedly stood at church sites. As Handley has argued, however, other stones (which could also mark burials) seem to have been located on the boundaries of emerging territories (Handley 1998). By linking the religion of the ruling class to the wider landscape they marked an initial step in its Christianisation.

Pottery and other objects imported from Gaul and the Mediterranean world also indicate overseas contacts. For Devon and Cornwall this seems to have been particularly important in the later fifth and sixth century. Dotted around the coastline are sites where archaeologists have discovered sherds of amphorae from the eastern Mediterranean and finewares from Turkey or north

Africa. It used to be argued that these might have resulted from just a few speculative trading trips (Thomas 1988), but continuing finds of a wide range of material and the longevity of some of the sites suggest that well-established, long-term relationships across the sea are much more likely (e.g. Turner and Gerrard 2004). The evidence from inscribed stones, burial practices (Petts 2004), and imports of pottery and other goods suggests that western Britain between *c.* AD 350–600 was a functioning, if distinctive, part of the Christian world of late Antiquity.

A flavour of the early Christian world of these western seaways can be had from the *First Life of St Samson*, composed in Brittany between the seventh and ninth centuries (Flobert 1997). The *Life* records that Samson was born into a noble family in south-west Wales (around the beginning of the sixth century), and was educated in the famous monastery school at Llanilltyd Fawr (Llantwit Major, Glamorgan). He became a priest and eventually a bishop, and travelled extensively: to Ireland in the company of pilgrims returning from Rome, to Cornwall, and to Brittany where his *Life* was subsequently written. As hagiography has led us to expect from early Celtic holy men, Samson performed miracles, corrected apostates, banished monsters, and founded monasteries. It is to Samson's biographer that we owe the earliest literary mention of south-western monasteries: the one that Samson established (unfortunately left unnamed, but perhaps near the south coast), and the community of *Docco*, later *Landocco*, now St Kew in Cornwall (Olson 1989; Thomas 1994, 223–36).

The name of *Docco* is virtually all we do know about the sites of the earliest churches in Devon and Cornwall. Not one church from the period before the ninth century has been excavated, and none survives as a standing building. Hints and scraps of archaeology provide tantalising glimpses of what may one day be learned. In Exeter, archaeologists working in the Cathedral Close during the 1970s discovered a small cemetery dating to the fifth and sixth centuries (Bidwell 1979). The site later became part of the Anglo-Saxon monastery where St Boniface probably received his education, and it is possible that these graves belonged to early members of that community. At Phillack, behind the dunes of the Hayle estuary in west Cornwall, there is an inscribed stone with a simple three-word text and another sculpted stone bearing a *chi-rho*, the monogram representing the first two letters of Christ's name (Okasha 1993, 210–17). Other evidence also hints there may have been an important early site here: a scrap of imported Mediterranean fineware, further sculpture from before the Norman Conquest, finds of burials outside the modern graveyard, and institutional links showing Phillack was the mother church of the early chapel at Gwithian (Thomas 1994, 197–200).

In this period Tintagel in Cornwall is the place about which we know most (Figure 10). This rugged headland on the north Cornish coast used to be regarded as a Celtic monastery, but recent writers prefer to see it as a secular centre occupied by the rulers of Cornwall between the fifth and seventh centuries (Ralegh Radford 1962; Thomas 1993). Excavations at Tintagel have produced more imported pottery than at all the other British findspots combined, and earthwork survey has revealed far denser concentrations of buildings than at any comparable site. On the cliffs beyond the citadel stands St Matheriana's, a Norman church in a great bleak graveyard. Excavations in the early 1990s revealed the remains of graves, patches of burning and broken sherds of imported Mediterranean pottery of the fifth and sixth centuries. It seems likely that the graves represent an early Christian cemetery, and Charles Thomas has suggested the other finds could be the remains of graveside meals in memory of the dead, a widespread practice in late Antiquity (Thomas 1994: 205–6).

We cannot yet be sure what sort of Christian community there might have been at Tintagel. There could have been a priest or two ministering to the

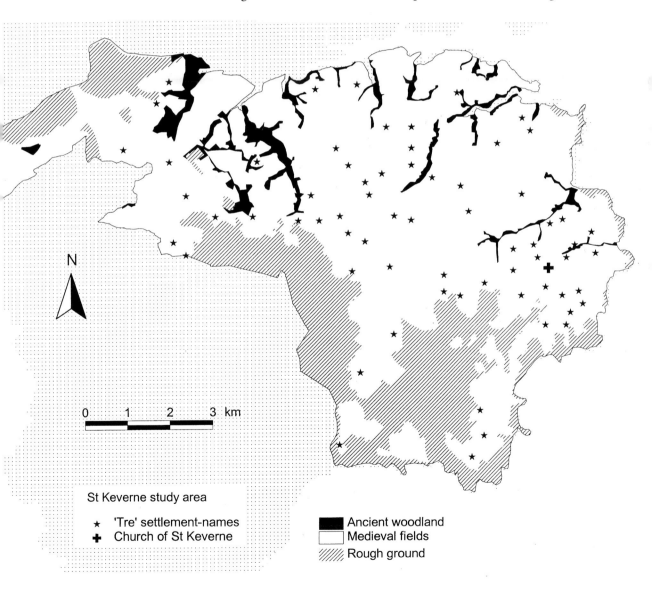

N

0 1 2 3 km

St Keverne study area

★ 'Tre' settlement-names
✚ Church of St Keverne

■ Ancient woodland
□ Medieval fields
▨ Rough ground

secular residents, or there might have been a whole enclave of monks with royal members like those mentioned by Gildas (see above). There is no doubt that the place lay at the heart of a network of communications extending far up into the Irish Sea and south to the Bay of Biscay and the Mediterranean. The Christian world of late Antiquity lay open to exploration by its rulers, and to judge from our present evidence they were the people who patronised Christianity in its earliest south-western phases.

We do not know the reasons why, but the citadel at Tintagel was left unoccupied after the seventh century. There were other important changes around the same time, such as the final abandonment of the old Romano-British 'rounds' (settlements enclosed by banks and ditches) and their replacement with open farmsteads (Rose and Preston-Jones 1995). The demise of Tintagel may be linked to these transformations in the wider landscape, but despite this the graveyard at St Matheriana's remained a stable feature into the Middle Ages. I have argued elsewhere that churches acted as foci for new patterns of life in the countryside from this time onwards (Turner 2006), and where they survived the ecclesiastical centres of late Antiquity probably provided models for them. In particular, there is a category of important early churches that probably became nuclei for the emerging medieval landscape. Once again there is little hard evidence for them and rarely any contemporary documentation, but scholars have identified around 20 in Cornwall and 25 in Devon from hints in later texts and surviving scraps of archaeology (Olson 1989; Orme 1996). Analogy with other parts of Britain and Ireland, later traditions, and the few early references we have in sources like the *First Life of St Samson* suggest many housed communities of monks or clerks. Where they can be located it seems that the most important early churches were normally sited in rich agricultural land and were surrounded by a dense scatter of farms and fields (Figure 11; Turner 2003).

Some of the important early churches may have provided links back to earlier landscapes by perpetuating the sites of ancient burial grounds. At Phillack and at Crantock (Cornwall) the medieval churches stood within extensive burial grounds that may have been continuously used since the later Iron Age (Olson 1982). Burial grounds provided places for meeting, for remembering and for dealing with the dead, and the founders of churches might have capitalised on these ready-made assembly points by explicitly linking burial practice and Christianity. Thomas' well-known model suggests that the normal sequence of church development was from unenclosed burial ground, to enclosed cemetery, to small church in its graveyard (Thomas 1971, 48–68). This may well have been common (Blair 2005), but the continuing lack of archaeological evidence means we must exercise caution before accepting it as universal (Petts 2002). Many burial grounds never acquired churches, including both examples from late Antiquity like Kenn (Devon) and others like Mawgan Porth (Cornwall), which was established only a century or so before the Norman Conquest (Weddell 2000; Bruce-Mitford 1997). There has been a tendency to try and push the foundation date of medieval churches in the South West

FIGURE 12
The cross-shaft fragments at Dolton (Devon).

back as far as possible, but there is currently little archaeological evidence to suggest origins for most of them before the seventh to ninth centuries (Turner 2006). In Cornwall, place-names containing the element **lann* are thought to represent churches with early medieval origins (the asterisk indicates a hypothetical early form of the word). The earliest record of a possible **lann* name in Cornwall is from the ninth century (Padel 1988, 108), and another ninth-century example comes from Brittany (Olson 1989, 23). Many place-names were used long before they were first recorded, and so many Cornish churches with **lann* names might well be earlier than this, but it is normally hard to date them more closely than the four or five hundred years after AD 500 (Padel 1985, 144). Circular or curvilinear churchyard boundaries have also been

identified as diagnostic of early sites on the grounds that these might represent the circuit of the earliest graveyard enclosure (Preston-Jones 1992). In particular, curvilinear churchyards with **lann* place-names and inscribed stones are thought to represent one of the earliest tiers of Christian sites. Of around 35 inscribed stones from Cornwall, 17 were first recorded at or close to churches or chapels, and of these 6 have **lann* place-names. We know from the *First Life of St Samson* that one of these (St Kew) was an important early site, and we suspect that others were too (e.g. Madron, Lanivet, Lewannick). However, there are few archaeologically dated churchyard enclosures in Devon, Cornwall or neighbouring regions like Wales, and more fieldwork needs to be undertaken before we can accept a curving enclosure boundary as evidence for an early foundation date (Pearce 2004, 148–67; Petts 2002).

By around AD 1050, however, the landscape of Devon and Cornwall was certainly dotted with numerous churches and chapels with a variety of different origins. Some were by now ancient but others were new; some were communities with extensive estates whereas others had no land or even burial grounds around them. Even the humblest of these sites were sometimes elaborated with monuments and might have had well-developed saints' cults. At Fenton Ia near Camborne (Cornwall), for example, excavations revealed a holy well chapel that may have antedated the Norman Conquest (Thomas 1967). An eleventh-century cross once stood nearby, and the chapel may have been the source of a carved late Saxon altar-slab (Okasha 1993). The little chapel of St Martin-in-Meneage, which did not even acquire burial rites until the fourteenth century, was perhaps home to as many as four different saints' cults in the course of the Middle Ages (Orme 2000, 184). It seems that the earliest church foundations acted as models for increasing numbers of minor churches throughout the period before the Norman Conquest. The differences between them have been obscured because the later sites gradually took on a range of similar functions to their forerunners, but they mostly operated on more local scales.

This understanding of the development of church sites is far from the old-fashioned image of remote and isolated 'Celtic' monks, but this only becomes a problem if we expect hermits and ascetics to be all we might find in the early Christian landscape. St Cuthbert's Northumbrian hermitage on Inner Farne was a different sort of place from the great monastery at Lindisfarne, but the two existed side-by-side. There might well have been a similar range of early sites in Devon and Cornwall, but if so we have yet to identify them securely. Olson has argued that the ninth-century *Life of St Paul Aurelian* might be referring to a Cornish hermitage when it mentions the *monasterium* of the saint's sister Sitofolla (Olson 1989, 21–3). St Samson's *First Life* describes how he lived for a period in a Cornish cave after killing the resident serpent (I.50; Flobert 1997). We do not know how long-lived such hermitages may have been, but some could have been elaborated with churches or other structures after they were first occupied. The two ruined churches at St Elidius' oratory (St Helen's, Scilly) may represent a site of this type, though it would be hard to argue that either dates to earlier than the eighth century (O'Neil 1964; Ratcliffe 1994, 23–49).

We know little of the pagan Romano-British religious sites of Devon and Cornwall. 'Fogous' – the narrow sinuous underground passages of west Cornwall – are a possible candidate, and to many people holy wells probably represent the quintessential 'Celtic' pagan survivals (Rattue 1995). The well-chapels at Constantine and St Levan are thought to be amongst the earliest standing Christian buildings in the peninsula, and it is not impossible that they were built to give new meanings to already ancient sacred places (Todd 1987). However, it has been hard to show continuity of practice at any such site, and holy wells might just as easily have gained their religious associations after the conversion to Christianity; they were after all a common and widely accepted part of medieval life all over Europe.

By the eleventh century, the landscape was sanctified by many different sorts of Christian holy places. We have seen how in the countryside the 'vocabulary' of religious places was established during the early Middle Ages. Though many sites were enlarged and embellished in the later Middle Ages, the essential categories remained largely stable: small monasteries, churches, chapels, burial grounds, holy wells, crosses. The remainder of this chapter concentrates

FIGURE 13
King Doniert's Stone and the Other Half Stone, St Cleer (Cornwall).
SAM TURNER

on one type of monument, crosses in stone, and looks into some of the ways they were used from the early Christian period to the later Middle Ages.

Crosses in the medieval countryside

The earliest monumental crosses in Devon and Cornwall are those cut onto inscribed stones. As discussed by Thomas, several of these are 'upright' *chi-rho* monograms with the cross arms formed by limbs of the *chi* and a looped-over head made from the top of the *rho* (Thomas 1994, 293–6). They proclaim the Christian identity of the communities whose memorial stones they adorn, in the same way as the simple equal-armed cross on a stone from Boslow, and the more intricate device on a monument from Madron in Cornwall (Okasha 1993). The role of stones such as these as boundary markers (mentioned above) foreshadows an important function of their successors, the sculpted stone crosses of the later Saxon period.

More than a century passed before large free-standing stone crosses began to appear in the South West. The earliest in the insular world are the great eighth-century examples from southern Ireland and Northumbria: Ahenny, Clonmacnoise, Bewcastle, and Ruthwell (Rynne 1998; O'Reilly 2003). The idea was taken up and developed in Devon and Cornwall in the late eighth or ninth century, and to this period we owe some of the region's most impressive monuments, like the cross-shaft fragment at Dolton (Devon, Figure 12) and King Doniert's Stone (Cornwall, Figure 13).

FIGURE 14
A medieval wayside
cross: Long Tom, St
Cleer (Cornwall).
SAM TURNER

Early crosses in Britain can often be linked to major ecclesiastical centres, and the same is true of the South West. Almost from the outset, though, it seems crosses fulfilled a variety of different roles. The first of these, and perhaps the most common, was the 'churchyard' cross. These were monuments set up within an ecclesiastical complex, often close to the church. They may have been used to define areas for different uses or to create boundaries between different social groups. In early medieval Ireland crosses were used to mark boundaries around the monastery (Bitel 1990, 64–6), and they could have been used in the same way in Devon and Cornwall. Unfortunately, it is virtually impossible to show that any churchyard crosses are in the same place now as they were a thousand years ago, and there is some record of movement in recent centuries for most. We can be sure, however, that monuments like the great ninth-century churchyard cross of St Neot or the slightly later crosses at St Buryan, Phillack, St Piran's, Padstow (Cornwall) or Colyton (Devon) would have played an important role in the lives of the communities around them.

In the wider medieval countryside, crosses had other roles, as waymarkers, boundary points and preaching crosses (Figure 14). Before going on to investigate some of these, we must also address an interesting difference between the two south-western counties. In Cornwall there are around 700 surviving medieval stone crosses – a huge number – and more are discovered every year (e.g. Turner 2004). By contrast, Devon has only about 300 monuments, despite being nearly twice the size of its western neighbour (source: Devon Sites & Monuments Record. For crosses, this is largely based on the work of E. N. Masson-Philips published between 1937 and 1987 in the *Transactions of the Devonshire Association,* e.g. Masson-Philips 1937; 1938). Although the monument at Dolton in Devon probably antedates the earliest Cornish examples, this difference in frequency does seem to have its roots in the early Middle Ages. There are over 50 crosses with distinctive pre-Norman decoration in Cornwall, whereas Devon has far fewer – perhaps just 10. It would be easy to see this difference in ethnic or religious terms, with the devout Celts of Cornwall setting up more crosses than the (rather less spiritual) English across the River Tamar. Easy perhaps, but surely wrong; the real reasons probably have much more to do with early medieval politics and the developing structure of territorial units. Once established, the different patterns of cross use seem to have lasted into the later medieval period.

Cornwall had only recently been incorporated into the kingdom of Wessex when most of the crosses were being set up. This political take-over probably involved the redistribution of estates from Cornish to English lords, and there may have been significant opportunities for enterprising thegns to acquire new lands. In Yorkshire, where similar processes were underway about the same time, certain types of stone monument are seen as expressions of the new elite's social aspirations (Carver 1998, 26). Some of the Cornish sculpture probably falls into this category, like the hog-back tombstones of Lanivet and St Tudy, and the Penzance market cross – recorded on Alfward's manor of Alverton in Domesday Book. In addition, new English royal manors were established at this time and new crosses were set up by their chapels, as at Roseworthy (Langdon 1896). Devon had been part of the kingdom of Wessex for much longer, and it seems likely that patterns of land-ownership here would have been more stable during the later Saxon period than in Cornwall.

There were particularly dense clusters of crosses in the landscape around some important Cornish collegiate churches such as St Neot and Bodmin. In marked contrast to most of late Saxon Wessex (including Devon), Cornwall still contained at the time of Domesday Book many small religious communities with substantial lands of their own. They may have had good reasons for marking out their territories: in the late Saxon landscape Christian monuments like crosses may have been used to articulate competing claims by new secular and old ecclesiastical powers over land and local authority.

Crosses were certainly sometimes used as boundary markers in early medieval Cornwall and Devon. We know of three separate examples from pre-Conquest charters, the official documents that were used to grant estates. The first is in a tenth-century description of the boundaries of an estate at Tywarnhayle (Cornwall; Hooke 1994; Sawyer 1968 (hereafter S) No. 684). The *cristelmael* ('Christ-image') mentioned by the charter is probably the surviving cross near St Piran's church, and the grant appears to represent encroachment onto an old ecclesiastical territory by secular powers (Olson 1989, 95). The Anglo-Saxon boundary clauses of the estates of Trevallack and Lesneage in the Lizard both use *crousgrua* as a boundary point (Cornish *crous* 'cross' + *gruah* 'hag, witch'; Hooke 1994; S755, S832). The cross, which is now lost, was located towards the edge of Crousa Common, about 2 km west of St Keverne churchtown. In Devon, the great surviving cross-shaft at Copplestone was first mentioned in a tenth-century charter boundary clause (Hooke 1994, 172; S795). It stood at the western limit of the territory associated with Crediton, which was the seat of a bishop in the tenth and eleventh centuries, and had first been granted for the construction of a monastery in the early eighth. In Cornwall there are other probably late Saxon crosses standing close to parish boundaries at Three Hole Cross (St Kew) and Carminow Cross (Bodmin; for a different view of these crosses see Blair 2005, 479–80).

Recent work by Ann Preston-Jones and Andrew Langdon on St Buryan in the far west of Cornwall has illuminated the ways crosses could be used in the later medieval period, after the Norman Conquest (Preston-Jones and Langdon 1997). The only late Saxon cross in the parish stands in the graveyard of St Buryan church, once a small monastery that had been refounded in the tenth century by the English king Athelstan (Hooke 1994, 22; S450) Virtually all the other 20 or so crosses stood alongside roads or paths. In the largely enclosed agricultural landscape of medieval Devon and Cornwall, this is no surprise: crosses in fields would only have been visible to those with access, and it seems logical that they would have been erected instead in places where they could be seen and venerated by the whole community. It is clear that the locations of many St Buryan crosses were significant for other reasons too. Some were by chapels or holy wells, and some marked the sites of fords; others stood near boundaries of different types. Up to seven of the crosses stand on land that was once heathland, and they may have had a dual function, being used to mark both paths across the rough ground and perhaps also a special medieval sanctuary zone associated with the church (Preston-Jones and Langdon 1997, 114–15). Three other churches in Cornwall possessed zones of privileged sanctuary in the later Middle Ages, and evidence of various sorts suggests they may all have been physically marked in some way. At Padstow, a fourteenth-century *Life* of St Petroc records that still-visible ditches had been dug to show the boundaries of the saint's land (Preston-Jones 1992, 120), and at Probus the 'Carvossa Cross' still marked the saint's liberty or sanctuary in 1301 (Preston-Jones and Langdon 1997). The final sanctuary was around the church of St Keverne, and during the later Middle Ages it probably encompassed the churchtown and the neighbouring holdings of Tregonning and Lanheverne (Henderson 1958, 256–6). If so, the Crousa Common cross named in the Anglo-Saxon charters may have stood on the heathland at its western boundary.

Wendy Davies has argued that from the beginning of the tenth century a special type of 'protected space' began to appear in the British Isles, normally associated with churches (Davies 1996). She suggests it was a '… response to increasing rather than decreasing ruler power …' and '… part of a general shift in attitudes to physical space …', when land became a commodity to be delineated and physically dominated (Davies 1996, 9–11). In several cases the zone of 'protected space' was marked by crosses, as at Ripon, Beverley and Hexham in northern England. In Ireland, Tomás Ó Carragáin has shown how the edges of the *termon* lands belonging to the monastery of *Inis Úasal* on the Iveragh peninsula were marked with boundary-crosses from as early as the eighth or ninth century (Ó Carragáin 2003, 137–41), and in Wales pre-Conquest monuments around Penmon and Dyserth could have marked ecclesiastical land and perhaps sanctuary (Edwards 1999, 14). Davies has suggested that the special powers of churches within their 'protected space'

may have developed as '… a defensive reaction against ruler aggression …' (Davies 1996, 11). The evidence suggests similar things were happening in Cornwall. The stimulus for this change probably resulted from the increasing power of the secular elite to grant land at the expense of long-established ecclesiastical communities.

Whilst we only have late and post-medieval records of 'protected space' in a few places, it seems likely that it would have been more widespread. Davies has argued that ecclesiastical communities used charters in the ninth and tenth centuries in a defensive way, to assert their rights over land that was increasingly under threat (Davies 1998). We can interpret the erection of prominent crosses on the borders of ecclesiastical land as another way churches tried to counter the power of the encroaching secular elite by marking out their territory.

Evidence from another area of Cornwall allows us to investigate in some detail the changing ways crosses were used. In the territory around St Neot there are the remains of at least seven monuments bearing decoration distinctive of the ninth to eleventh centuries. Three of these are at medieval parish churches (St Neot, Cardinham, and a cross head fragment at St Cleer). One was found reused in a post-medieval cottage at Bofindle, Warleggan (Langdon 1996), and the remaining three in open ground close to roads but some distance from any settlements. The King

Doniert Stone and the Other Half Stone were first recorded around 1600 standing in their present position (Okasha 1993, 213), and before its recent move during a road-building scheme the Fourhole Cross had stood on the boundary of St Neot parish since at least the eighteenth century (Figure 15; Langdon 1996).

The four monuments that are not at medieval churches stand in a rough ring around St Neot. All four stand astride important routeways, on or close to land that was formerly rough grazing ground (Turner 2003). One of their functions was certainly to act as waymarkers, like many of the later medieval crosses in the area. Bearing in mind the charter evidence discussed above, however, we might also suggest that they functioned as boundary markers for an early territory associated with St Neot's church. Fourhole Cross still stands on the parish boundary, and the Bofindle fragment and the King Doniert and

FIGURE 16
(opposite left)
The inscribed stone at
Cardinham (Okasha
1993, 88–90; Thomas
1994, 265).
SAM TURNER

FIGURE 17
(opposite right)
The Cardinham Cross
(Cornwall).
SAM TURNER

Other Half Stones were only 500 m or so beyond it. Analogy with St Buryan, St Keverne, and Probus suggests this territory could have been the core of the church's estate and a zone of protected space.

The fate of some of the decorated late Saxon crosses may illustrate ways that early arrangements were changed in the later medieval period. Rosemary Cramp has argued that early medieval sculpture seldom strays far from its original site, but it seems possible that reuse in the fabric of churches might be an exception, comparable perhaps to the reuse of Roman stones as building material (Cramp 1975; Eaton 2000). Such relocation could have taken place whilst local churches and their parishes were becoming firmly established in the centuries either side of the Norman Conquest. It is likely that there were symbolic as well as practical aspects to reusing earlier crosses in medieval churches, just as there was an ideological justification for the destruction of crosses in the post-medieval period (Moreland 1999). The practice was widespread throughout England (see e.g. Tweddle *et al.* 1995, *passim*). The pre-Conquest crosses at Cardinham, St Just-in-Penwith, Gulval, St Erth, Ludgvan and Sancreed (Cornwall), and at Colyton, Braunton and Sidford (Devon) were all found incorporated into the medieval fabric of parish churches; those at Quethiock, St Teath and Phillack (Cornwall) had been used in churchyard boundaries (Langdon 1896).

The parish of Cardinham near St Neot provides an interesting case-study. The date Cardinham church was founded is uncertain, but several early monuments were found built into its medieval fabric in the nineteenth century, including an inscribed stone and an intact late Saxon cross. A probably post-Conquest cross head was also discovered and stuck onto the top of the inscribed stone in 1896, creating the rather odd-looking monument visitors see today (Figures 16 and 17; Okasha 1993, 88). The original location of these monuments is not known. They could have stood next to an early church at Cardinham, but it is clear that in the later Middle Ages they were no longer valued as they had been before and so were built into the church. Crosses were, however, still being set up and used in the parish, including the four that marked the boundaries of the church's glebe. These were first recorded in an early seventeenth-century description of the glebe land, which was:

> … bounded on the east with lands in the tenement of George Rowe near adjoining to a crosse called Wydeyeat Cross, in the west with the lands of Cardinham adjoining to a crosse called Peaches Cross, in the north with the lands of the lords of the manner of Cardinham adjoining to a cross called Poundstock Cross. In the south with the lands of the same adjoining to a crosse called Averie's Cross. (Henderson *EC*, 75–83)

Two of these late medieval crosses survive at Wydeyeat Cross and Poundstock Cross (Figure 18; Langdon 1996, 26–7). It seems possible that the medieval priests of Cardinham were imitating the earlier practice of more powerful churches like St Neot, Crediton, St Keverne or their neighbour Bodmin when they used crosses to mark out their little territory, and it is possible

FIGURE 18
Wydeyeat Cross,
Cardinham (Cornwall).
SAM TURNER

that the incorporation of earlier monuments into the church fabric marked a stage in the reorientation of their medieval landscape. Other crosses used as boundary stones are mentioned in a perambulation of Cardinham parish of 1613 including 'Greedetch Cross', 'Prease Cross' and 'White Crosse', the last of which may be the monument known today as Peverall's Cross (Henderson *EC, 75–83;* Langdon 1996, 16). All these crosses had a number of functions: not only were they waymarkers and boundary stones, but they probably also acted as foci for local acts of religious piety and devotion. It seems that this range of functions was established during the early Middle Ages and endured until the Reformation.

Conclusion

Most of the medieval parish churches in Cornwall and Devon were founded during the early Middle Ages. It seems likely that there would have been a variety of ways that foundation could happen; churches began, for example, as burial grounds, as small hermitages, or as manorial chapels. Despite half a century of work, it remains unclear how many church-sites genuinely date to the fifth or sixth centuries rather than the later Saxon period. Some early Christian sites appear to have survived the end of late Antiquity in Devon and Cornwall during the seventh century (e.g. St Matheriana's, Tintagel), but based on our current understanding of the archaeological and historical evidence it seems likely that the majority of church sites first appeared between the seventh and tenth centuries, with some even later. The apparent similarities between so many medieval churches in the region may mask divergent origins, and archaeological investigation is probably the only way to solve these problems.

It seems increasingly likely that the essential foundations of the medieval landscape were laid in the period between the seventh and ninth centuries. The developing networks of Christian sites must have formed an essential part of daily life in the countryside. Like medieval crosses, the monasteries, hermitages, churches, chapels and holy wells of Devon and Cornwall could have had many different roles in this landscape. They were not just sites of religious veneration, but also meeting places and markers showing how people understood, divided and controlled the landscape. Until our own understanding of these matters is much more secure, we should make the most of every opportunity to carry out research into the region's medieval religious archaeology.

Acknowledgements

I am grateful to Jeremy Paterson for his advice on translating Gildas' *On the Destruction of Britain* 1.28, and to David Petts for his comments on an earlier version of this chapter.

References

Bidwell, P. (1979) *The Legionary Bath House and Basilica and Forum at Exeter*, Exeter City Council and University of Exeter, Exeter.

Blair, J. (2005) *The Church in Anglo-Saxon Society*, Oxford University Press, Oxford.

Bruce-Mitford, R. (1997) *Mawgan Porth: A Settlement of the Late Saxon Period on the North Cornish Coast*, English Heritage, London.

Carver, M. (1998) 'Conversion and politics on the eastern seaboard of Britain: some archaeological indicators' in *Conversion and Christianity in the North Sea World*, ed. B. Crawford, University of St Andrews, St Andrews, 11–40.

Carver, M. (2003) 'Northern Europeans negotiate their future' in *The Cross Goes North: Processes of Conversion in Northern Europe, AD 300–1300*, ed. M. Carver, York Medieval Press, York, 3–13.

Cramp, R. (1975) 'Anglo-Saxon sculpture of the Reform period' in *Tenth Century Studies,* ed. D. Parsons, Phillimore, London, 184–99.

Davies, W. (1996) "Protected space' in Britain and Ireland in the middle ages' in *Scotland in Dark Age Britain*, ed. B. Crawford, University of St Andrews, St Andrews, 1–19.

Davies, W. (1998) 'Charter-writing and its uses in early medieval Celtic societies' in *Literacy in Medieval Celtic Societies*, ed. H. Pryce, Cambridge University Press, Cambridge, 99–112.

Dodds, J. (1990) *Architecture and Ideology in Early Medieval Spain*, Pennsylvania State University Press, Pennsylvania.

Eaton, T. (2000) *Plundering the Past. Roman Stonework in Medieval Britain*, Tempus, Stroud.

Edwards, N. (1999) 'Viking-influenced sculpture in north Wales: its ornament and context', *Church Archaeology* **3**, 5–16.

Gerrard, J. and Collins, R. eds (2004) *Debating Late Antiquity in Britain AD 300–700*, BAR British Series 365, Oxford.

Farmer, D. ed. (1990) *Bede: Ecclesiastical History of the English People*, Penguin, Harmondsworth.

Flobert, P. (1997) *La Vie Ancienne de Saint Samson de Dol*, CNRS, Paris.

Handley, M. (1998) 'Early medieval inscriptions of western Britain: function and sociology' in *The Community, the Family and the Saint: Patterns of Power in Early Medieval Europe,* eds J. Hill and M. Swan, Brepols, Turnhout, 339–61.

Handley, M. (2001) 'The origins of Christian commemoration in late antique Britain', *Early Medieval Europe* **10(2)**, 177–99.

Handley, M. (2003) *Death, Society and Culture: Inscriptions and Epitaphs in Gaul and Spain, AD 30–750,* BAR International Series 1135, Oxford.

Harris, A. (2003) *Byzantium, Britain and the West,* Tempus, Stroud.

Henderson, C. n.d. *Materials for a Parochial History of East Cornwall,* unpublished manuscript (*c.*1924–1933), Royal Institution of Cornwall Courtney Library, Truro.

Henderson, C. (1958) 'The ecclesiastical history of the 109 parishes of west Cornwall', *Journal of the Royal Institution of Cornwall* n.s. **3.2**, 211–382.

Hooke, D. (1994) *Pre-Conquest Charter Bounds of Devon and Cornwall,* Boydell, Woodbridge.

Langdon, A. (1896) *Old Cornish Crosses,* Joseph Pollard, Truro.

Langdon, A. (1996) *Stone Crosses in East Cornwall,* Federation of Old Cornwall Societies, Truro.

Lapidge, M. and Herren, M. (1979) *Aldhelm: the Prose Works,* Brewer, Cambridge.

Masson-Philips, E. (1937) 'The ancient stone crosses of Devon, part 1', *Transactions of the Devonshire Association* **69**, 289–342.

Masson-Philips, E. (1938) 'The ancient stone crosses of Devon, part 2', *Transactions of the Devonshire Association* **70**, 299–340.

Moreland, J. (1999) 'The world(s) of the cross', *World Archaeology* **31(2)**, 194–213.

Ó Carragáin, T. (2003) 'A landscape converted: archaeology and early church organisation on Iveragh and Dingle' in *The Cross Goes North: Processes of Conversion in Northern Europe, AD 300–1300,* ed. M. Carver, Boydell, Woodbridge, 127–52.

Okasha, E. (1993) *Corpus of Early Christian Inscribed Stones of South-West Britain,* Leicester University Press, London.

Olson, L. (1989) *Early Monasteries in Cornwall,* Boydell, Woodbridge.

O'Neil, H. (1964) 'Excavation of a celtic hermitage on St Helen's, Isles of Scilly, 1956–58', *Archaeological Journal* **121**, 40–69.

O'Reilly, J. (2003) 'The art of authority' in *After Rome,* ed. T. Charles-Edwards, Oxford University Press, Oxford, 141–89.

Orme, N. (1996) *English Church Dedications,* Exeter University Press, Exeter.

Orme, N. (2000) *The Saints of Cornwall,* Oxford University Press, Oxford.

Padel, O. (1985) *Cornish Place-Name Elements,* English Place-Name Society vol. 56–7, Nottingham.

Padel, O. (1988) *Cornish Place-Names,* Alison Hodge, Penzance.

Pearce, S. (2004) *South-western Britain in the Early Middle Ages,* Continuum, London.

Petts, D. (2002) 'Cemeteries and boundaries in western Britain' in *Burial in Early Medieval England and Wales,* eds S. Lucy and A. Reynolds, Society for Medieval Archaeology, Leeds, 24–46.

Petts, D. (2004) 'Burial in western Britain, AD 400–800: late antique or early medieval?' in *Debating Late Antiquity in Britain, AD 300–700,* eds J. Gerrard and R. Collins, BAR British Series 365, Oxford, 77–87.

Preston-Jones, A. (1992) 'Decoding Cornish churchyards' in *The Early Church in Wales and the West,* eds N. Edwards and A. Lane, Oxbow Books, Oxford, 104–24.

Preston-Jones, A. and Langdon, A. (1997) 'St Buryan crosses', *Cornish Archaeology* **36**, 107–28.

Ralegh Radford, C. (1962) 'The Celtic monastery in Britain', *Archaeologia Cambrensis* **111**, 1–24.

Ratcliffe, J. (1994) *Fieldwork in Scilly, July 1993,* Cornwall Archaeological Unit, Truro.

Rose, P. and Preston-Jones, A. (1995) 'Changes in the Cornish countryside, AD 400–1100' in *Landscape and Settlement in Britain AD 400–1066,* eds D. Hooke and S. Burnell, University of Exeter Press, Exeter, 51–68.

Rynne, E. (1998) 'Ireland's earliest 'Celtic' high crosses: the Ossory and related crosses' in *Early Medieval Munster: Archaeology, History and Society*, eds M. Monk and J. Sheehan, Cork, Cork University Press, 125–37.

Sharpe, R. (1995) *Adomnán of Iona: Life of St Columba*, Penguin, Harmondsworth.

Stevens, W. (1999) 'Easter controversy' in *The Blackwell Encyclopaedia of Anglo-Saxon England*, eds M. Lapidge, J. Blair, S. Keynes and D. Scragg, Blackwell, Oxford, 155–7.

Thomas, C. (1967) 'Fenton Ia chapel, Troon', *Cornish Archaeology* 7, 78–9.

Thomas, C. (1971) *The Early Christian Archaeology of North Britain*, Oxford University Press, Oxford.

Thomas, C. (1981) *A Provisional List of Imported Pottery in Post-Roman Western Britain and Ireland*, Institute of Cornish Studies, Redruth.

Thomas, C. (1988) 'The context of Tintagel: a new model for the diffusion of post-Roman Mediterranean imports', *Cornish Archaeology* 27, 7–26.

Thomas, C. (1993) *Tintagel: Arthur and Archaeology*, Batsford/English Heritage, London.

Thomas, C. (1998) *Christian Celts: Messages and Images*, Tempus, Stroud.

Todd, M. (1987) *The South West to AD 1000*, Longman, London.

Turner, S. (2003) 'Making a Christian landscape: early medieval Cornwall' in *The Cross Goes North: Processes of Conversion in Northern Europe, AD 300–1300*, ed. M. Carver, Boydell and Brewer, Woodbridge, 171–94.

Turner, S. (2002–3) 'A medieval cross from Lidwell, Stoke Climsland', *Cornish Archaeology*, 41–42, 161–64.

Turner, S. (2006) *Making a Christian Landscape: The Countryside in Early Medieval Cornwall, Devon and Wessex*, University of Exeter Press, Exeter.

Turner, S. and Gerrard, J. (2004) 'Imported and local pottery from Mothecombe: some new finds amongst old material at Totnes Museum', *Devon Archaeological Society Proceedings* 62, 171–5.

Tweddle, D., Biddle M. and Kjølbye-Biddle, B. (1995) *Corpus of Anglo-Saxon Stone Sculpture, Vol 5: South-East England*, British Academy, London.

Weddell, P. (2000) 'The excavation of a post-Roman cemetery near Kenn', *Devon Archaeological Society Proceedings* 58, 93–126.

Winterbottom, M. (1978) *Gildas: the Ruin of Britain and Other Documents*, Phillimore, Chichester.

CHAPTER 4

Cornish Strip Fields

Peter Herring

This, the first of two connected chapters on fields in this volume, considers what strip fields and their enclosure reveal about medieval Cornwall; the second pursues a range of issues through presentation and discussion of the well-preserved field system at Brown Willy.

Cornwall's medieval landscape

The 1994 Historic Landscape Characterisation established that extant or former 'Anciently Enclosed Land' (AEL) covers 67 per cent of Cornwall (Figure 19). AEL is the agricultural heartland with farming settlements first documented before the seventeenth century (and mainly before the fourteenth century) and field patterns of either medieval or prehistoric origin, albeit often altered in the later medieval and post-medieval periods (Cornwall County Council 1996; Herring 1998). The beauty, interest and distinctiveness of Cornwall's landscape, away from coast, moor and mine, is largely dependent on the AEL. Its twisting lanes, tree-lined hedges and small fields with their variety of land uses create a fabric upon which the wayside crosses, medieval churchtowns and shrunken hamlets seem fixed in an apparently natural way, such is the coherence of the pattern they make (Figure 20).

The fields derived from prehistoric antecedents tend to be on and around the West Penwith, Lizard and Bodmin Moor uplands (Cornwall County Council 1996), leaving well over half of Cornwall with medieval-derived AEL. Even off the moors prehistoric settlements and field patterns tend to underlie the countryside (increasingly visible through aerial photography, geophysical survey and watching briefs during pipeline and road works). With the exception of irregular slips and plots at the margins of field systems – mainly hams, marshes, meadows and crofts – the bulk of the medieval pattern is clearly derived from former strip fields, still recognisable either as groups of enclosed strips or as furlongs, or 'cropping units', the enclosures that originally contained the strips.

Of the 67 per cent of Cornwall that was AEL at its greatest extent 250 or so years ago, 57.5 per cent still survives as working farmland with coherent and understandable patterns of boundaries and lanes. The remainder has mainly been lost to twentieth-century boundary removal, urbanisation, and parks

FIGURE 19
A simplified representation of the later medieval Cornish landscape as derived from the 1994 Historic Landscape Characterisation (for which see Cornwall County Council 1996). This shows the extents of Anciently Enclosed Land (where most rural settlements and field systems discussed in this paper were located), Rough Ground (largely common grazing), Recently Enclosed Land (which was probably also rough ground in the medieval period), and the steep-sided valleys that would have held most of Cornwall's woodland. If produced at a larger scale, medieval towns, roads and bridges, castles and estate centres, deer parks etc. could be added to generate a more complete image of later medieval Cornwall.

Cornish Strip Fields and gardens. Cornwall has, therefore, an essentially ancient landscape, especially as much of what lies beyond the AEL also has an historic character established by prehistoric and medieval land use. Rough ground – upland or coastal rough grassland and heaths, or towans (dunes) – still covers 5.7 per cent and another 5.7 per cent comprises steep valleys, much with anciently established woodland. Even the remaining 23 per cent, post-medieval or

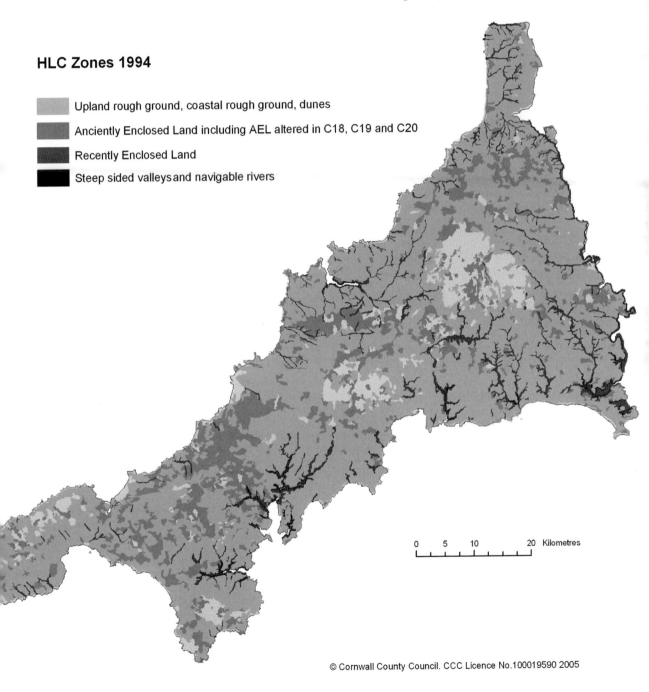

HLC Zones 1994

Upland rough ground, coastal rough ground, dunes

Anciently Enclosed Land including AEL altered in C18, C19 and C20

Recently Enclosed Land

Steep sided valleys and navigable rivers

0   5   10   20 Kilometres

© Cornwall County Council. CCC Licence No.100019590 2005

45

modern landscape elements, is coherent and understandable in terms of the medieval landscape. Formerly more extensive rough ground is visible in the 17.5 per cent now covered by straight-sided fields, taken in during the last few centuries. The remainder (just 5.5 per cent) comprises modern conifer plantations, reservoirs, or industrial, recreational and military land, all clearly superimposed on former land uses that can be established from earlier maps (Herring 1998, 40–1).

Field and boundary systems reflect society directly; each component had a reason, meaning or function, and each system an agricultural logic bound by economic, social, cultural, ritual and customary constraints. Cornwall's landscape is therefore a relatively easily read later medieval 'document' that reveals much about economy, society and culture. Palimpsests – later patterns of boundaries – confuse us no more when reading this 'document' than do the barriers we face when trying to understand other medieval written documents – partiality, omission, uneven coverage, unclear language and uncertain meaning. Cornish medieval written records do provide valuable material enriching interpretation of landscape evidence, but they tend to be less useful to rural historians than those of some other parts of Britain, due mainly to the nature of Cornish manors, the form of documentation they produced, and most significantly because most agricultural activity occurred in the largely undocumented hamlet. This chapter uses all the sources of landscape history to model change in medieval Cornwall.

FIGURE 20
A typical area of Anciently Enclosed Land in Lanreath parish; slightly sinuous hedges with mature woody vegetation, mainly following the lines of medieval strip field systems' cropping unit boundaries.
PETER HERRING

Individualism and communalism: twentieth-century research

Previous studies of medieval field systems reveal much about changing preoccupations in Cornish studies (Herring 1986, volume 1; summarised here). Work has often been frustrated by resistance to an acknowledgement that most of Cornwall contained at some stage in the medieval period small farming communities organised into hamlets whose fields were common, open and subdivided into strips. This resistance has usually centred on a romantic certainty that the Cornish 'Celtic' character has been built on individualism that saw farming households working their small plots of land separately.

Little room has been allowed for the possibility that medieval life was more complex than either simple communalism or simple individualism, but instead comprised a dynamic relationship at hamlet level between the two. The hamlet embodied the cooperation and sharing that enabled households of varying health, age and ability to survive, but also constrained the vigour of an ambitious individual or household; hamlets therefore contained a perpetual tension between communalism's conservatism and safety on the one hand and the risk-taking of more ambitious households on the other. Of course such was also the case up-country, beyond west Somerset, in the land of villages and much more extensive and closely regulated open fields, but it is in Cornwall (and also in Devon and Somerset) that the tensions between the cooperative group and its constituent individuals, and the changes they contribute to, can be most clearly seen. The relationship between household and hamlet is made visible archaeologically at Brown Willy and in most other Cornish hamlets by the placing away from the hamlet's 'communal' central townplace of the 'private' household elements (mowhays with ricks of deadstock, yards for livestock).

Late nineteenth- and early twentieth-century deference to cultural and environmental determinism stifled discussion of Cornish strip-field systems. Those around towns were ascribed 'alien', Saxon origins (Henderson 1935, 67); field systems, like settlements, were considered cultural, even racial attributes (see Gray 1915, 3–6, 71, 157). Being a 'Celtic' country, Cornwall was assumed to have always possessed the Celt's isolated farms, the *Einzelhöfe* (Meitzen 1895, cited in McCourt 1971, 126–7), and their associated enclosed field systems. Any strip fields that were recognised as such were seen as either foreign implants or late developments, confined to the English-derived towns and the margins such as cliff-tops and reclaimed land (Henderson 1935).

The shift from cultural to geographical determinism in the 1920s merely replaced questionable assumptions with more respectably logical and functional ones, leaving interpretations essentially unchanged. So Demangeon in 1928 (cited in Uhlig 1961, 287) explained the *Einzelhöfe* by arguing that Highland areas, where 'Celtic' patterns persisted, had pastoral economies that required individual farmers to live close to their fields. In a work that has influenced popular Cornish history ever since (e.g. Balchin 1983; Payton 1996,

Pounds was able to write, on the basis that his reading of Domesday Book suggested early medieval Cornwall was extensively pastoral, that

> Such conditions required that settlements should be widely spaced, and should each consist of at most a very small group of home- steads. This purely agricultural reasoning seems best to explain the dispersed settlement of Cornwall, as of other Celtic lands. Around each farmstead were its fields, small, roughly square patches, enclosed by walls, rudely built of the local material (Pounds 1945, 110).

Pounds and A. L. Rowse had, in fact, already documented several medieval strip-field systems around Cornish hamlets surviving into the sixteenth and seventeenth centuries (Pounds 1944, 116–20; Rowse 1941, 33–6).

Recognition in the 1940s and 1950s that medieval subdivided field systems were widespread in south-west England was accelerated by H. P. R. Finberg's work. After demonstrating that Braunton Great Field was indeed medieval, he presented documentary evidence for open fields throughout Devon and on modern maps found strip patterns, 'the fossilised remains of strip cultivation', in 18 out of a randomly sampled 24 Devon parishes (Finberg 1949, 182; 1952, 279).

A few years later Flatrès, comparing Cornish fields with those of Ireland, Wales and Man, used Victorian Tithe Maps and large-scale Ordnance Survey maps to show how widespread were enclosed *'champs laniérés'* (strip fields) (Flatrès 1957, figs 37 and 39). As most strip fields were associated with hamlets with Cornish *tre-* prefixes rather than villages with Saxon names, Flatrès proposed a native, pre-Saxon origin for the Cornish strips. In his scheme *'champs ouverts'* (open fields), predominant in the early medieval period, were spontaneously (*spontané*) enclosed in the thirteenth and fourteenth centuries, but as the Cornish strips were neither racially nor environmentally deter- mined, Flatrès suggested that 'il est donc nécessaire de chercher la raison de ces champs (laniérés) dans la domaine de la géographie humaine,' – 'it is therefore necessary to search for their explanation in human geography' (Flatrès 1957, 362–5).

Maurice Beresford (1964) used fourteenth-century Duchy of Cornwall records to confirm that many rural settlements were indeed hamlets, and William Ravenhill produced a map in a similar style to those of Flatrès showing fossilised strips scattered throughout Devon and Cornwall (Shorter *et al.* 1969, fig. 26; Figure 21). Neither worker produced an interpretative model, but Charles Thomas suggested that west Cornish strip fields were more closely related to Welsh share-lands than to English open fields (Fowler and Thomas 1962, 78).

Completion of Harold Fox's PhD thesis on the field systems of Devon and Cornwall (1971), and the publication of John Hatcher's on the economy and society of the later medieval Duchy of Cornwall (1970a), provided two substantial academic documentary studies, but both works paid little regard to non-documentary sources of information. Archaeology was used infrequently,

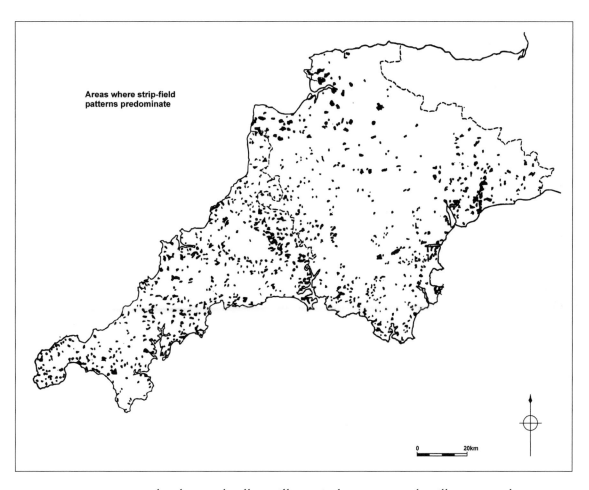

Areas where strip-field
patterns predominate

0   20km

and only anecdotally or illustratively, an approach still commonplace among
historians at that time. Both also viewed their subjects from a Midlands
England perspective.

Fox applied to Devon and Cornwall concepts derived from Midlands two-
and three-field systems. Dealing with the debate over pressure on pasture
as a stimulus to reorganisation of 'immature' field systems, he deemed the
south-western systems 'imperfectly developed' (Fox 1971, 39–51). Fox did,
however, review a wider range of documentation to confirm that subdivided
or strip fields were widespread in medieval Cornwall and Devon. He also
examined the process and chronology of early enclosure of these subdivided
fields (Fox 1971, 52–133; 1975). Hatcher compared the administration and
socio-economic structure of the Duchy estates with the 'classic' Midlands
manors and was impressed by the Duchy's 'non-manoralism'; but he did not
explain the local form (Hatcher 1970a; 1970b). In his review of the medieval
Cornish rural economy, Hatcher disappointingly followed the earliest workers:
cultural and geographical determinism produced isolated farms within several
enclosures (Hatcher 1970a, 17), and no open fields (Hatcher 1970b, 1).

Nevertheless, in the late 1970s, when the research underpinning this chapter was commenced, it was more generally accepted that most early-fourteenth-century Cornish farmers lived in small hamlets rather than isolated farms. Many hamlets had subdivided open-field systems arranged around them, whose origins 'must be sought before the mid-thirteenth century' (Fox 1971, 62). It was appreciated that most subdivided fields in Cornwall (and Devon) were enclosed considerably earlier than in most of England, mainly in the thirteenth to fifteenth centuries, although enclosure chronologies and reasons for it varied across the South West. Compared with the Midlands' carefully organised subdivided fields, the south-western ones were relatively easy to enclose. Lacking strict grazing regulations and having long ley periods within convertible husbandry regimes enabled households to more easily arrange to consolidate and enclose their holdings (Fox 1971; 1975).

Thirty years after Norman Pounds had summarised pre-war ideas, the orthodoxy had completely changed. Instead of solitary, cattle-owning Celts, the medieval Cornish were seen as sociable, living in nucleations, with their arable lands intermixed in subdivided fields and their cattle and sheep grazing either in those open fields not under hay and crops or with their co-tenants' animals on the commons. Successively more detailed investigations and observations had produced a more accurate representation of medieval rural Cornwall.

A disappointing feature of most post-war studies of Cornish field systems, however, is that they identified, described, and interpreted forms only; few used this material to discuss rural life in medieval Cornwall more generally. As a result the work remained marginal, and vulnerable to being overlooked by those developing different agendas.

The postgraduate thesis upon which this chapter is based (Herring 1986) used analytical landscape history to model medieval Cornish farming communities. It included detailed survey and analysis of one of Britain's best preserved medieval farming landscapes, Brown Willy (see Chapter 5); at the same time other archaeological surveys were also recording surviving or relict strip fields elsewhere on Bodmin Moor and in other marginal landscapes, as at Treskilling, Luxulyan (e.g. Johnson and Rose 1994; Preston-Jones and Rose 1986, fig. 8). This work has subsequently been extended to record outfield strips in West Penwith, on Kit Hill and at Godolphin, and strip lynchets on the north Cornish coast (Cornwall and Scilly Historic Environment Record for West Penwith surveys; Herring and Thomas 1988; Herring 1997; Taylor 2002; Dudley 2003).

Meanwhile Andrew Fleming built on the work of Jones (1973) to model the household, neighbourhood group and community as universal lower tiers of pre-industrial rural social organisation and in doing so noted that 'the single peasant farm of recent European history is of course the product of particular historical circumstance' (Fleming 1984, 11), such as that outlined below for later medieval Cornwall. More recently Harold Fox and Oliver Padel have reconsidered the detail of later medieval land tenure and the enclosure of Cornish strip field systems, mainly through analysis of the Arundell archives. They too regard the hamlet as 'a settlement type of ancient origins' (Fox and

Padel 2000, xciii), an observation that can be confirmed in the archaeological record of prehistoric and early medieval Cornwall, where tight or loose groupings of households are common, but where there is still (bearing in mind the difficulty in confirming that single dwellings never had near neighbours) no definitively solitary rural settlement site, the eastern Romano-British courtyard house site at Bosigran, Zennor, being perhaps the only possible candidate (Herring 1987; forthcoming).

In the 1990s the medieval period was drawn into the 'new' Cornish Studies, an approach to culture that privileges views of Cornwall's past that emphasise feelings of Cornish identity, often recognised through difference from and even resistance to their nearest neighbours, the English. Unfortunately this has led some strands of Cornish medieval studies back down the old cultural determinism cul-de-sac.

The more recent work on hamlets and fields has been largely overlooked and we can once again read that 'Celtic' Cornwall had few strip fields and that these were alien imports (e.g. Payton 1996, 95–6; 2004). Hatcher's discussion of the non-manorialism of the medieval Duchy estates is used to provide academic support to a neo-Celtic aversion to strip fields as the work of the English, an attitude derived ultimately from earlier twentieth-century workers. Communalism, cooperation and strip fields are kept out of presentations of Cornish culture that emphasise the individual. Consequently medieval Cornwall is filled again with 'a class of independent and potentially mobile peasant ... a precursor of the independently-minded small tenant farmer which came to characterise Cornwall in later centuries, and indeed which is still much in evidence today' (Payton 1992, 49–50).

More interesting would be recognition by the new generation of historical synthesists that Cornwall did indeed have its own forms of nucleations, estates and strip-field systems. It is true that the evolution and form of all three seem to have been shared by much of Devon and west Somerset, but it is equally true that these are all very different from their English versions. In the South West there were generally nucleated hamlets rather than villages. Estates were markedly different from textbook Midland English manors with their labour services and closely maintained customs, though they still had a significant influence on many aspects of rural life. Finally, south-western strip-field systems were small-scale and supported convertible husbandry rather than the classic English two- or three-field rotations, although they were still based on communalism, allotment and cooperation. To pursue these similarities would do little violence to a need to maintain the continuity of Cornwall's difference from large parts of England, but it would enrich our understanding and, of course, would fit with the landscape, archaeological and historical evidence. It would also reclaim for the modern Cornish the cooperative roots of their numerous sociable and communal ways of living and the institutions that support them, and would help reduce the influence of the essentially romantically constructed individualistic Celt.

Tenurial status of farming communities

We do not have a particularly clear view of Cornish peasants earlier than the patchy documentation of the thirteenth and fourteenth centuries. The Brown Willy case study presented below interprets a change from carefully measured strips in the earliest (possibly pre-Norman) core part of the field system to more irregular strips beyond as reflecting a change from allotment to shareholding, and so from imposition of land division on the hamlet by the lord or their steward to organisation of land by members of the hamlet. Other examples of measured strips and of very regular-looking strip patterns scattered throughout Cornwall indicate that lordly imposition of allotment on bond tenants was possibly once widespread, but the existence of at least as many patterns which appear to be fundamentally irregular, like the system at Brown Willy's neighbour, Garrow, also shows that shareholding between households in a relatively autonomous hamlet was also common. An important recent review of later medieval Cornish land organisation indicates that shareholding was the norm in Cornwall's surviving hamlets by the end of the later medieval period (the fourteenth to sixteenth centuries) (Fox and Padel 2000, lxxxiii–xciii).

The Cornish manor, the countryside's principal administrative entity, was, as Hatcher had noted, different from the typical English one. Although the documentary evidence from many Cornish estates is limited, it seems that labour services were less important than in Midlands England, money payments probably more so, and most Cornish estates were not single units but instead broken into several parts.

The 1086 Domesday survey asked only how many slaves (*servi*), villagers (*villani*) and smallholders/cottagers (*bordarii/cotarii*) each manor contained. Blisland, on the west side of Bodmin Moor, had 12 slaves, 40 villagers and 20 smallholders (Thorn and Thorn 1979, 1.6). Some or all of the slaves worked on the lord's demesne (Finberg 1969) while the villagers and smallholders, sixty in all, were perhaps precursors of the free and conventionary tenants that dominate later medieval Cornish records.

Free tenants had the higher status, inherited tenancies by right (having paid homage and relief to the lord), and could quit them too. Males inherited alone, through primogeniture, but females inherited jointly, hence the tendency for subdivision of holdings and the movement of them between families on the marriage of these daughters (Fox and Padel 2000, lvi). Free tenants' rents were normally fixed (and so tended to become less valuable to the lord through time), and the land they rented was recorded in the fiscal terms of Cornish acres and their quarters, or ferlings, rather than as measured units (Fox and Padel 2000, liv). This last feature suggests that the lands of free tenements in hamlets were shared rather than allotted.

Conventionary tenants on the other hand, were, from the lord's point of view, 'the real "meat" of the manor' (Fox and Padel 2000, lvi) as their rents (usually paid on the four quarter days) could be increased when tenants changed and they were obliged to perform more duties (often commuted to further money payments). They also paid an entry fine on taking up the tenement, their family paid a heriot (usually the best beast or monetary equivalent) on the tenant's death and a farleu if the tenancy had to be abandoned before due time. They were obliged to attend the manorial court and grind their corn at the lord's mill. Conventionary tenants were named from the *conventio*, or 'agreement', by which they held their land, which on Earldom and then, after 1337, Duchy of Cornwall manors was made anew every seven years as tenants bid for properties, 'in as near a free market in land as existed on such a large scale anywhere in England at this time, with assessions resembling auctions' (Hatcher 1970a, 56). Such assessions were not universal in Cornwall; they do not seem to have occurred on the Arundell manors (Fox and Padel 2000, lviii), but there are fifteenth-century references to ten- and twenty-year assessions on the lands of Launceston Priory (Hull 1987, xxxix–xl) and an early-seventeenth-century custumal of Blisland manor stated that customary tenants 'had a license in court to let for 7 years', but held their tenements by customary descent (Maclean 1873, 88). 'The bondman who can persuade his lord to grant him a lease is transformed at once … into a conventionary tenant, holding by deed; and as the prior of Otterton [Devon] noted in 1260, he is apt thenceforth to consider himself a free man' (Finberg 1969, 251).

Conventionary holdings on Duchy estates were measured in customary 'English acres' (i.e. measured with the 18-foot Cornish rod – see Chapter 5) and their acreages at named places were often either identical or proportional because they were allocated on the basis of shareholding (see Table 2 and Fox and Padel 2000). As individual conventionary tenants had no security of tenure, messuages (house, outbuildings and yard) were let with the land; hence their appearance in the Caption of Seisin of 1337. Of the 741 messuages mentioned in 1337, 674 (91 per cent) were rented by conventionary tenants, seven by free tenants (5 in one manor, Calstock) and 60 by villeins (*nativi de stipite*). These villeins were, as elsewhere in England, true bondspeople tied to their holdings (Hatcher 1970b, 60–1). The Duchy by the fourteenth century, was allowing villein holdings to lapse; whenever one came in hand it was transferred to the pool of conventionary holdings where competition forced rents up (Hatcher 1970a, 61–2), hence the intermixing of conventionary and villein holdings where acreages of villein and conventionary holdings were usually identical (see Table 1).

Conventionary tenure was common in later medieval Cornwall and parts of Devon (Ugawa 1962, 634; Carew 2004, 38v; Hatcher 1970b, 2) although conditions of tenure often varied from those in Duchy manors. That these other conventionaries were again lease-holding derivatives of villeins is suggested at Blisland, where, in 1420, the term conventionary lapsed back to villein (*nativi*) (Maclean 1873, 87), and confirmed at Tavistock Abbey (Finberg 1969, 251).

As noted above, by the fourteenth century Cornish tenements were organised on the basis of shareholdings within individual hamlets and what might best be called their townlands, an Irish term that captures the essence of

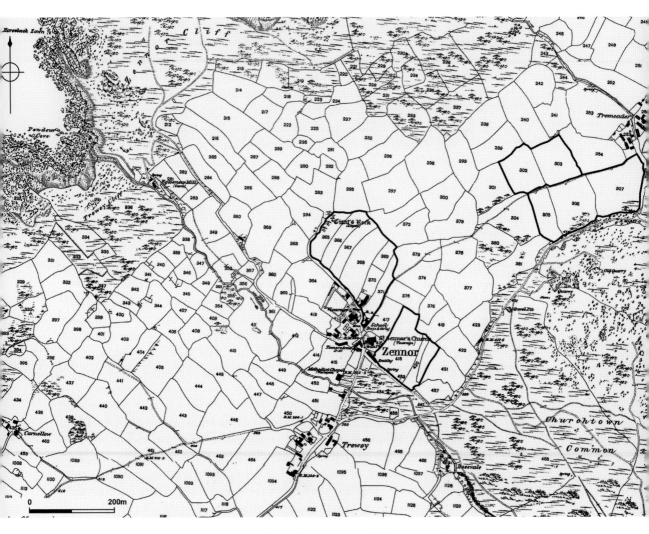

FIGURE 22
Zennor churchtown,
otherwise known as
Treveglos, with two
blocks of medieval
strips superimposed
on prehistoric fields
picked out by bolder
outlines. Fieldwork
confirmed that
those fields similarly
highlighted further
east at Tremeader were
also reorganised into
strips. (Based on 1st
edition OS 25-inch
map of 1876.)

what a Cornish *tre* 'estate, farmstead' (Padel 1985) probably originally represented, a block of varied farmland that supported a settlement (see Evans 1957, 28). The lord expected a hamlet with townland to yield a total rent and this was then perceived as a 'common pool to which tenants contributed differing amounts … according to their number and capacity to pay' (Fox and Padel 2000, lxxxvii). Shares of rent were worked out according to divisions of total land, hence the matching of proportions of land tenants held with rents they paid, and hence also the maintenance of strip-field systems. Shareholding arrangements would vary as hamlets grew and shrank (as seen on the ground at Brown Willy and in the records of Earldom, Duchy, and Arundell estates), but they were always easy to establish on the ground if landholdings could be worked out at hamlet level by allocation of the field system's numerous small and measurable strips (Fox and Padel 2000, lxxxviii–lxxxix).

Evidence of shareholding of land is remarkably common in later medieval and post-medieval records in Cornwall. Fox and Padel (2000, xc) note how

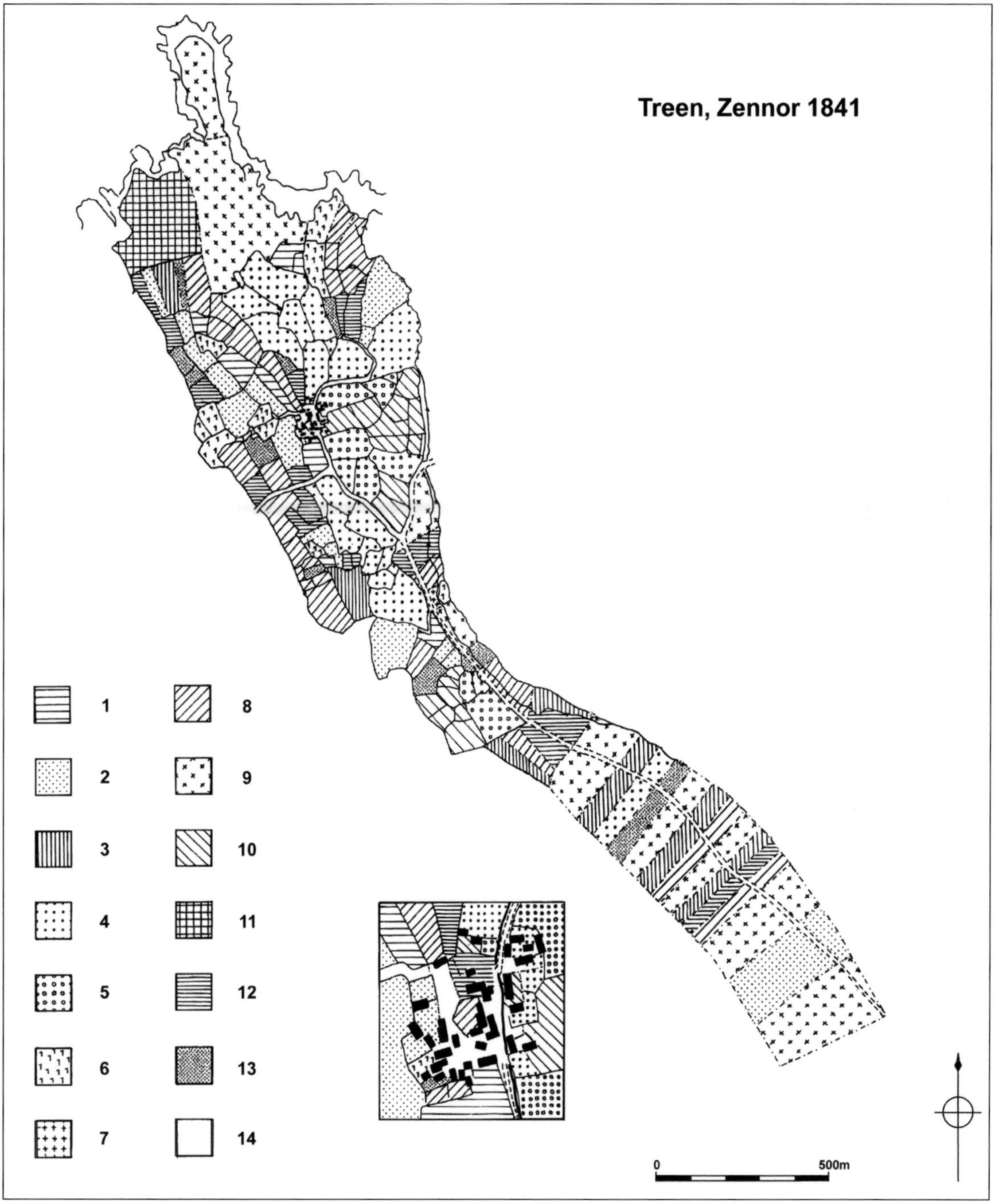

FIGURE 23
Extract from the 1841 Tithe Apportionment Map for Zennor parish showing the ribbon shaped townland of Treen. The coastal promontory of Gurnard's Head (used for cliff grazing) is north of the hamlet set on the coastal plateau. This lies below the southern downlands that were subdivided by low banks into strips. The fourteen tones represent different occupiers whose holdings were intermixed in a typically medieval way, even in the plateau fields that were established in later prehistory. See Table 2 for the nine shareholdings at Treen sixty years earlier.

holdings in sixteenth- and seventeenth-century leases were often described as being 'in the vill and fields of' a named place. There are even more explicitly descriptive examples, such as the 1610 lease by Richard Gedye of 'the syxth parte in six partes devyded or to be devyded of and in one great close of land called Abbotts Hender otherwise Hender Parke in the mannor of Treglaston' (RIC, PE/38/A).

Fox and Padel (2000, lxxxix–lc) also draw attention to shareholding (in fifths) at Zennor churchtown in the 1616 Glebe Terrier. Recent archaeological survey confirms that two small groups of strips were indeed laid out here, overlying the lynchets of prehistoric brick-shaped fields (Herring 1987; Figure 22). In fact most of Zennor's prehistoric field systems are partially overlain by medieval strip fields, usually set close to the hamlets, but the extent of intermixing visible in the 1840 Tithe Apportionment shows that the prehistoric fields were also reused in shareholding schemes, echoing their possible original design from nearly two thousand years before the later medieval period (see below). Further 'outfield' strips were also often established on open moorland above the main field systems (e.g. Bosigran, Treen (Figure 23), Boswednack and Kerrow). There are references to shareholding in postmedieval leases for Zennor tenements, for example the 1708 lease to David Eddy of 1/8 and 1/32 of Bosigran, the origin of the 1/32 being a quarter of a tenement which was itself half of the quarter share held in 1627 by James Udye [Eddy] (CRO, X110/13/1). We also have detailed records of late-eighteenth-century shareholding for the whole parish in the form of Rev William Borlase's remarkable 'Tithe Book' (CRO, X110/23). Shareholdings are set out most clearly for the year 1781 (tabulated below). The amounts of annual tithe payments were generally tied to the shareholdings. One surprising factor is the clustering of surnames in particular hamlets (especially Treen, Bosigran, Boswednack and Trevail), as if shareholding was associated with a form of partible inheritance.

Table 1 *Sizes of holdings on tenements in the manor of Helstone-in-Trigg in 1337 (data extracted from Hull 1971)*

	Free Tenants (Cornish acres)	Conventionaries (Customary acres)	Villeins (Customary acres)
Treclago	3		
Trethin	1		
Windsor	1		
Longstone	1		
Trenuth	1, 1, 1		
Penpethy	½, ½		
Bodulgate	2, ½, ½		
Treueou	1, 1		
Trevenning	3		
Trecarne	1		
Treworra	2		
Fenteroon	1		

	Free Tenants (Cornish acres)	Conventionaries (Customary acres)	Villeins (Customary acres)
Rostarlock	1		
Hendrawalls	1		
Penhale	½		
Camelford	1		
Tregarth	1		
Trevarledge	2		
Michaelstow	1	18	20
Tregreenwell	½	12, 12	
Treynchout	1½	19, 19	
Pencarrow	2½	13, 16	
Fentonadle	½, ½	8, 8, 9, 15	15
Treveighan		17, 20, 20, 20, 20, 20, 20	20
Trewen		9½, 9½, 19, 19, 19	
Tregawne		16, 16	
Helstone		7½, 8½, 10, 10, 10, 10, 10, 15	20
Kenningstock		15, 15	
Tremagnena		20, 20	20
Trevillick		18, 18	
Trefrew		33	
Trevia		14, 14½, 14½, 14½, 15, 15,	
Crowdy		20	
Fenterwanson		11, 18, 20, 20	
Treforda		11, 18	
Trestithen		19, 19, 20	
Tregoodwell		9, 9, 9, 9, 18, 18, 18, 18	
Trewalder		21, 22, 22, 22	22
Castle Goff		32	
Tredarrup		8, 8½, 17	

Table 2 *Shareholding arrangements in Zennor in 1781 (second and third columns derived from CRO, X110/23)*

Hamlet	Shares	Surnames	Notes
Treen	1/4, 1/8, 1/8, 1/8, 1/8, 1/12, 1/16, 1/16, 1/24	Thomas (x4), Perry (x2) Christopher, Stevens, Eddy	Outfield strips and strips near hamlet. (See Figure 23 for the 1841 field system.)
Bosigran	1/2 (divided into four), 1/4, 1/6, 1/12	Eddy (x6), Stevens	Outfield strips and strips near hamlet. Eddy family recorded at Bosigran since at least 1627. (RIC, HHJ/6/23)
Boswednack	1/4, 1/8, 1/8, 1/8, 1/8, 1/8, 1/8, 1/8	Thomas (x3), Berryman, Davy, Stevens	Outfield strips and strips near hamlet.
Gear	1/2, 1/2	Osborn, Hollow	
Carne	1/4, 1/4, 1/5, 1/5 and 1/10	Berryman, Michell, Philips, Osborn*	
Churchtown (Treveglos)	1/5, 1/5, 1/5, 1/5, 1/10, 1/10	Stevens (x2), Berryman, Donithorn, Richards, Philips	Vicar had another 1/5 for house and glebe. Strips near hamlet.

Hamlet	Shares	Surnames	Notes
Tremedda	1/4 and 1/24, 1/8, 1/6, 1/6, 1/6, 1/6, 1/12	Michell (x2), Berryman, Quick	One Michell and Quick held sixths from two landlords. Strips near hamlet.
Tregerthen	1/3 and 1/9, 2/9, 1/6, 1/6	Michell (x2), Stevens, Richards	Strips near hamlet.
Trendrine	1/2, 1/4, 1/4	Osborn, Hollow, Quick, Baragwanath	Osborn and Hollow shared the half.
Wicca	1/2, 1/2	Quick, Osborn	
Porthmeor	1/3, 2/9, 1/12	Berryman, Eddy, Murrish, Phillips	Not all shares seem to be recorded.
Boscubben	1	Richards	A single holding.
Trevail	Not stated	Stevens (x4), Curnow (x2), Osborn, Sweet	Annual payments indicate that shareholding was in place, probably based on fifths.

Early enclosure of strip fields on Brown Willy and in Cornwall

Most enclosure of Cornish strip fields took place so many hundreds of years earlier than in Midlands England that relatively few open fields survived by the late sixteenth century. Harold Fox has outlined some of the enclosure process and its chronology and has used documentary sources to describe how the consequent field systems of 'closes' were used (Fox 1971; Fox and Padel 2000, lxviii–lxxvii). The following section considers how Brown Willy's hamlet and strip-field system were transformed by the later thirteenth century into three farms each with enclosed fields, and discusses how typical the processes visible there seem to have been in Cornwall.

Its famously diversified economy (tinning, fishing, shipping, shipbuilding, quarrying and textile industries) provided medieval Cornwall's agriculture with extensive markets (Hatcher 1969, 209). Early-fourteenth-century expansion of Cornish tinning masks the still earlier importance of tin stream-works in Fawymore (the stannary district roughly coterminous with Bodmin Moor), then already in decline, having peaked in the previous two centuries (Hatcher 1973, 20–1; Gerrard 1986). That the twelfth and thirteenth centuries apparently coincide with an expansion of Brown Willy's settlement and field system is probably significant; if farmers there were not part-time tinners themselves, they were almost certainly supplying the local tinning industry's market for foodstuffs.

By the mid or later thirteenth century several conditions that would increase the likelihood of Brown Willy's communal system breaking down were in place. There was tension in communal systems between households, the basic economic units, and the cooperative unit, the hamlet. Moreover, the replacement of the assessed landholding system with a shareholding system at Brown Willy before 1275, probably accompanying a change from bond to free tenure, led to a relaxation of organisational dependence on the manor, and a consequent increase in autonomy of the hamlet and its component households.

Practical agricultural decisions would probably then have been made at hamlet meetings, Cornish manors no longer concerning themselves with such matters. Finally, Fawymore's tinning industry provided a local market for agricultural produce and thus an opportunity for the basic economic units, the households, to improve economic security and status, and amass sufficient capital to effect real change in their situation (see Turner 1984).

These conditions probably played a part in the disintegration of Brown Willy's hamlet before 1275. External causes usually called on to explain settlement abandonment in the next century, climatic deterioration and pestilence (Kershaw 1973; Postan 1975), would not apply.

Brown Willy's fully developed strip-field system had probably also become unwieldy; outfields had taken arable to over one kilometre from the hamlet (see Figure 35). Reorganisation to create several farmsteads would improve the field system's productivity (and increase tenants' income) by drawing more of the arable into relatively intensive cultivation (see also Dodgshon 1980, 130; Turner 1984, 40–1). It seems likely that a shared appreciation of all this eventually brought the Brown Willy households together to reallocate the land into consolidated blocks according to each household's share, and then led to the creation of new farmsteads. As loss of communal rights (most notably common grazing of the fields) is a consequence of enclosure, the agreement of the whole settlement to the reorganisation would have been a necessity (Dahlmann 1980, 147).

The location of the new settlements of Slades and Higher Brown Willy within the pre-existing field system and not at its periphery, as in assarting settlements (e.g. Taylor 1984, 181), is significant. The only alternative mechanism to a reorganisation such as that suggested above that could have produced such a settlement pattern – the placing of three new farmsteads on an abandoned hillside – is shown to be unlikely by the early reference to Slades.

There is ample place-name evidence for other splitting of townlands on or around Bodmin Moor (and indeed throughout Cornwall) by the thirteenth and early fourteenth centuries (i.e. before plague and climatic deterioration). By 1231 Gunan, in Altarnun, had split into Overgunan and Nithergunan (Gover 1948, 48); Muchelworthe (i.e. Great Worth), in St Neot, was distinguished by 1241 (Gover 1948, 292); Little Lanke, St Breward, by 1278 (Gover 1948, 105); South and West Carne, and West Hendra, Altarnun by 1302 (Gover 1948, 44–5); and West Rose, St Breward, by 1339 (Gover 1948, 292). That these splittings resulted from processes similar to those modelled for Brown Willy can only be suggested, and without further research it is unclear whether such splittings were accompanied by enclosure of the former open field systems still visible in each case as either fossilised strips or cropping units.

Consolidation by landholders of groups of strips by exchanges and their enclosure into separate fields which were then withdrawn from common grazing regimes has been identified in later medieval records (Finberg 1952, 277; Flatrès 1957, 373; Fox 1971, 53–5). In 1295–96, for example, lands were being exchanged, under the lord's license, in the Duchy manor of

Helstone-in-Trigg (Fox 1971, 54). That subdivided fields were reorganised to become enclosed field systems in medieval Cornwall, rather than better-organised subdivided field systems (see Dodgshon 1980, 108–32), in medieval Cornwall is probably partly also a function of the size of the original hamlets. Small groups of households would be more likely to come to radical agreements than the larger group in villages, where the inherent conservatism of the open field inhibited change (as set out in Dahlmann 1980).

Many Cornish subdivided field systems were only partially reorganised during enclosure, so that small bundles of strips or even individual strips were enclosed. Most have now been finally consolidated into individual farms, but in the 1840s, when the Tithe Maps were produced, many were still associated with nucleated hamlets, and the holdings of individual tenant farmers were still intermixed (Figures 27, 28 and 29). These are the fossilised strips mapped

FIGURE 24

Metherell in Calstock manor and parish as mapped in the 1880s (1st edition OS 25-inch map). Primary lines and lanes allow us to identify the fifteen or more cropping units whose strips were still clearly visible after their partial consolidation and enclosure. This was one of the largest hamlets in Calstock (fifteen holdings recorded in 1337) and it may have been more difficult for the landholders to come to arrangements to enclose more rationally than in smaller hamlets, such as Marsland and Cory (Figure 32). Note the numerous reversed-J shaped strips.

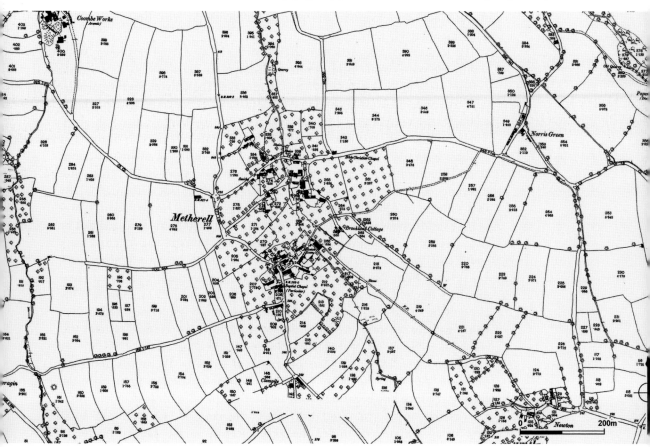

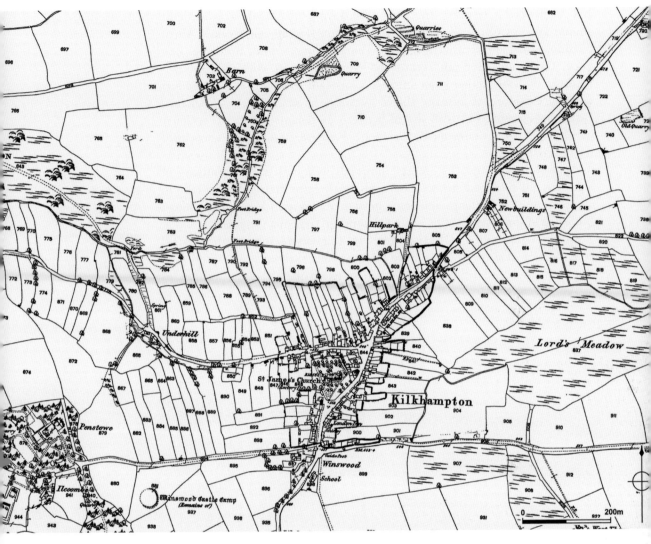

FIGURE 25

Kilkhampton, an early fourteenth-century town surrounded by a well-defined enclosed strip field system and with cropping-unit fields (probably formerly subdivided into strips, some with the same reversed-J curve as many of the strips) to the north and south. As at Metherell (Figure 24), the large number of tenants probably made a more rational enclosure of the core strips more problematic. Some strips appear to have been reused as burgage plots. (1st edition OS 25-inch map, c. 1880.)

by Flatrès and Ravenhill and tend to be associated with larger hamlets where agreements to entirely reorganise the fields may have been harder to achieve.

For example, the most clearly defined fossilised strips in Helstone-in-Trigg in 1881 (OS 1:2500) were at those settlements with the largest groups of holdings recorded in the 1337 Caption of Seisin: Trevia (seven holdings), Treveighan and Tregoodwell (both eight) and Helstone (nine). Likewise, in Calstock manor, the four most clearly defined strip patterns are at Metherell (Figure 24; fifteen holdings in 1337), Harrowbarrow (nine), Latchley (eight) and Chilsworthy (seven). The very well-defined fossilised strip patterns around some of Cornwall's towns (Kilkhampton (Figure 25), Week St Mary, Helston, Marazion, Redruth, Tregony, Penryn, Grampound, Boscastle, East Looe, Camelford, Bodmin, Truro and Mitchell), most with the reversed-J curves of fields rather than burgage plots, are probably also a product of early enclosure of systems shared between larger numbers of tenants. Forrabury's stitches were still shared between 21 tenants in 1842 (Forrabury parish Tithe Apportionment; Dudley 2003, Figure 8) and remain unenclosed today (Figure 26).

Pendrift in Blisland (Figure 27) illustrates well both the intermixing of holdings and fossilised strips. These had clearly been arranged originally in cropping units or furlongs and some possess the reversed-J curves of plough (rather than spade) cultivation. At neighbouring Tregenna (Figure 27), and at Bowithick (Altarnun) and Treclago (Advent) (Figures 28 and 29), the original consolidation of strips had continued further before their enclosure, producing larger, block-shaped fields that nevertheless retain parallel sides and are, as at Pendrift, clearly arranged into cropping units. At Tregenna, Treclago and

Medieval Devon and Cornwall

FIGURE 26
The surviving unenclosed strip field system on Forrabury Common, from the north from Willapark. Enclosed strips can be seen on the distant slopes.
PETER HERRING

62

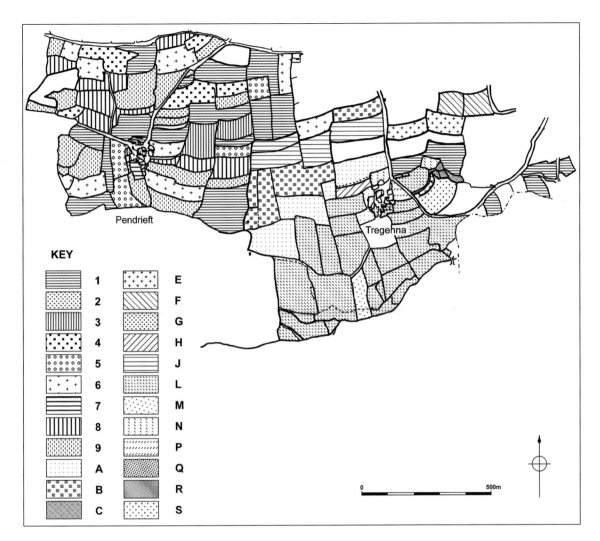

KEY

1	E
2	F
3	G
4	H
5	J
6	L
7	M
8	N
9	P
A	Q
B	R
C	S

Pendrieft

Tregenna

0   500m

FIGURE 27
Extract from the 1839
Blisland parish Tithe
Apportionment Map
showing (through
tones) the intermixing
of holdings in the
adjoining enclosed
strip field systems
of Pendrieft (now
Pendrift) and
Tregenna. Note
the greater degree
of grouping of the
holdings at Tregenna
and the probably
consequent removal of
narrower strips.

Bowithick the reorganisation of holdings extended to the grouping together of several fields so that most farmsteads held consolidated blocks of land.

Considerable numbers of hamlets shrank to single farmsteads through the engrossment of particularly successful tenants, often in the fourteenth and fifteenth centuries (see Fox 1983, 40; Herring and Thomas 1993), which again provided farmsteads with the opportunity to rearrange enclosures to best suit their own convertible husbandry schemes (Fox 1971, 102–4). Although the lines of some strip boundaries, the low balks, were occasionally reused (as at Slades and Higher Brown Willy), most were swept away and usually only the stock-proof cropping unit boundaries survive. For large parts of Cornwall's AEL, this is the pattern that has prevailed through the later medieval and post-medieval centuries.

Most engrossment or hamlet shrinkages resulted in the solid yeoman farms so lovingly described in neighbouring Devon by W. G. Hoskins; a few became 'the homes of small gentry or "squireens"' (Hoskins 1954, 74); and fewer still

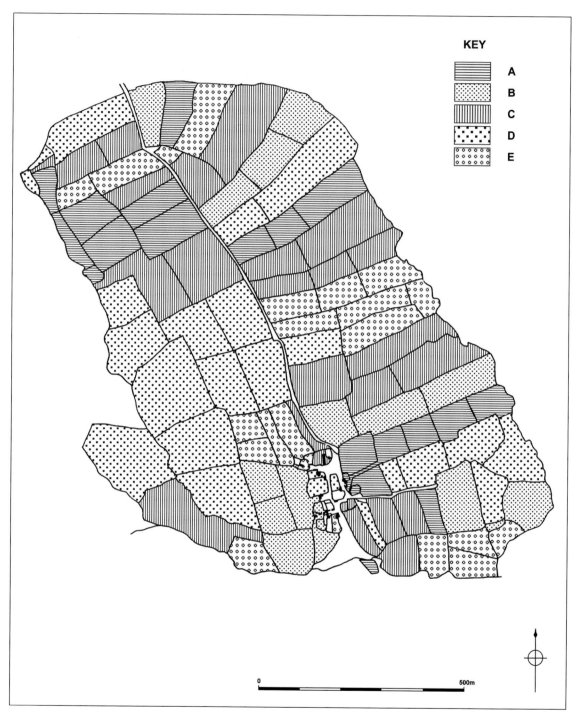

KEY

A
B
C
D
E

0   500m

FIGURE 28

Extract from the 1840 Altarnun parish Tithe Apportionment Map showing (through tones) the intermixing of holdings in the enclosed strip field system of Bowithick. Like at Tregenna (Figure 27), the grouping together of holdings enabled farmers to not only remove more strip boundaries but also to reorganise the patterns through insertion of cross-boundaries and so make more manageable field shapes.

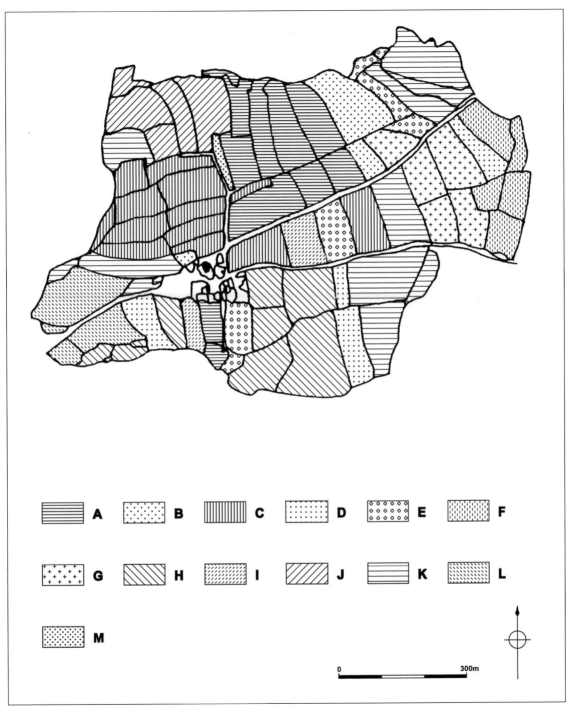

FIGURE 29

Extract from the 1841 Advent parish Tithe Apportionment Map showing (through tones) the intermixing of holdings in the enclosed strip field system of Treclago. The largest groupings are those closest to the hamlet whose integrity may have been partly maintained by the centripetal force of the smaller landholdings being also more scattered.

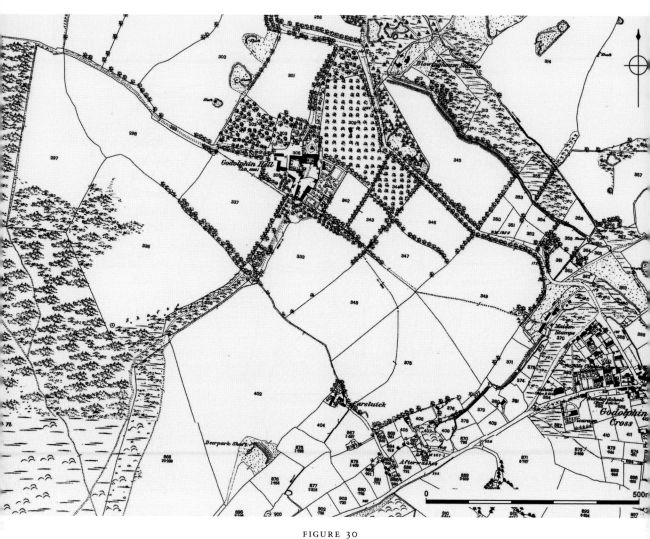

FIGURE 30

Godolphin in Breage as mapped in the later nineteenth century (1st edition OS 25-inch map, c. 1880). Large rectilinear fields created to the north-west and south-east of the house in the early post-medieval period were fitted into compartments of the later medieval deer park so that virtually no trace is left of the preceding subdivided field system, whose edges are visible archaeologically on the heathy hill to the west.

became the seats of the gentry. Godolghan, or Godolphin, in west Cornwall was transformed by one of the original Godolghan households with the help of tinning wealth and the spur of great ambition from a hamlet with outfield strips on the hill above to a 'castle' with massive deer park by the early four-teenth century. Then in the early post-medieval period, when the family had moved on to the London scene it became a classic barton (normally an estate's home farm) with very large ten- to fifteen-acre fields in the former parkland that retain only the slightest traces of their open-field precursors (Herring 1997; Figure 30). Similar 'barton' field systems can be identified scattered throughout lowland Cornwall and Devon.

66

Fossilised strips and cropping units

Many former strip fields are visible on modern or late-nineteenth-century Ordnance Survey maps, Tithe Maps and estate plans. They appear either as patterns of long parallel-sided fields or roughly square or rectangular fields whose slightly sinuous sides are also fossilisations of medieval field boundaries, either much larger bundles of strips or the cropping units that enclosed them. Development of some of these 'cropping unit' systems from strips can be followed through map regression, or through archaeological recording (earthwork or geophysical survey) of former strips (as at Brown Willy; Figure 36). They are typically sub-rectangular with cross-contour sides usually slightly curving (following the lines of the strips they once contained), but with tops and bottoms often straighter, also often not quite so parallel (see Figures 24, 25, 28, 29, 31 and 32).

While many strips in Somerset and further east followed the contour and created strip lynchets as soil built up along their downhill sides, in Cornwall they almost always ran up and down the slope; rare exceptions include the famous strip lynchets on the north coast on Forrabury and Bossiney Commons (Figure 26; Wood 1963; Taylor 2002; Dudley 2003).

There is little variety in strips in Cornwall. Away from relict, excavated and

FIGURE 31
Trevarrian in St Mawgan in Pydar parish with clearly defined enclosed strip fields to the west of the hamlet and 'cropping unit' fields to the east. Further east again are the fields of Tolcarne Merock, also of 'cropping unit' type, which had strips 'intermingled' within them as late as 1575 (Fox and Padel 2000, 217). (1st edition OS 25-inch map, c. 1880.)

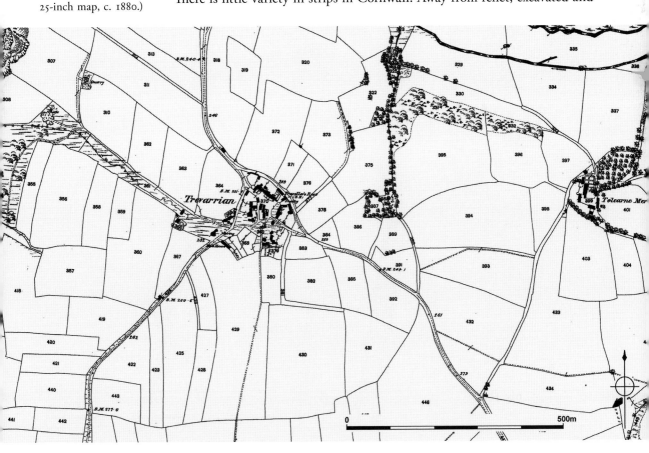

geophysically surveyed field systems it is no longer possible to measure original strip widths, but it is usually possible to measure their lengths and most fall in the range of 450 to 650 feet (137 to 198 m). Some north coast strips are a little longer and straighter (some at Trevarrian, St Mawgan in Pydar, reach 850 feet, 260 m (Figure 31).

Ley farming and ploughing

Numerous former strip-field systems are still sufficiently well defined for their cropping units to be counted (see Figure 24, for example). As many field patterns were disturbed by boundary removal in the last century, the First Edition Ordnance Survey 25-inch maps (made around 1880) were used to

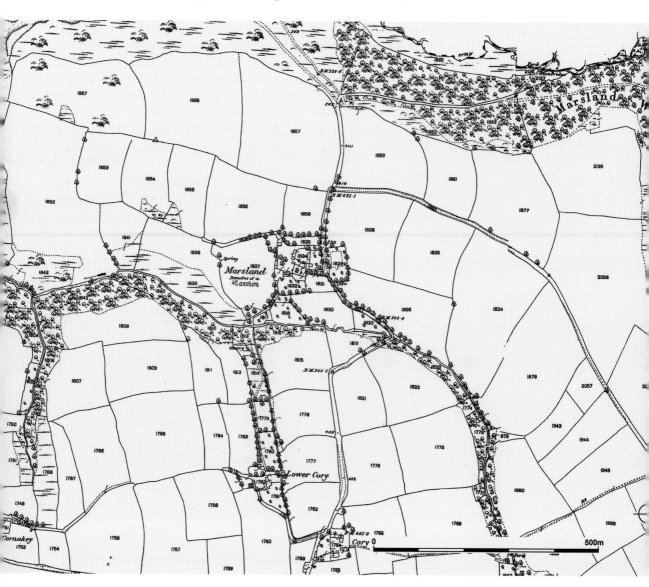

record 150 systems scattered across Cornwall from Morwenstow to Rame, St Keverne to Sennen. Numbers of cropping units ranged from six to seventeen, but most (127, or 85 per cent) fell between eight and thirteen, with 10.36 being the average number. Original numbers were probably a little higher as there has been some loss of field pattern definition since the later medieval period.

Very few townlands in Cornwall therefore resemble the two- or three-field systems of the English Midlands, with their intensive rotations incorporating recuperative fallows. Instead Cornwall's strip fields were designed to accommodate the ley or convertible husbandry regime described below in the Brown Willy case study. In any one year in a typical Cornish field system, just two or three of the ten or so units would be under the spade or plough, the remaining seven or eight being used for hay and grazing, the grass having been undersown with the last crop of the two- to four-year cycle, leaving no fallow – the newly sown grass being immediately incorporated into the hamlet's pastoral sector the following year. Each year one of the cropping units would be undergoing preparation for cultivation – beat-burning from late spring, the ashes mixed with dressing from yards, beaches and ditches later in summer, and either wheat or rye sown in late September or early November respectively in the first year, with spring-sown barley or oats in the cycle's later years. All this work would have been done cooperatively, in common, although the produce of each strip and each animal would have belonged to individual tenants or households (Figure 33).

Many fossilised and surveyed strips have distinctive curving shapes, almost always reversed-J curves when viewed from the bottom of the slope (see Figures 24, 25 and 31 for examples). There are virtually no J-curves in Cornwall and only a handful of systems have the reversed-S or aratral curve of ox-team ploughing – the Forrabury stitches (Wood 1963, Figure 26) are a rare example and, as noted, are among very few Cornish strips that follow the contour. As reversed-J strips are curved at just their downhill ends, it must be inferred that the plough producing them worked the steep Cornish slopes in one direction only, downwards (cf. Eyre 1955, 86). Ridge and furrow is still to be seen in some relict strips away from spade-ridging country; see Chapter 5. To produce this by ploughing downhill only, the plough's mouldboard could not have been fixed, but instead had to be able to turn sods to both left and right and so would have been a relatively sophisticated 'one-way plough'. One-way ploughs are apparently unrecorded in Cornwall before the early nineteenth century (Jewell 1981, 102–4), though they did exist in later medieval England (Fussell 1966, 182). The existence in Cornwall of previously unsuspected medieval one-way ploughs, perhaps lighter than ox ploughs but still drawn by teams to create the reversed-J curves, may be proposed. The lack of J-curves suggests these field shapes are not simply a response to local topography, but that the Cornish ploughs were, like the English ploughs that produced the reversed-S, always turned to the left at the end of their run.

FIGURE 32
Marsland and Cory in Morwenstow parish have excellent examples of 'cropping unit' fields derived from the removal of strips. Their boundaries retain the reversed J lines formed by the medieval plough. (1st edition OS 25-inch map, c. 1880.)

FIGURE 33

A reconstruction (by Rosemary Robertson, with guidance from the author) of Lanhydrock churchtown and fields in the fifteenth century, based on detailed measured survey of the surviving medieval strips preserved in post-medieval parkland (see Thomas 1998, fig. 3). The Bodmin to Liskeard road passing through the churchtown is also accurately plotted, but the disposition of longhouses, mowhays and townplace is conjectural, as are the patterns of strips attached to the distant hamlets of Cutmadoc (left) and Newton, although their reconstruction is based on surviving cropping unit boundaries.

The season is midsummer, with a late hay harvest (right of church and in front of Cutmadoc) and late beat-burning (centre left), but early ripening of grain (foreground and centre). Fewer fields are shown under grass than would probably have been the case. Cooperative working is shown in the hay fields, beat-burning and charcoal making, and communalism in the intermingling of houses and amenities in the hamlets and the common use of the fields.

Origins of Cornish strip fields

The development of strips in Cornwall may not be 'a mute process of which we have no evidence' (Rowse 1941, 36); the evidence we do have may be circumstantial and the use of it tentative, but a model can be developed that places the origins of Cornish strips firmly in the early medieval period.

A complementary paper (Herring forthcoming) follows the development of prehistoric Cornish fields from later Neolithic ovoid enclosures, through earlier Bronze Age accretive fields and middle Bronze Age extensive co-axial fields organised by communities of several neighbourhood groups, all understandable in relation to increasing pressure on the common grazing land lying beyond their edges.

As pressure on commons continued to develop the co-axial fields were in turn replaced some time early in the first millennium BC by a new pattern, now dominated by brick-shaped fields (see Figure 34 for an example). These may have had the holdings of associated groups of households intermixed through them in a proto-medieval way, the 'bricks' being regular in shape and size to enable communities to agree their essential equality and so use them in a form of shareholding. Crops and livestock seem to have been regarded as the household's own separate 'property'; each courtyard house in West Penwith's Romano-British hamlets has rooms best interpreted as dwelling, animal house and various stores and workshops, the latter seemingly containing livestock and deadstock belonging to the individual household (e.g. Christie 1978).

This type of field system seems to have survived through the best part of 1,500 years – including the millennium-long period when many hamlets were enclosed in 'rounds'. If creation of the rounds' banks, palisades and ditches was akin to having a licence to crenellate, this probably signalled to contemporaries a differentiation in status between those living in rounds and the other open or undefended settlements, and signals to us the existence of a higher level of rural society that could accord hamlets such licence, presumably receiving some kind of tribute in return. We can therefore suggest that proto-estates were developing in later prehistoric Cornwall and that their later Iron Age locus (but not necessarily their permanent home) was probably the hillfort (Herring forthcoming).

This brief review of the later prehistoric situation is relevant as the origin of Cornwall's strip fields is to be sought in the pre-Norman period (expanded on elsewhere; Herring 1999). The strip system at Trerice, St Dennis, was sufficiently mature by 1049 to have been both divided into two and also to have determined the line of a highway (Herring and Hooke 1993). Roman period fields at Trenowah, near St Austell, were replaced on the establishment of the settlement (probably pre-Norman), by strips (Johns 1995). At Brown Willy itself a complex strip field system with considerable chronological depth visible in its surviving remains had already been transformed and overlain by three individual farms some time before 1275 (Herring 1986); the origin of this field

FIGURE 34

Bosigran in Zennor has 'brick-shaped' later prehistoric fields in the western part of its field system. These appear to have been worked in the Romano-British period by households living in a hamlet of four (or more) courtyard houses, the households' holdings possibly scattered through the fields in a similar way to that in medieval and early modern times (as at nearby Treen in 1841; Figure 23); the regularity of the fields enabling allotments or share holdings to be more easily agreed. A less extensive pattern of later prehistoric fields in the eastern part appears to have been associated with a very unusual example of a single farmstead, the fields' irregularity apparently due to the lack of need for shareholding. In the early medieval period the hamlet of Bosigran was established between the two prehistoric settlements. Its households attached bundles of medieval strips to the southern perimeter of the prehistoric fields and also established groups of outfield strips on the downlands to the south. (From Herring 1987.)

system, with its core of carefully measured strips, must be sought at the latest in the tenth or eleventh centuries (see Chapter 5).

When we consider what might be the possible context in pre-Norman Cornwall for the revision of large parts of a settled landscape with substantially built field boundaries into an entirely new pattern with larger open fields subdivided into strips, we are drawn to the major changes that occurred around the sixth or seventh century AD. This was when the rounds seem to have been systematically abandoned (Quinnell 2004, 243–4), or even emptied. As far as we can tell Cornwall's new early medieval settlements, those that replaced the rounds, were still hamlets, many now with the *tre* 'farming estate' (?townland) names. At around this time Cornwall's main high status sites, including Tintagel and St Michael's Mount, seem also to have been abandoned. Ceramic styles, key indicators of cultural affinities, also changed; local Romano-Cornish wares were replaced by Gwithian and grass-marked ones and imported Mediterranean pottery by south-western French (Quinnell 2004, 243). These and other changes may have been coincidental, but it seems more realistic to suggest that they were interconnected and also related to the adoption in Cornwall of a new ideology – Christianity – that underpinned not just a change in ritual and belief, but also affected more fundamentally the ways that people related to each other and to authority, including the ways in which land was owned, held and organised. 'Render unto Caesar the things that are Caesar's' underpinned tribute/rent payment while parables like the loaves and fishes and exhortations like 'Love thy neighbour as thyself' underpinned shareholding and communalism.

Adoption of strips by people accustomed to intermixing within 'common' brick-shaped fields can be considered a relatively small step if, as has been suggested in the Brown Willy case study, the principal original quality of strips was not their ability to accommodate a plough, but their possession of a measurable and assessable dimension, the width. This allowed both 'lord' and land-holder to have closer control of allotment or shareholding, the 'lords' to more efficiently 'charge' (rent or service) for access to land, the co-tenants or shareholders to have a greater sense of equity in their arrangements.

Individualism and communalism

Significant implications for our understanding of Cornwall flow from an awareness that its prehistoric, medieval and later rural landscape contained thousands of hamlets, visible from the Middle Bronze Age (Johnson and Rose 1994; Nowakowski 1991). Groups of households, tight-knit in Iron Age and Romano-British West Penwith, may have been more loosely grouped in other parts of later prehistoric Cornwall (Andy M. Jones, pers. comm.), but were nevertheless still neighbourhood or cooperative groups. The single household settlement is a rarity not only in prehistoric, but also medieval Cornwall, until the arrival, around the thirteenth century, of the externally driven and commercially founded processes that stimulated the hamlet disintegration, splitting and engrossment outlined above. Ironically, the 'Celtic' isolated farmer can be seen to be a product of the influence of the English market for tin and cloth.

Recognising the importance of resource sharing and cooperation between member households of hamlets is crucial to understanding the development of Cornwall's landscape and society. The cooperative group or hamlet was generated from below, by its constituent households, to satisfy basic agricultural and human needs, and not imposed from above, hence its ubiquity, universality and enduring presence in Cornwall for over 3,000 years (Herring 1986). Communalism and cooperation included collective and flexible use of labour; the needs of the busiest seasons or most onerous tasks, like harvest-time and beat-burning, determining the strength of cooperative ties. Collective and flexible use of equipment and facilities included sharing ploughs, wells, mills and corn-driers. Trerice Mill was 'common' (not manorial) in 1049, and the scarcity of manorial mills recorded in Domesday Book for Cornwall may suggest how widespread such arrangements were (Herring and Hooke 1993). Collective rights to extensive or special resources included rough ground (for grazing and obtaining fuel and bedding), woods, meadows and sanding ways. The neighbourhood or cooperative group is visible not only in the grouped buildings and enclosures and shared spaces of the hamlet, but also on the land. Field systems are not only the places where the oats, barley and wheat were grown, and the hay saved. They are also the historically meaningful products of the complex relationships between the household, with its individual holding, and the cooperative group, the facilitating level of rural society.

Secondary forms of communalism reinforced commitment to the group. Redistribution of specialist products like honey, baskets, pottery, clothing and so on between member households would have established dependencies while hamlet-level decision-making systems will have helped fix peoples' responsibilities and relationships. Commitment of household members to the hamlet was reinforced by the shared pleasures of music, dancing, poetry, food and drink (Herring 1986). Couching a presentation of Cornish peasant life in concepts and words suggestive of friendliness, communalism and even happiness does not weaken it; on the contrary, it helps further to explain how its essence was sustained for so long.

As the communal and cooperative way was the norm throughout farming Cornwall it comes as little surprise to see similar communalism, cooperation and risk-spreading in the organisation of labour and equipment in other walks of medieval Cornish life, for example when streamworking, mining and fishing. Richard Carew, at the turn of the seventeenth century, noted how once a tinwork was, 'found and bounded, looke how many men doe labour therein, so many Doales or shares they make thereof, and proportionably divide the gaine and charges' (Carew 2004, 13v). He also recorded the methods of seine fishing for pilchard. To each Seine, 'there commonly belong three or four boats, carrying about six men apeece', men who Carew wrote, 'complayne with open mouth' about the 'prejudice to the Commonwealth of fishermen' caused by opportunistic individuals 'droving' pilchards with square nets hung athwart the tide (Carew 2004, 32r–v).

All this allows us to acknowledge that the present-day interdependence of Cornish households, including farming ones, has deep roots. For many farmers such interdependence was last made routinely visible in the sharing between farms of labour and equipment at hay and corn harvest (largely lost on the introduction of round bales); it is resurfacing in the groups of farmers supporting machinery rings and even the groups making regular use of particular agricultural contractors. This modern farming and these modern relationships are located within, and to a great extent maintain that beautiful, distinctively Cornish landscape that we see was created by earlier relations between individual farmers and the communal groups of which they were part. It is not just a place of great beauty, but a place full of great meaning to the Cornish.

Acknowledgements

Thanks to Dr Sam Turner for commissioning this piece, to Professor Andrew Fleming for supervising the original work, and to Professor Harold Fox, Veronica Chesher, Peter Rose, Cathy Parkes, Nicholas Johnson, Carol Vivian and many others for discussing Cornish strip fields over the years.

References

Balchin, W.G.V. (1983) *The Cornish Landscape* (2nd edition), Hodder and Stoughton, London.

Beresford, M.W. (1964) 'Dispersed and grouped settlement in medieval Cornwall', *Agricultural History Review* **12**, 13–27.

Carew, R. (2004) *The Survey of Cornwall* (first published 1603), republished by Devon and Cornwall Record Society, Exeter.

Christie, P.M. (1978) 'The excavation of an Iron Age souterrain and settlement, Carn Euny, Sancreed, Cornwall', *Proceedings of the Prehistoric Society* **44**, 309–434.

Cornwall County Council (1996) *Cornwall Landscape Assessment, 1994*, a report prepared by Landscape Design Associates and Cornwall Archaeological Unit.

Curwen, E.C. (1927) 'Prehistoric agriculture in Britain, *Antiquity* **1**, 261–89.

Dahlmann, C.J. (1980) *The Open Field System and Beyond, A Property Rights Analysis of an Economic Institution*, Cambridge University Press, Cambridge.

Dodgshon, R.A. (1980) *The Origin of British Field Systems: An Interpretation*, Academic Press, London.

Dudley, D. and Minter, E.M. (1962–63) 'The medieval village at Garrow Tor, Bodmin Moor, Cornwall', *Medieval Archaeology* **4–5**, 272–94.

Dudley, P. (2003) *Forrabury Strips, Forrabury and Minster, Cornwall, An Archaeological Assessment*, Cornwall County Council, Truro.

Evans, E.E. (1957) *Irish Folk Ways*, Routledge and Kegan Paul, London.

Eyre, S.R. (1955) 'The curving plough-strip and its historical implications', *Agricultural History Review* **3**, 80–94.

Finberg, H.P.R. (1949) 'The open field in Devonshire', *Antiquity* **23**, 180–7.

Finberg, H.P.R. (1952) 'The open field in Devon' in *Devonshire Studies*, eds W.G.Hoskins and H.P.R.Finberg, Jonathon Cape, London, 265–88.

Finberg, H. P. R. (1969) *Tavistock Abbey; A Study in the Social and Economic History of Devon* (second edition), David and Charles, Newton Abbot.

Flatrès, P. (1957) *Geographie Rurale de Quatre Contrees Celtiques: Irlande, Galles, Cornwall and Man*, Rennes.

Fleming, A. (1984) 'The prehistoric landscape of Dartmoor: wider implications', *Landscape History* 6, 5–19.

Fowler, P. J. and Thomas, A. C. (1962) 'Arable fields of the pre-Norman period at Gwithian, Cornwall', *Cornish Archaeology* 1, 61–84.

Fox, H. S. A. (1971) 'A Geographical Study of the Field Systems of Devon and Cornwall', PhD thesis, University of Cambridge.

Fox, H. S. A. (1975) 'The chronology of enclosure and economic development in medieval Devon', *Economic History Review* 28.2, 181–202.

Fox, H. S. A. (1983) 'Contraction: desertion and dwindling of dispersed settlement in a Devon parish', *31st Annual Report of the Medieval Village Research Group*, 40–2.

Fox, H. S. A. and Padel, O. J. (2000) *The Cornish Lands of the Arundells of Lanherne, Fourteenth to Sixteenth Centuries*, Devon and Cornwall Record Society, New Series, Volume 41.

Fussell, G. E. (1966) 'Ploughs and ploughing before 1800', *Agricultural History*, 40, 177–86.

Gerrard, G. A. M. (1986) *The Early Cornish Tin Industry – An Archaeological and Historical Survey*, PhD thesis, University of Wales.

Gover, J. E. B. (1948) *The Place-names of Cornwall*, unpublished TS held at the Royal Institution of Cornwall, Truro.

Gray, H. L. (1915) *The English Field Systems*, Harvard University Press, U.S.A. (Reprinted 1969, by Merlin Press, London.)

Hatcher, J. (1969) 'A diversified economy: later medieval Cornwall', *Economic History Review* 22, 208–27.

Hatcher, J. (1970a) *Rural Economy and Society in the Duchy of Cornwall 1300–1500*, Cambridge University Press, Cambridge.

Hatcher, J. (1970b) 'Non-manorialism in medieval Cornwall', *Agricultural History Review* 18, 1–16.

Hatcher, J. (1973) *English Tin Production and Trade before 1550*, Clarendon Press, Oxford.

Henderson, C. (1935) *Essays in Cornish History*, Clarendon, Oxford.

Herring, P. (1986) 'An exercise in landscape history. Pre-Norman and medieval Brown Willy and Bodmin Moor', M.Phil thesis, Sheffield.

Herring, P. (1987) *Bosigran, Zennor, archaeological survey*, National Trust and Cornwall Archaeological Unit, Truro.

Herring, P. (1997) *An archaeological and historical assessment of Godolphin, Breage*, Cornwall County Council, Truro.

Herring, P. (1998) *Cornwall's Historic Landscape, Presenting a Method of Historic Landscape Characterisation*, Cornwall County Council, Truro.

Herring, P. (1999) 'Farming and transhumance in Cornwall at the turn of the first millennium AD, part 2', *Journal of the Cornwall Association of Local Historians*, **Autumn 1999**, 3–8.

Herreng, P. (forthcoming) 'Commons, fields and communities in prehistoric Cornwall' in *Recent Approaches to the Archaeology of Land Allotment*, A. Chadwick, BAR (International Series), Archaeopress, Oxford.

Herring, P. and Hooke, D. (1993) 'Interrogating Anglo-Saxons in St Dennis', *Cornish Archaeology*, 32, 67–75.

Herring, P. and Thomas, N. (1988) *The Archaeology of Kit Hill*, Cornwall County Council, Truro.

Herring, P. and Thomas, N. (1993) *Stratton Hundred, Rapid Identification Survey*, Cornwall County Council, Truro.

Hoskins, W. G. (1954) *Devon*, Collins, London.

Hull, P. L. ed. (1971) *The Caption of Seisin of the Duchy of Cornwall*, Devon and Cornwall Record Society NS 17, Torquay.

Hull, P.L. ed. (1987) *The Cartulary of Launceston Priory*, Devon and Cornwall Record Society NS 30, Torquay.

Jewell, A. (1981) 'Some Cultivation Techniques in the South-West of England' in *Agricultural Improvement: Medieval and Modern, Exeter Papers in Economic History No 14*, ed. W. Minchinton, University of Exeter, Exeter, 95–111.

Johns, C. (1995) *An archaeological evaluation of the St Austell NE distributor road*, CAU, Truro.

Johnson, N. and Rose, P. (1994) *Bodmin Moor: an Archaeological Survey. Volume I: The Human Landscape to c. 1800*, English Heritage, London.

Jones, G.E. (1973) *Rural Life, Patterns and Processes*, Longman, London.

Kershaw, I. (1973) 'The Great Famine and Agrarian Crisis in England, 1315–1322', *Past and Present* **59**, 1–50.

Maclean, Sir J. (1873) *Parochial and Family History of the Deanery of Trigg Minor, Cornwall Vol. 1*, Nichols, Bodmin.

McCourt, D. (1971) 'The dynamic quality of Irish rural settlement' in *Man and his Habitat*, eds R.H. Buchanan, E. Jones, and D. McCourt, Routledge and Kegan Paul, London, 126–64.

Nowakowski, J.A. (1991) 'Trethellan Farm, Newquay: the excavation of a lowland Bronze Age settlement and Iron Age cemetery', *Cornish Archaeology* **30**, 5–242.

Padel, O. (1985) *Cornish Place-Name Elements*, English Place-Name Society vol. 56/57, Nottingham.

Payton, P. (1992) *The Making of Modern Cornwall*, Dyllansow Truran, Redruth.

Payton, P. (1996) *Cornwall*, Alexander Associates, Fowey.

Payton, P. (2004) *Cornwall, A History*, Fowey.

Postan, M.M. (1975) *The Medieval Economy and Society: An Economic History of Britain in the Middle Ages*, Penguin, Harmondsworth.

Pounds, N.J.G. (1944) 'The Lanhydrock atlas and Cornish agriculture about 1700', *Rep. Roy. Cornwall Poly. Soc.* **11**, 113–25.

Pounds, N.J.G. (1945) *The Historical Geography of Cornwall*, PhD thesis, University of London.

Preston-Jones, A. and Rose, P. (1986) 'Medieval Cornwall', *Cornish Archaeology* **25**, 135–85.

Quinnell, H. (2004) *Excavations at Trethurgy Round, St Austell: Community and Status in Roman and Post-Roman Cornwall*, Cornwall County Council, Truro.

Rowse, A.L. (1941) *Tudor Cornwall, Portrait of a Society*, Jonathon Cape, London.

Shorter, A.H., Ravenhill, W.L.D. and Gregory, K.J. (1969) *South West England*, Nelson, London.

Taylor, C.C. (1984) *Village and Farmstead*, George Phillips, London.

Taylor, S.R. (2002) *Tintagel East, archaeological and historic landscape assessment*, Cornwall County Council, Truro.

Thomas, N. (1998) *Lanhydrock Park, a survey of an historic landscape*, Cornwall County Council, Truro.

Thorn, C. and Thorn, F. (1979) *Domesday Book: 10 Cornwall* (from a translation by O. Padel) Phillimore, Chichester.

Turner, M. (1984) *Enclosures in Britain 1750–1830*, MacMillan, London.

Ugawa, K. (1962) 'The economic development of some Devon manors in the thirteenth century', *Transactions of the Devonshire Association* **94**, 630–83.

Uhlig, H. (1961) 'Old hamlets with infield and outfield systems in western and central Europe', *Geografiska Annaler* **43**, 285–312.

Wood, P.D. (1963) 'Open field strips, Forrabury Common, near Boscastle', *Cornish Archaeology* **2**, 29–33.

CHAPTER 5

Medieval Fields at Brown Willy, Bodmin Moor

Peter Herring

Remarkably well-preserved medieval and early post-medieval field systems and settlements on Brown Willy, St Breward, on Bodmin Moor, were surveyed by the author in 1981–82 at a scale of 1:1000 or larger (as appropriate). All features and relationships were closely described and analysed to develop a complex relative chronology and interpretative framework (Herring 1986). This chapter includes the fruits of further related research plus two decades of reflection, and concentrates on describing and discussing those aspects of the Brown Willy complex that throw light on wider Cornish issues.

The hill and its more distant past

Brown Willy, from Cornish *bron gwennili* (*bron* 'rounded hill', literally 'breast', and *gwennili* 'swallows', the summer birds (Padel 1985, 32, 117–18), has a two-kilometre-long spine with four separate tor-topped peaks, the highest (419 m, 1375 feet) to the north (Figure 35). These mean that it is only breast-shaped when viewed from the north and south; the large Bronze Age summit cairn then resembles a nipple. From its peaks clitter pours unevenly down concave slopes leaving some areas relatively stone-free; patches of marsh along the De Lank river and its tributary have been streamed in medieval and later times for tin.

Midway along each side, below the steepest ground, are scatters of probably Middle Bronze Age round houses with associated small curvilinear enclosures (Johnson and Rose 1994, map i). The western side also has a fine group of transhumance huts of probably early medieval date, whose seasonal occupants, possibly teenaged girls (if other north-west European summer grazing systems are guides), seem to have experimented with cultivation by laying out sketchy strip fields (Herring 1996). All these features, both natural and cultural, would have been visible to later occupants of the hill, and stories were no doubt weaved around them, providing them with meanings (Altenberg 2003).

FIGURE 35
Brown Willy from the
south-west showing the
western flank on which
the subdivided field
system lies.

PETER HERRING

The Fields, phase 1: colonisation

The next detectable medieval phase, after transhumance, involved laying out
the core of the main western strip-field system (Figures 36 and 37). It is not
possible without excavation to determine whether the one followed directly on
from the other, with those sketchy strips associated with the transhumance
huts successful enough to encourage the transhumants or their landlords to
establish a permanent settlement. Nor is it possible to provide a close date for
the new strips, although they are likely to be from towards the end of the first
millennium AD (see below).

The earliest strips, in what the author labels the North-West (NW) and the
South (S) Fields, are laid out on relatively low-lying, well-drained and clitter-
free ground on the hill's western flank, and are much more regular than others
on the hill. As they have straight and perfectly parallel sides, the strips in each
Field maintain a single orientation. All eleven in the NW Field depend from
the straight perimeter boundary to their east which curves around the north-
east corner to become the northern boundary. This is not parallel with the

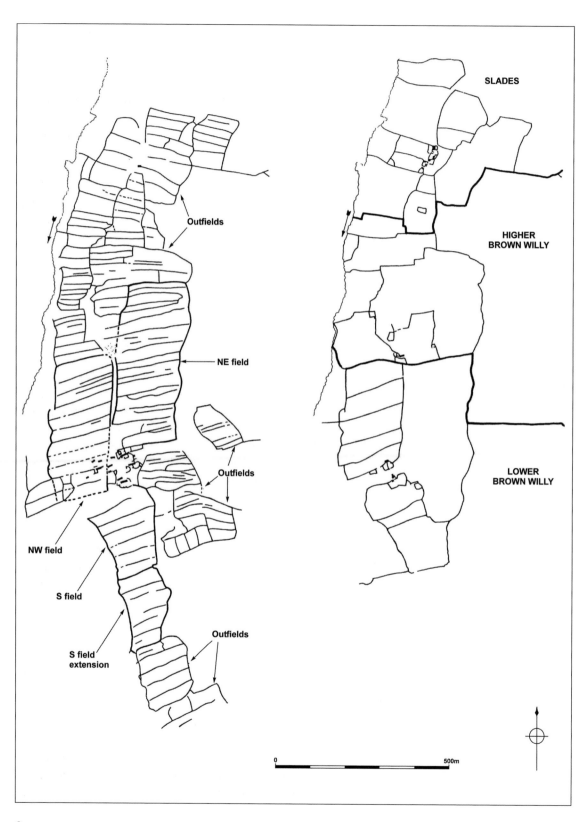

Outfields

NE field

Outfields

NW field

S field

S field
extension

Outfields

SLADES

HIGHER
BROWN WILLY

LOWER
BROWN WILLY

0   500m

penultimate strip boundary, giving the most northerly strip a splayed shape. The strips are not attached to the eastern perimeter perpendicularly, as might be expected, but at 65 degrees, repeating the angle of the Field's south-eastern corner. The impression gained is that the Field's perimeter was laid out first, and then this primary enclosure was carefully subdivided, starting from its southern, settlement end. Similarly splayed end strips caused by subdivision of a primary enclosure can be seen at Brown Gelly, St Neot (Johnson and Rose 1994, fig. 75) and Bray Down, Altarnun.

The NW Field's western boundary is not as straight as the eastern due to uneven development of cultivation lynchets at strip bottoms. The two long sides of the Field are consequently not strictly parallel and strip lengths, and areas, vary a little. Strip widths, however, are, with the exception of the northern splayed strip, all exactly the same; when measured from crest of bank to crest of bank, all are 33 m wide.

Although all six of the S Field's strips are again exactly 33 m wide, their lengths, and thus their areas, are, like those of the NW field, not equal. Differences are not large, however, and may have been perceived or accepted as being negligible as strips run disproportionately into an area of clitter and pre-existing round houses, reducing inequalities in cultivable areas.

Strip boundaries themselves, where not damaged by later farming or fossilised as Cornish hedges, are unfaced stone banks significantly less massive than the perimeter banks (Figure 38). There is no reason to doubt that they retain their original form and scale, being typically 1.0 to 1.3 m wide, and 0.3 to 0.5 m high in the NW Field (similar to the low banks revealed beneath many Cornish hedges during sectioning in lowland Cornwall; Bull 1999). Their stones are the size (0.1 m to 0.4 m) normally turned up during cultivation and found in the small clearance heaps scattered through the field system. The zones devoid of clearance heaps alongside the banks confirm these were not only line markers but also linear clearance heaps. Similar low stone and earth balks forming boundaries of medieval and modern strip fields have been recorded in Ireland, Scotland, north and south Wales, and England (McCourt 1953, 72; 1954–55; 372–3; Whittington 1973, 537; Jones 1973, 437–73; Davies 1956, 94; Taylor 1975, 86, respectively). Stock could graze freely over them when the fields were not under crops or hay grass.

The consistency of the strips' widths, 33 m (108 feet), and their parallel sides, indicate that equality in their size was important to those who laid them out. Medieval distances were measured in rods, also known as poles or perches (Dilley 1975, 174), whose customary lengths varied throughout the country (Jones 1979, 14). The Cornish customary rod was 18 feet (5.5 m) long (Hull 1971, lix and 107), as was that of neighbouring Devon (Finberg 1969, 30; Fleming and Ralph 1982, 113). The NW and S Field strips incorporate this local measure; each is precisely six Cornish rods wide. Elsewhere on Bodmin Moor a field of regular parallel strips on Bray Down includes eight whose widths are 22 m (i.e. four Cornish customary rods) and two at 33 m (six rods) and on Brown Gelly another field is divided into parallel straight-sided strips

FIGURE 36
The western fields of Brown Willy in the mid thirteenth century (left) and around 1800 (right). The three medieval 'infields' are picked out by bolder lines; their names are the author's inventions.
Broken lines at the southern end of the NW Field indicate earlier measured strips (existence confirmed by deturfing) which were overlain, probably before 1275, by the two western longhouse farmsteads of the hamlet. Bold lines delineate the properties of the three separate early-nineteenth-century holdings.
So few medieval boundaries were reused that only the north-western fields of Lower Brown Willy reveal their strip-field origins. (From Herring 1986, figs 37 and 84; also Johnson and Rose 1994, fig. 70.)

FIGURE 37

The mid-thirteenth-century hamlet at Brown Willy as reconstructed by Rosemary Robertson, with guidance from the author, and based on detailed measured survey of the surviving well-preserved remains (Herring 1986, fig. 61). Cattle are being driven from a lane between strip fields into the communal townplace, the open ground shared by all Brown Willy's farmsteads. The building shown slate-roofed with a gabled chimney (top right) is a communal corn-drying barn.

Four of the hamlet's six farmsteads are shown, each with a longhouse (thatched buildings emitting smoke), and each with ancillary buildings (additional cowhouses, stores, etc), mowhays (with ricks of corn, hay, turf (peat) and bracken), and gardens. Note how these 'private' structures and spaces are arranged to be away from the communal space, suggesting a dynamic, potentially tense relationship between individual households and the group as a whole. The hamlet was to explode and resolve itself into three separate settlements spaced through the reorganised fields within a generation or two of this scene.

RECONSTRUCTION © ROSEMARY ROBERTSON

of 22 m, or four rods' width. The newly enclosed land was therefore carefully divided into separate parcels through use of a regionally accepted measuring device. Staves nine feet long were probably used to lay out each Cornish 'landyard', as the rod was known locally (Hull 1971, lix).

A customary acre calculated with an 18-foot rod contains 5760 square yards

(4 × 40 rods), compared with the 4840 square yard statute acre (a rod of 16 feet 6 inches). It has been demonstrated that sizes of actual parcels of land in medieval England tended not to be whole acres (Clark 1960, 91–2), so it is not surprising that the Brown Willy strips are also not exactly one customary acre. Those in the NW Field cluster around 1.2 customary acres and in the S Field range from 0.79 to 1.14. Insensitivity to equality of strip areas compared with widths is typical of medieval land surveyors, who found it difficult to convert precise linear measurements into equally precise areal ones. Indeed, 'for purposes of land measurement and ownership it was the width of the parcel which mattered; once this was known the area could be estimated' (Jones 1979, 15). The strips within each of Brown Willy's two Fields were thus laid out to be regarded as equal.

Such careful mensuration suggests allotment and at Brown Willy can be associated with the hamlet of longhouse farmsteads situated between the two Fields. As two farmsteads were built within the NW Field, making the three southernmost strips redundant as units of land allotment and thus post-dating them, it seems that the strips were originally laid out by (or for) the occupants

83

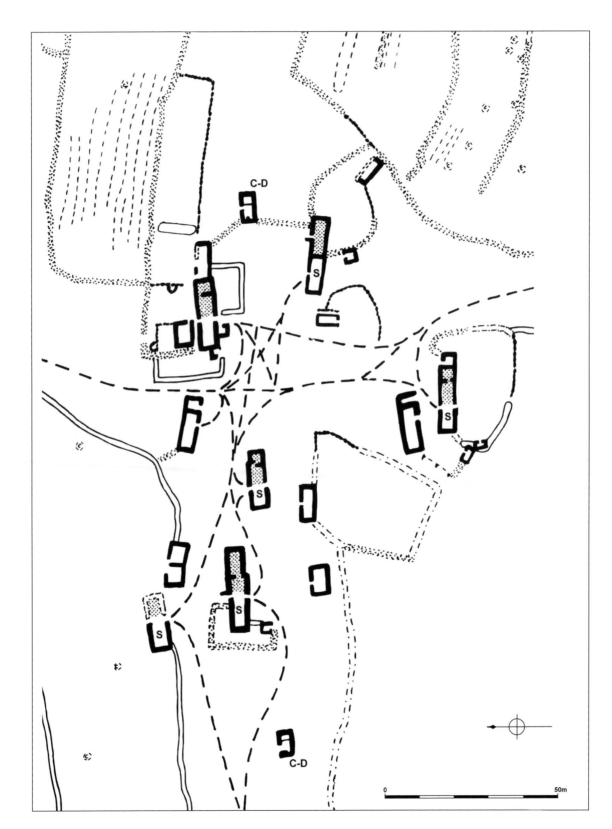

C-D

S

S

S

S

S

C-D

0   50m

of some (or all) of the other four farmsteads slightly further uphill, outside the NW Field. This first medieval settlement was sensibly located, close to a spring and central to the most attractive arable land, but in an area of relatively dense clitter. Valuable land was thus not wasted. Two farmsteads reused ovoid prehistoric enclosures for mowhays, gardens etc; these pre-existing features helped attract the first permanent medieval settlers to the site.

If the ubiquitous stone was the building material from the start, and not turf (cf. Beresford 1979; Henderson and Weddell 1994), it may be argued that the extant longhouse ruins are either the remains of the first houses or are on the sites of them. Farmstead enclosures are less likely to have been rebuilt than houses and indicate that the first settlement contained a maximum of four farmsteads, and probably just three (see Herring 1986 for details). Each had its own small enclosure, two reused prehistoric ovoid ones and a new recti-linear one of similar area (Figure 39). The three farmsteads were very alike, each having similar-sized houses, cowhouses and small enclosures and were arranged around a central area or townplace that was presumably communal. The buildings themselves, however, were apparently all carefully located so that their associated (private) enclosures and their later outhouses were placed away from this communal area. This sort of arrangement, suggestive of a degree of tension between the individual households and the small community that formed the hamlet, was continued throughout the development of the hamlet, and can also be identified in most other surviving medieval hamlets on Bodmin Moor.

The earliest record of lordship over Brown Willy is as late as 1385–86, when an Inquisition Post Mortem revealed that it was held of Fawton manor (Maclean 1873, 380). Fawton, to the west of St Neot churchtown, was the *caput* manor of West Wivelshire hundred, an important early medieval estate possessing seven leagues by four of pasture in 1086 (Thorn and Thorn 1979), certainly sufficient to have included Brown Willy. Carefully measured strips, associated with a nucleated hamlet, strongly suggest that Brown Willy's first medieval settlement was not that of a single colonising free tenant (cf. Miller and Hatcher 1980, 34) but a group of planted bond tenants, presumably estab-lished by Fawton manor (see Austin 1985, 73–5, for the status of colonising farmers). Places like Bray and Brown Gelly had similar origins.

Hamlets with less regular subdivided fields, such as Garrow (St Breward), whose field system has no carefully measured strips (Figure 40), may have originally contained free tenants, the strips being used to mark shareholdings, rather than allotments, as in other regions of highland Britain (Jones 1961, 114–16; 1981, 202–5; Thomas 1978, 273; McCourt 1971, 129–32).

Of course, reasons for colonisation would change over the centuries and vary according to the economic and organisational characters of individual estates or manors. The freeing of slaves and the rationalisation of demesne economies may have been important early stimuli to colonisation (Finberg 1976, 214–23). The lord's benevolence, expressed by the extent and nature of the freedom granted, depended on the economic benefits that he could

FIGURE 39
The full extent of the medieval longhouse hamlet at Brown Willy (north to left). Stippling and 'S' identify the dwelling areas and shippons (cow-houses) of the longhouses. The earliest three farmsteads were those to the east. A network of broken lines represents the routes taken by cattle from the shippons through the communal townplace to the Fields and pastures. Two peripheral buildings marked C–D were communal corn-dryers. (From Herring 1986, fig. 61.)

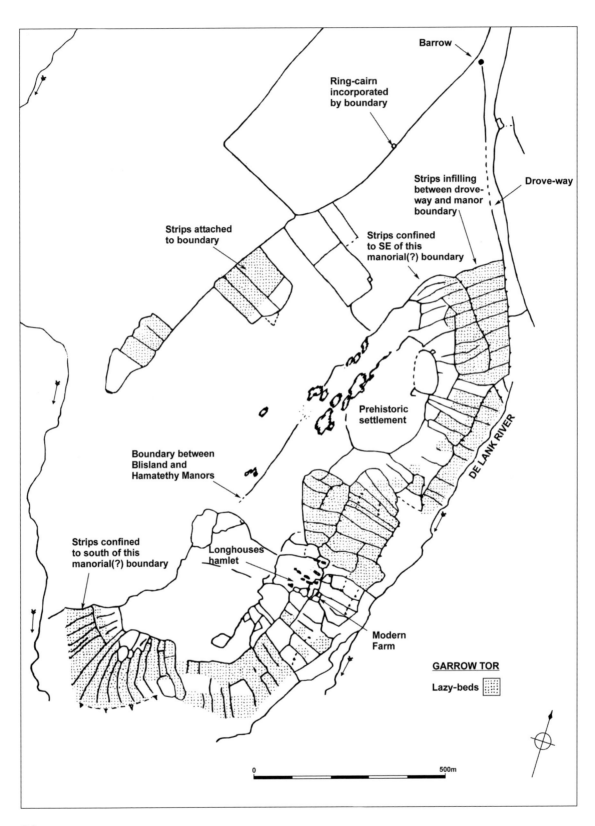

Barrow

Ring-cairn
incorporated
by boundary

Strips infilling
between drove-
way and manor
boundary

Drove-way

Strips attached
to boundary

Strips confined
to SE of this
manorial(?) boundary

Prehistoric
settlement

DE LANK RIVER

Boundary between
Blisland and
Hamatethy Manors

Strips confined
to south of this
manorial(?) boundary

Longhouses
hamlet

Modern
Farm

GARROW TOR

Lazy-beds

0   500m

obtain. Lords with extensive demesnes might insist on regular labour services from freed slaves, now serfs, in consideration for messuage and land; others, perhaps with smaller demesnes and greater reliance on a money economy, might demand regular money rent (Finberg 1976, 217–20). Since Brown Willy is *c.* 12 km (*c.* 7.5 miles) from Fawton, it is unlikely that regular labour services were demanded; a money rent was more likely.

Other stimuli to medieval colonisation included rising population levels and consequent pressure on agricultural economies and thus land, especially if agricultural technology remained essentially stagnant (Postan 1975, 35–8). More locally, the tin industry, based on surface working of alluvial and eluvial deposits, would have concentrated on moorland valleys. Fragmentary documentary evidence suggests those on Fawymore were worked early, and were perhaps already declining through the exhaustion of easily worked deposits by the later thirteenth century (Maclean 1874, 189; see also Gerrard 1986). Supplementing income by tinning would make moorland settlements more economically attractive. Perhaps equally importantly, any full-time tinners would also provide a local market for food products (see Austin *et al.* 1989).

The Fields, phase 2: extension, expansion and new fields

When two groups of less regular strips were added to the field system, called here the South Field Extension and the North East (NE) Field, less attention was given to keeping them regular; the NE Field's long sides were made fairly parallel, as if to maintain reasonably equal strip lengths. Strip widths as well as lengths and areas do vary, however, and although most of the strips have fairly parallel sides, all are sinuous (to take account of heavy clitter) and a number are splayed. These strips were not designed to ensure equal allotment of land between tenants, as in the NW and S Fields. Instead, it seems to have been sufficient that strips could be regarded as fairly equal or proportional, suggesting that the basis of land division had changed from allotment between bondsmen to shareholding between members of a group who had attained a degree of autonomy from the manor, at least in agricultural decision making.

A track 9.5 m wide between the NW and NE Fields connected the settlement with pastures to the north and led towards a ford between Brown Willy and Fernacre, to the west. Deturfing of a fragment of the NW Field's original perimeter boundary revealed a substantial stony bank relatively massive compared to the strip divisions, 1.5 m wide with orthostats defining a face. If a tumbled dry stone wall or Cornish hedge, this perimeter (and by extension also those of the other Fields) was stock-proof.

The area enclosed as strips was more than doubled in this extension phase, from 19.37 to 40.29 customary acres. Four subdivided fields, discrete enclosed sets of strips, had thus been created around a centrally placed settlement. The Fields did not all have the same area. It is likely that some

FIGURE 40
Sketch plan, based on aerial photographs supplemented by fieldwork, of the medieval field system on Garrow Tor with most prehistoric features omitted to retain clarity. Note the irregularity of the strip fields close to the longhouse hamlet compared with those on Brown Willy (Figure 36). (From Herring 1986, fig. 65.)

form of rotation was undertaken in which each Field (or perhaps just half of the larger NE and NW Fields) was used communally each year by the farmers.

The Fields, phase 3: further extension; outfields, more farmsteads, pasture boundaries

Outfields

Groups of small irregular outfield strips established beyond the edges of the phase 2 field system were either accreted onto pre-existing Fields or attached to other earlier outfield groups, many within extensions of ring fences against the rough grazing north of the field system (Figure 43). A few others were detached, including one on the hill's eastern side. Where sequences among outfield groups can be detected, the earliest were in less marginal locations, in terms of distance from the hamlet and ease of cultivation (lower altitude, less clitter etc.).

Outfield groups typically consist of round-cornered enclosures that were cleared, bounded by banks and finally subdivided, again by banks, into three, four, five or six strips. Although widths, lengths and areas vary, and shapes are fairly irregular, with sinuous sides, there seem to have been attempts to equalise the perceived dimensions of the strips within each group, as far as constraints of clitter, slope and pre-existing features allowed. As in the more irregular strips of phase 2, these outfields indicate a shift from manorial or external allotment to communal or internal shareholding. The numbers of strips within each outfield group presumably corresponded to that of house-holders who worked together to clear the ground. Each had their own strip, perceived to be equal to the others. It is significant, then, that groups with five or six strips tend to be on the field system's margins while the groups with four or fewer strips are nearer its nucleus. Groups of four were probably created when the hamlet had just four farmsteads, outside the NW Field. Those with five or six strips, on the other hand, were probably laid out after the hamlet had expanded to six farmsteads and had extended onto the NW Field's southern strips.

The outfields contain ridge and furrow and clearance heaps and are lynchetted on their downhill sides; all were cultivated. Outfields on Brown Willy comprise 46.88 customary acres, although the damaged groups in the area of the later medieval Slades farmstead may have brought the original total up to around 55 customary acres.

Cultivation ridges

The narrow ridge and furrow – 2.0 to 2.5 m wide between furrows – recorded in the outfields is also found in many strips of the NE Field and S Field Extension, but any in the NW and S Fields has been lost to post-medieval cultivation in this, the most favourable part of Brown Willy for arable farming.

FIGURE 41
A portion of the medieval NE Field at Brown Willy showing narrow ridge and furrow or lazy-beds, clearance heaps and relatively sinuous stony banks. (The three eastern structures are early medieval transhumance huts and the western one is a prehistoric round house.) (From Herring 1986, map xxi.)

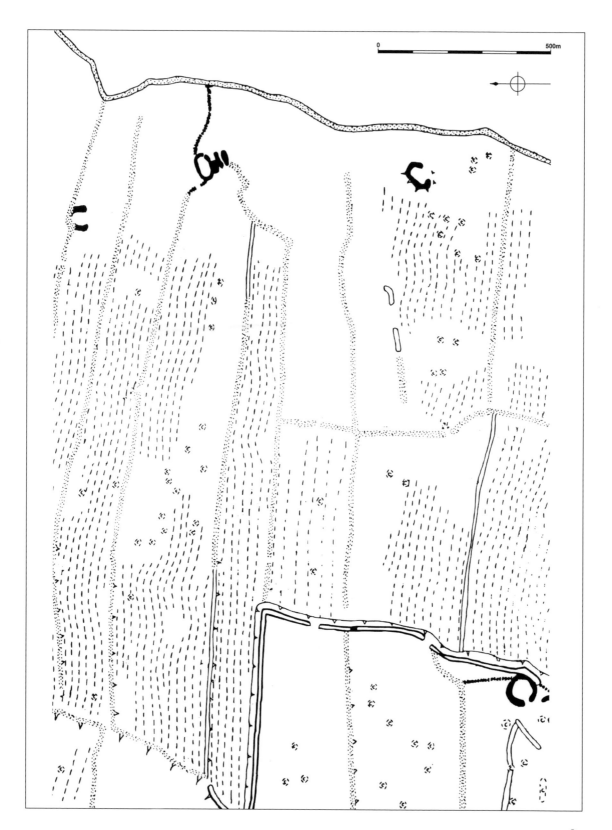

Suggestions have previously been made that medieval ridge and furrow on Garrow and at Stuffle, both the same width as on Brown Willy, was spade-dug rather than created by ploughing (Dudley and Minter 1962–63, 278; Austin *et al.* 1980, 2). There is much to support these claims. The stoniness of the granite-based soil and the numbers of earthfast boulders and clearance heaps in many areas of narrow ridge and furrow argue against the use of even a very light plough. Collis attributed medieval ridges of similar character on Shaugh Moor and Wotter, Dartmoor, to the spade for this reason (Collis 1983, 53). Much of the Brown Willy ridge and furrow is within light and medium clitter (Figure 41) and it is found elsewhere on Bodmin Moor in surprisingly rocky areas (e.g. Garrow Tor, Brown Gelly and Fox Tor). Irish spade-dug 'lazy-beds' are often in rocky areas (O'Donachair 1970, 49).

Spade-dug furrows or trenches drain built-up seed-beds, effectively increasing soil depth. This is of particular importance in areas like Bodmin Moor where soils are generally shallow (Crawford 1962, 244). Spade digging also raises nutrients from lower soil profiles and thus improves fertility (Evans 1957, 143). Another indirect benefit is the removal of the need to maintain draught animals (O'Donachair 1970, 49).

FIGURE 42
Lazy-beds within medieval strip fields at Trezibbett, Altarnun.
PETER HERRING

90

Lazy-bed cultivation (Figure 42) is labour intensive and, while yields are higher than those of plough-cultivation, area by area, they are less when yields per units of labour are compared (Crawford 1962, 245). It might be argued, then, that areas of narrow ridge and furrow on Brown Willy and Bodmin Moor are too large to have been spade dug. Much surviving ridge and furrow, however, is within relatively small outfields. With a ley husbandry rotation, in any given year Brown Willy probably had just a few outfields cultivated, plus one (or half of one) of the main Fields, giving a total annually cultivated area of less than 10 customary acres. Although undeniably hard work (see O'Siochain 1975, 13), such an area would have been manageable given that the field system was worked by several households. Lengths of patches of narrow ridge and furrow on Bodmin Moor compare well with Irish lazy-beds (cf. O'Donachair 1970, 50).

Widths of lazy-beds are also very similar. On Bodmin Moor they average 2.38 m, while Gawne (1970, 65) notes that Dartmoor ridge and furrow is 'nearly always' 7 feet 6 inches wide (i.e. 2.3 m). Measured Irish lazy-bed ridges average 1.83m wide (O'Donachair 1970, 50), to which 0.6 m should be added for the 'furrows' (Evans 1957, 144) to obtain average widths of 2.43 m.

Although Cornish medieval documentation of all husbandry practices is sparse, there are references to spades. An early twelfth-century Scilly grant included five 'bescates' – 'the amount of land that can be dug with a spade in one day' (Finberg 1969, 15) and, from north-west Bodmin Moor, comes an early-fourteenth-century Duchy reference to the necessity in Helstone-in-Triggshire to 'dig over by hand those places which could not satisfactorily be ploughed' (Hatcher 1970, 9).

Narrow ridge and furrow can be made by ploughing. Eighteenth- and nineteenth-century ploughed wheat ridges could be just 7 to 9 feet (2.13 to 2.74 m) wide (Worgan 1811, 54) and as narrow as 4 feet (1.22 m) in the seventeenth century (Stanes 1964, 284). Ridge and furrow averaging 3.1 m wide in field XXI at Gwithian, dated via material in the soil to the ninth to eleventh centuries, was apparently ploughed (Fowler and Thomas 1962, 72–3) although Taylor (1981, 15) has remarked that the excavators' conclusions are 'questionable'. The Gwithian ridges are not really too long to be lazy-beds (Fowler and Thomas 1962, 73); the headlands are no more than 'plausible' (Fowler and Thomas 1962, 70 and fig. 19); the ridging's irregularity may just be a function of poor preservation as no ridge was higher than 6 inches (0.15m) (Fowler and Thomas 1962, 68); and lack of spade-cuts in furrows (Fowler and Thomas 1962, 73) can be explained by trenches being regularly cleaned out with shovels. Almost all medieval strips on Bodmin Moor are straight-sided (as are significant numbers in lowland Cornwall); the reversed-J strips that are common in lowland Cornwall are rare on the uplands (see Chapter 4). Examples include those at the southern end of Garrow and the fossilised strips of Pendrift, Blisland (Figures 40 and 27), and these on the stony moorland soils are useful for helping us appreciate how light and manoeuvrable the ploughs that created them would have been. To conclude, it is suggested here

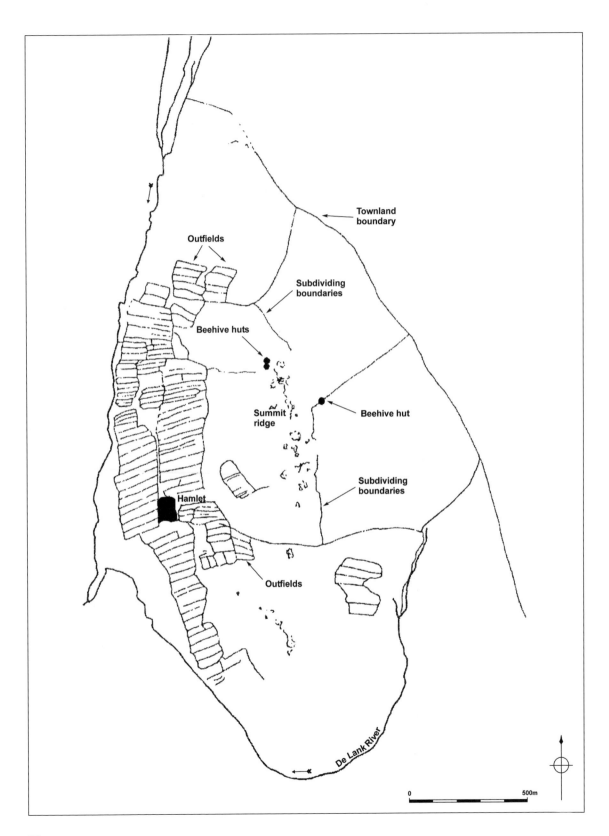

Outfields

Townland
boundary

Subdividing
boundaries

Beehive huts

Summit
ridge

Beehive hut

Subdividing
boundaries

Hamlet

Outfields

De Lank River

0   500m

that the medieval narrow ridge and furrow on Bodmin Moor was largely made with spade and shovel.

This discussion of cultivation method is important as it might seem reasonable to attribute the basic medieval strip shape to the need for a long, efficient, plough-run (e.g. Hoskins 1970, 83; Pearce 1981, 182). Spade cultivation, likely to have preceded ploughing in Cornwall, would not in itself require plots to be strips. We have seen, however, that strips facilitate land-allotment and land sharing as widths can be easily measured and areas then estimated. That the Brown Willy strips (and others on Bodmin Moor) were primarily so shaped for allotment purposes is confirmed by the otherwise illogical enclosing of patches of light, medium, and certainly unploughable clitter in many strips. Also, in terms of their dating, strips need not be tied to the advent of the plough.

Pasture boundaries

Long stock-proof boundaries, built to complement the De Lank river and its tributary, which curve around three sides of the hill, enclose Brown Willy in a ring fence. This separates a discrete block of land from the surrounding hills and moors and their commons, within which the establishment and development of the settlement and field system took place. Others later split up the rough pasture within this ring fence beyond the strip-field system. Some of the dividing boundaries pre-date certain outfield groups attached to them (Figures 43 and 44).

One dividing boundary on the hill's east side is of particular interest as it post-dates a ruined beehive hut (Figure 45). Two similar beehive huts high on the western side have another boundary running to within 30 m of them. Panoramic views of pasture commanded by all three huts and their careful positioning, obtaining maximum possible shelter for such exposed spots, suggest they were shelters for people tending stock on rough pastures in the period before pasture-dividing boundaries were built (Nowakowski and Herring 1985). Their small size makes it unlikely that the huts were anything other than refuges in inclement weather. Herders would normally live in the longhouse settlement, and would only dash for the cover of these huts if the weather turned when they were out tending animals – the eastern hut is a good half-hour's walk from the hamlet.

The boundaries themselves, where not refurbished, vary in construction according to availability of materials. All, however, are still quite large features, often with substantial ditches, and appear to have been stock barriers. They divide the hill's rough pasture into large blocks that probably had no proprietorial significance, not being associated with separate farmsteads. Instead, attachment of subdivided outfield groups to two boundaries indicates that the rough land was still held in common. Pasturing rights would also have been held in common and the land was presumably parcelled up by mutual agreement to give the community the potential to control the grazing animals with stock-proof boundaries rather than with the full-time and

FIGURE 43
Brown Willy townland. Streams define its western, southern and south-eastern sides, but a built stock-proof stone-faced bank defined its eastern and northern sides. The land not subdivided into strips was used as a form of private common, managed with the help of herds (whose shelters, beehive huts survive) until pasture boundaries broke the land up into blocks. Note that these boundaries pre-date at least three of the outfield groups. (From Herring 1986, fig. 37.)

communally-supported herds who had used the beehive huts. One system of stock control in these commons that were private to the hamlet appears to have been replaced by another.

Other long pastoral boundaries on Bodmin Moor (and other upland areas in Cornwall) served similar functions. Ring fences enclosing whole townlands are common in St Breward (Leaze, Garrow, Casehill, Candra, Stannon, Louden etc). Boundaries subdividing a townland's pasture, as at Brown Willy, are rarer but can be seen at Garrow, Casehill (both St Breward) and Codda (Altarnun). Enclosure of large blocks of rough pasture by long boundaries, attached to the ring fences of identifiable hamlets, or farms, is visible at Rowden, Stannon, Candra (all St Breward) and Carkees (Blisland). Some of these enclosures of commons would have been, like at Brown Willy, associated with the original medieval colonisation, but their effect was the same: the alienation of common pasture rights from the other tenants of moorland manors.

The lord's obligation to protect all their tenants' common rights was made law by the 1235 Statute of Merton (Richardson 1974, 25). A probable compromise between these obligations and a wish to intensify moorland exploitation may well have involved the lord denying rights of common on manorial waste to tenants of new settlements; their rough pasture would then be confined to that within their ring fences. The 1288 lawsuit between Henry Cauvel of

FIGURE 44
Pasture boundaries on the eastern side of Brown Willy. The more substantial ones are post-medieval, but that extending to the right centre edge of the image is one of the medieval boundaries that divided the rough ground within the townland's ring fence into large blocks (Figure 43).
PETER HERRING

FIGURE 45
Medieval herd's
shelter, in the form
of a beehive hut, on
the eastern side of
Brown Willy. It was
built entirely of stone,
the roof of corbelled
granite slabs.
PETER HERRING

Louden and Hamatethy manor confirmed that Cauvel had no pasture rights
on the manorial commons (Maclean 1873, 355); the now tumbled pasture
boundary that encloses Louden Hill was presumably built to enclose Cauvel's
privately held rough pasture. Tracks through these new blocks of 'private
common' (shared between the tenants of the hamlets that had annexed
them) permitted the passage of the stock of the other manorial tenants to the
remaining blocks of manorial common.

Brown Willy's medieval farming economy

Being so marginal, emphasis may have been placed on the pastoral side of
Brown Willy's agricultural economy, at least in terms of creating market-
able surpluses to pay the Fawton rent and other obligations. Calculations of
the arable area, however, suggest that it did not differ significantly from less
marginal parts of Cornwall. The total area of the NW, NE and S Fields was
40.29 customary acres. If we assume that division between households was
equal (and cowhouse and yard capacities suggest it probably was; see Herring

95

1986), this area when split three ways would give the primary farmsteads 13.43 customary acres each; and 10.07 customary acres if quartered when the fourth farmstead was built. When the outfields are added the grand total of 95.29 customary acres can be divided by the maximum number of farmsteads, six, to produce 15.88 customary acres per farmstead. If peripheral outfield groups with more than four strips are removed, and the revised total (80.64 customary acres) divided by four farmsteads, a respectable 20.16 customary acres per farmstead is obtained. This compares favourably with the customary acreages of typical Helstone-in-Trigg holdings which, in 1337, ranged from 15 to 22 (see also Hatcher 1970, 23; cf. Thomas 1975, 33–4). Brown Willy's medieval agricultural economy may, therefore, be rather more similar to other less well-preserved systems in lowland Cornwall than at first expected.

Exposure and rainfall would have reduced the likelihood of completing satisfactory wheat harvests (Colyer 1982–83, 55–7), while barley would have barely tolerated the acid soils (Beresford 1979, 143; cf. Austin 1980, 54). Oats, however, can stand acidity, high rainfall and low summer temperatures (Colyer 1982–83, 55) and has thus always been the main grain crop of the 'Atlantic fringe' (Uhlig 1961, 288). Charred oat grains were found within a corn-drying barn at Houndtor, Dartmoor (Beresford 1979, 143). A now virtually extinct strain of oats, pillas (*Avena nuda*), was, until the early-fourteenth-century improvement of the 'large oat', probably the major grain crop on Cornish marginal grounds like Brown Willy (see Finberg 1969, 95–6). It made good straw (Worgan 1811, 66) and was an important fodder crop, as well as being 'the oatmeal of the poor' (Jenkin 1945, 378–9). Pillas also obtained a higher price than oats (Finberg 1969, 95–6), which was always the cheapest medieval grain (Bridbury 1985, 3). Another crop which was tolerant of poor conditions and could make reasonable prices was rye, the main bread grain of the medieval poor (Finberg 1969, 98); it was as important as wheat in the early-fourteenth-century Devon markets (Ugawa 1962, 635).

Rye would have been confined to the margins of field systems, or to beat-land (which, as we will see, was bare anyway in the first winter), not because its value was less than that of oats or pillas but because it was winter-sown (see Stanes 1964, 291; Finberg 1969, 109). In-bye land would have been invaluable for overwintering, in common, unhoused stock (yearlings, sheep etc); and farmers would probably have been reluctant to lose a large proportion of this to a winter crop. Winter stocking of the in-bye land was also a vital part of the manuring cycle (see Evans 1939, 34; McCourt 1954–55, 371; Jones 1961, 116). Oats or pillas, being spring-sown, would therefore have been the main crop of the inbye land.

The rotation practised in the strips of Brown Willy, as elsewhere in medieval and post-medieval Cornwall and Devon, was probably a form of convertible or ley husbandry. A two- or three-year course of cropping was followed by three to ten years of ley grass, with no clean fallow (see Fox 1971, 102; Jewell 1981, 95–7). The length of medieval south-western leys is little known (Fox 1971, 41–3) and agricultural writers from the seventeenth to the nineteenth centuries could not agree on either real or ideal leys (see Fox 1971, table 3.4) although their average was seven years, producing a nine- or ten-year rotation.

Any rotation proposed for Brown Willy must incorporate the three main Fields, or more likely their six halves, include either a two- or three-year cropping course, and have a suitable number of years of rejuvenating ley. It must allow crops to be taken each year, but must not have two large Fields under crops in any one year – this would overstretch labour and also put pressure on grass and hay production. A further complication is that in the early summer of the year before cropping began a ley field was withdrawn from the grass sector to undergo intensive ground preparation, almost certainly involving 'beat-burning'.

In April or May a biddax (a broad-bladed mattock) or breast-plough (a human-pushed skimming share) was used to pare off the turf (Jewell 1981, 98). It was turned with titch crooks until dry (Dodgshon and Jewell 1970, 82) when it was heaped into 'beat-burrows' and fired with wisps of rough straw (Chope 1918, 274). The ashes were then scattered over the ground, reducing its acidity, mineralising nitrogen compounds, and increasing phosphoric nutrients (Hatcher 1970, 12–13). Beat-burning was extremely hard work; a person would expect to clear just one acre in a week (Jewell 1981, 99). To lighten the load it would probably have been done communally, 'a kind of harvest work, bustle, bustle, for a month or six weeks' (Worgan 1811, 67–8). All arable land in the south-west would have been subjected to beat-burning from the medieval period until well into the nineteenth century; it not only increased the soil's fertility, but also greatly eased the passage of spade or plough, and removed weeds and pests (Dodgshon and Jewell 1970, 84–6).

Only the more intensively cropped lands, probably just the three Fields at Brown Willy, would receive cowhouse dung (Uhlig 1961, 288–9). Whether soil-sweetening seasand (see Borlase 1932) was brought all the way to Brown Willy in the medieval period is debatable (see Hatcher 1970, 13–14); but if it was, its expense would ensure that it too was confined to the more intensively cropped lands.

Whatever the details of Brown Willy's rotations, there would have been unevenness in the ley in those years when fields were taken out for ground preparation. Although most hay would have been made in valley-bottom meadows, a significant amount came from ley fields. When these were reduced the hamlet would have looked elsewhere for hay ground, probably to the 'outfields'. More importantly, the decrease in crop yields over the second and third years of cultivation would put stress on any system that required fairly consistent annual production for subsistence and for sale to pay money obligations; again the farmers would have turned to the outfields to accommodate extra crops. The outfields, which were gradually increased in number partly because their leys would probably have been longer (receiving less manure and dressing), provided the field system with the flexibility to adapt to favourable market conditions and to increases in the settlement's subsistence demands, and also provided areas where seed corn might be grown (pers. comm. Carol Vivian).

Though secondary to the main Fields, Brown Willy's outfields therefore had an important function in the arable system, reflected in the size of lynchet that developed at their bottoms. These outfields differed from those recorded by Fox in Devon and Cornwall which were cropped very sporadically (as infrequently as every 40 years) to produce 'bonus' crops and were returned to rough pasture between uses (Fox 1971, 165–205; 1973).

The minimum size of the stock element in Brown Willy's economy can be estimated by calculating how many cattle could be accommodated in the hamlet's cowhouses. A maximum of 60 cattle can be postulated overwintering indoors when all six farmsteads were operating (Herring 1986, 112–13). The herd may have been smaller when there were just four farmsteads, being dependent not only on the carrying capacity of the land but also on the availability of labour for dairying and so on. Apart from housed cattle (the most visible archaeologically), yearlings and other hardy stock would probably have been overwintered on the in-bye land. Sheep, for instance, would be wintered outdoors, their close nibbling and manuring benefiting the grass, and would be taken to shelter only in the worst weather.

That sheep were part of the Brown Willy economy is suggested by the width (9.5 m) of the track between the NW and NE Fields. Medieval sheep (and goats) were kept mainly for their milk (Ryder 1984, 23) although in Devon and Cornwall a wool industry detectable in the twelfth century (Finberg 1969, 150–1) was flourishing, in small-scale enterprises, by the thirteenth (Fogwill 1954, 89; Seward 1970, 29; Pearce 1981, 231).

An infield-outfield system on Brown Willy

The Brown Willy fields discussed here form a good example of an 'infield-outfield' system, as redefined by Robert Dodgshon in the light of detailed studies from throughout the British Isles (1980, 83–103; cf. Whittington 1973, 532–6). Only the relatively intensively cropped land was 'assessed' by the lord and defined by measured units; land beyond this, although appended to holdings in the assessed land, was 'non-assessed' (Dodgshon 1980, 85–94). Holdings in the former were normally originally in bond tenure, as was probably the case at Brown Willy; enclosures in the non-assessed land (either several or communal) were a form of freehold and when they were subdivided this was done on the basis of shareholding (Dodgshon 1980, 96), as in Brown Willy's outfields and phase 2 Fields.

As Brown Willy's hamlet grew, the only means of expanding the arable was outwards into the non-assessed sector. This inevitably altered the balance between assessed and non-assessed land, placing increasing emphasis on shareholding. Indeed, the final expansion of the hamlet itself onto assessed land (by placing farmsteads 5 and 6 on the southern strips of the NW Field) demonstrates a significant eclipse of assessment principles by those of shareholding and (presumably with the lord's blessing) an associated change from bond to free tenure. Brown Willy was recorded as a free tenement of Fawton by 1450 (Royal Institution of Cornwall library, Charles Henderson's *East Cornwall Book*, 410a).

The wider economy

As noted above, the Brown Willy farmers were not involved in simple subsistence agriculture, although they were no doubt able to feed and clothe themselves. They were drawn into wider economies to raise cash to fulfil monetary obligations. In medieval Cornwall, with its small demesnes, manorial labour services were very limited and money rents were generally paid instead (Hatcher 1970, 64–7). Additional manorial dues would include payment of heriots on land-holders' deaths and entry fines on taking up holdings (Fox and Padel 2000). Combined, manorial obligations could be onerous, sometimes representing c. 50 per cent of a peasant's total annual product (Postan 1975, 140). A further 10 per cent of the holding's crops and newborn livestock were taken as tithes for the upkeep of the parish church and its priest (Miller and Hatcher 1980, 108). Added to these were the occasional royal taxes (Postan 1975, 140).

Such oppressive obligations not only forced peasants to at least double the production required for subsistence, they also made it difficult for them to accumulate sufficient wealth to effectively improve their economic position. On the other hand, they brought the peasants into the market-place and into the business of making money, even profits. With this came the potential, given more favourable regional or local economic conditions, for individual households to increase their material wealth at differing rates, undermining the links of communalism, cooperation and basic equality among households in neighbourhood groups.

The Fields, phase 4: disintegration and shrinkage of the hamlet and field system

In 1275 four inhabitants of Brown Willy, namely 'Will's de Teake de Brenwenely, Nich's de Brenweneky, Jocelinus de Brenweneky, Will's fil' Gunnore de Bronkenely', were accused at the Launceston Assize of disseising 'Steph'm de Trewent' of his tenement 'in Fawymore' (probably in Trewint Moor, immediately south of Brown Willy). Among those standing bail for the accused were two more men from Brown Willy, 'Nich'm de Brenwenelyn ... et David de Bronewenely', making six men 'of Brown Willy' in all. Also standing bail was 'Rembaldus de la Lade', that is, of the new farmstead of Slades, imposed on the northern end of the Brown Willy strip field system (TNA:PRO, Just 1/1224, m.7).

Although caution must be taken when using such references to date archaeological features, it is reasonable to accept that the increase from four to six farmsteads ante-dates 1275 if the six men were all householders. The reorganisation of the settlement and fields that accompanied the creation of Slades must have occurred before 1275, and that included revision of outfield groups with six strips (i.e. indirectly indicating that the settlement had indeed reached six households by then).

This becomes, of course, a crucial date for the whole medieval complex on Brown Willy, as many important features and episodes thus pre-date 1275 (for details see Herring 1986). Not only were there four distinct phases in the medieval settlement before the increase to six farmsteads, including the change from single longhouses to multi-building farmsteads and then an increase from three to four farmsteads, but the three Fields were also laid out in two main phases before 1275 with a sufficient interval between each for the requirement for careful mensuration to lapse; then the bulk of the outfields (with four strips) were laid out; and the use of the pastures changed from herding to fencing. In fact, most of the recognisably medieval features on Brown Willy pre-date this final expansion of the settlement before 1275. There seems no doubt that this long sequence of significant changes pushes the date of origin of the Brown Willy settlement and field system back to long before the thirteenth century and quite possibly to before the Norman Conquest.

Later medieval and post-medieval developments

Probably at the same time that Slades farmstead was established, i.e. before 1275, a second farmstead, later called Higher Brown Willy, was created halfway between it and the original hamlet (Lower Brown Willy). Squat, rectangular fields, uphill to this farmstead's east, were created through cross-bank subdivision of NE Field strips and there were similar reorganisations of the outfield strips around Slades. At Lower Brown Willy a smaller group of households may have continued a reduced form of communal farming; there is no sign of early reorganisation of the fields here, and the pairing up and enclosing of strips in the NW Field is likely to be later, from around the turn of the seventeenth century. At this time new farmhouses of small yeoman farmer quality were built at each of the three settlements. Lower Brown Willy appears to have been reduced to just two farmsteads by this date and it may be that one worked the land north of the former hamlet and the other that to the south. An extent of Slades in 1639 reveals that a mixed economy was maintained there; the property included twenty acres of 'land' (i.e. arable), five of meadow (probably best pasture, close to the farmstead, for hay and for nursing young or sick animals), and forty of pasture (probably that beyond the arable fields) (R.I.C., HF/8/27). The pastures were reorganised with well-built dry stone walls with jutting copes (indicating that sheep were kept). They were mainly built along new lines, ignoring most of the medieval pasture walls.

These were marginal farms and the post-medieval period saw times when one, two or all three were abandoned and later reoccupied. Slades was the last to be inhabited, in the 1940s. Now the medieval field system has been fenced around and forms part of the private in-bye land of Brown Willy Farm, based at Fernacre Farm.

The post-medieval field systems reused some of the lines of the medieval Fields and strips so that it would have been possible to suggest that there was a former strip system here even without the detailed earthwork survey (Figure 36), but it required critical analysis of a detailed survey to draw meaningful stories out of the place.

Acknowledgements

Peter and Piers Throssell, owners of Brown Willy, allowed me to survey the hill from 1981 to 1984. I would like to thank Jacky Nowakowski, Andrew Fleming, Cathy Parkes, Professor Harold Fox, Peter Rose, Nicholas Johnson, Sandy Gerrard, Carol Vivian and Andrew Jewell for helpful conversations about Brown Willy over the years.

References

Altenberg. K. (2003) *Experiencing Landscapes. A Study of Space and Identity in Three Marginal Areas of Medieval Britain and Scandinavia*, Lund Studies in Medieval Archaeology 31, Almqvist and Wiksell International, Stockholm.

Austin, D. (1980) 'Farms and fields in Okehampton Park, Devon: the problems of studying medieval landscapes', *Landscape Archaeology* 2, 39–57.

Austin, D. (1985) 'Dartmoor and the upland village of the South-West of England' in *Medieval Villages*, ed. D. Hooke, O.U.C.A. Monograph No. 5: Oxford, 71–9.

Austin, D., Greeves, T., Daggett, R., Gerrard, S., Davidson, J. and Lawson, A. (1980) *Colliford Reservoir, Bodmin Moor, Cornwall. Interim Report of Excavation and Fieldwork in 1980*, unpublished typescript, University of Lampeter.

Austin, D., Gerrard, G.A.M. and Greeves, T.A.P. (1989) 'Tin and agriculture in the Middle Ages and beyond', *Cornish Archaeology* 28, 5–251.

Beresford, G. (1979) 'Three deserted medieval settlements on Dartmoor, a report on the late E. Marie Minter's excavations', *Medieval Archaeology* 22, 98–158.

Bridbury, A.R. (1985) 'Thirteenth-century prices and the money supply', *Agricultural History Review* 33.1, 1–21.

Borlase, W. (1932) 'The use of sea sand on soils in Cornwall', *Journal of the Royal Institution of Cornwall* 23, 440–50.

Bull, E. (1999) *Cornwall's field boundaries*, unpublished report, Cornwall County Council, Truro.

Chope, R.P. (1918) 'Some old farm implements and operations', *Transactions of the Devonshire Association* 50, 268–292.

Clark, H.M. (1960) 'Selion size and soil type', *Agricultural History Review* 8, 91–8.

Collis, J.R. (1983) 'Field Systems and boundaries on Shaugh Moor and at Wotter, Dartmoor', *Proceedings of the Devon Archaeological Society* 41, 47–61.

Colyer, R.J. (1982–83) 'Crop husbandry in Wales before the onset of mechanisation', *Folk Life* 21, 49–70.

Crawford, I.A. (1962) 'Feannagan taomaidh (lazy-beds)', *Scottish Studies* 6.2, 244–6.

Davies, M. (1956) 'Rhosili open field and related South Wales field patterns', *Agricultural History Review* 4.1, 80–96.

Dilley, R.S. (1975) 'The customary acre; an indeterminate measure', *Agricultural History Review* 23, 173–5.

Dodgshon, R.A. (1980) *The Origin of British Field Systems: An Interpretation*, Academic Press, London.

Dodgshon, R A. and Jewell, C.A. (1970) 'Paring and burning and related practices with particular reference to the south-western counties of England' in *The Spade in Northern and Atlantic Europe*, eds A. Gailey and A. Fenton, Ulster Folk Museum, Belfast, 74–87.

Dudley, D. and Minter, E.M. (1962–63) 'The medieval village at Garrow Tor, Bodmin Moor, Cornwall', *Medieval Archaeology* **4–5**, 272–94.

Evans, E.E. (1939) 'Some survivals of the Irish open field system', *Geography* **24**, 24–36.

Evans, E.E. (1957) *Irish Folk Ways*, Routledge & Kegan Paul, London.

Eyre, S.R. (1955) 'The curving plough-strip and its historical implications', *Agricultural History Review* **3**, 80–94.

Finberg, H.P.R. (1969) *Tavistock Abbey; A Study in the Social and Economic History of Devon* (2nd edition), David and Charles, Newton Abbot.

Finberg, H.P.R. (1976) *The Formation of England 550–1042*, Paladin, St Albans.

Fleming, A. and Ralph, N. (1982) 'Medieval settlement and land use on Holne Moor, Dartmoor: the landscape evidence', *Medieval Archaeology* **25**, 101–37.

Fogwill, E.G. (1954) 'Pastoralism on Dartmoor', *Transactions of the Devonshire Association* **86**, 89–114.

Fowler, P.J. and Thomas, A.C. (1962) 'Arable fields of the pre-Norman period at Gwithian, Cornwall', *Cornish Archaeology* **1**, 61–84.

Fox, H.S.A. (1971) 'A geographical study of the field systems of Devon and Cornwall', PhD thesis, University of Cambridge.

Fox, H.S.A. (1973) 'Outfield cultivation in Devon and Cornwall: a reinterpretation' in *Husbandry and Marketing in the South-West, Exeter Papers in Economic History* **8**, ed. M. Havinden, University of Exeter, Exeter, 19–38.

Fox, H.S.A. and Padel, O.J. (2000) *The Cornish Lands of the Arundells of Lanherne, Fourteenth to Sixteenth Centuries*, Devon and Cornwall Record Society, New Series, Volume 41.

Gawne, E. (1970) 'Field patterns in Widecombe parish and the Forest of Dartmoor', *Transactions of the Devonshire Association* **102**, 49–69.

Gerrard, G.A.M. (1986) *The Early Cornish Tin Industry – An Archaeological and Historical Survey*, PhD thesis, University of Wales.

Hatcher, J. (1970) *Rural Economy and Society in the Duchy of Cornwall 1300–1500*, Cambridge University Press, Cambridge.

Henderson, C.G., and Weddell, P.J. (1994) 'Medieval settlements on Dartmoor and in west Devon: the evidence from excavations', *Devon Archaeological Society Proceedings* **52**, 119–40.

Herring, P. (1986) 'An exercise in landscape history. Pre-Norman and medieval Brown Willy and Bodmin Moor', unpublished M.Phil thesis, University of Sheffield.

Herring, P. (1996) 'Transhumance in medieval Cornwall' in *Seasonal Settlement*, ed. H.S.A. Fox, University of Leicester, 35–44.

Hoskins, W.G. (1970) *The Making of the English Landscape*, Penguin, Harmondsworth.

Hull, P.L. ed. (1971) *The Caption of Seisin of the Duchy of Cornwall*, Devon and Cornwall Record Society NS 17, Torquay.

Jenkin, A.K.H. (1945) *Cornwall and its People*, Dent & Sons, London.

Jewell, A. (1981) 'Some cultivation techniques in the South-West of England' in *Agricultural Improvement: Medieval and Modern, Exeter Papers in Economic History No 14*, ed. W. Minchinton, University of Exeter, Exeter, 95–111.

Johnson, N. and Rose, P. (1994) *Bodmin Moor. An archaeological survey. Volume 1: The Human Landscape to c. 1800*, English Heritage and The Royal Commission on the Historical Monuments of England, London.

Jones, A. (1979) 'Land measurement in England, 1150–1350', *Agricultural History Review* **27**, 10–18.

Jones, G.R.J. (1961) 'The tribal system in Wales: a re-assessment in the light of settlement studies', *Welsh Historical Review* **1**, 111–32.

Jones, G. R. J. (1973) 'Field Systems of North Wales' in *Studies of Field Systems in the British Isles*, eds A. R. H. Baker, and R. A Butlin, University Press, Cambridge, 430–79.

Jones, G. R. J. (1981) 'Early customary tenures in Wales and open-field agriculture' in *The Origins of Open-field Agriculture*, ed. T. Rowley, Croom Helm, London, 202–25.

Maclean, Sir J. (1873) *Parochial and Family History of the Deanery of Trigg Minor, Cornwall Vol. 1*, Nichols, Bodmin.

Maclean, Sir J. (1874) 'The tin trade of Cornwall in the reigns of Elizabeth and James, compared with that of Edward I', *Journal of the Royal Institution of Cornwall* **4**, 187–90.

McCourt, D. (1953) 'Traditions of Rundale in and around the Sperrin Mountains', *Ulster Journal of Archaeology* **3** ser **16**, 69–83.

McCourt, D. (1954–55) 'Infield and outfield in Ireland', *Economic History Review* 7, 369–76.

McCourt, D. (1971) 'The dynamic quality of Irish rural settlement' in *Man and his Habitat*, eds R. H. Buchanan, E. Jones, and D. McCourt, Routledge and Kegan Paul, London, 126–64.

Miller, E. and Hatcher, J. (1980) *Medieval England – Rural Society and Economic Change 1086–1348*, Longman, London.

Nowakowski, J. A. and Herring, P. C. (1985) 'The Beehive huts on Bodmin Moor', *Cornish Archaeology* **24**, 185–96.

O'Danachair, C. (1970) 'The use of the spade in Ireland' in *The Spade in Northern and Atlantic Europe*, eds A. Gailey, and A. Fenton, Ulster Folk Museum, Belfast, 49–56.

O'Siochain, C. (1975) *The Man from Cape Clear*, Mercier Press, Dublin.

Padel, O. (1985) *Cornish Place-Name Elements*, English Place-Name Society vol. 56/57, Nottingham.

Pearce, S. M. (1981) *The Archaeology of South West Britain*, Collins, London.

Postan, M. M. (1975) *The Medieval Economy and Society: An Economic History of Britain in the Middle Ages*, Penguin, Harmondsworth.

Richardson, J. (1974) *The Local Historian's Encyclopaedia*, Historical Publications, New Barnet.

Ryder, M. L. (1984) 'Medieval sheep and wool types', *Agricultural History Review* **32.1**, 14–28.

Seward, D. (1970) 'The Devonshire cloth industry in the early seventeenth century' in *Industry and Society in the South-West* ed. R. Burt, Exeter Papers in Economic History **No. 3**, University of Exeter, Exeter, 29–50.

Stanes, R. G. F. (1964) 'A georgicall account of Devonshire and Cornwalle, Samuel Colepresse (1667)', *Transactions of the Devonshire Association* **96**, 269–302.

Taylor, C. C. (1975) *Fields in the English Landscape*, Dent, London.

Taylor, C. C. (1981) 'Archaeology and the origins of open-field agriculture' in *The Origins of Open-Field*, ed. T. Rowley, Croom Helm, London, 13–21.

Thomas, C. (1975) 'Peasant agriculture in medieval Gwynedd', *Folk Life* **13**, 24–37.

Thomas, C. (1978) 'The rural landscape of north Wales in the later Middle Ages', *Geographia Polonica* **38**, 271–7.

Thorn, C. and Thorn, F. (1979) *Domesday Book: 10 Cornwall* (from a translation by O. Padel), Phillimore, Chichester.

Ugawa, K. (1962) 'The economic development of some Devon manors in the thirteenth century', *Transactions of the Devonshire Association* **94**, 630–83.

Uhlig, H. (1961) 'Old hamlets with infield and outfield systems in western and central Europe', *Geografiska Annaler* **43**, 285–312.

Whittington, G. (1973) 'Field systems of Scotland' in *Studies of Field Systems in the British Isles*, eds A. R. H. Baker, and R. A. Butlin, University Press, Cambridge, 530–79.

Worgan, G. B. (1811) *General Review of the Agriculture of the County of Cornwall*, Board of Agriculture, London.

CHAPTER 6

Castles and the Medieval Landscape

O. H. Creighton and J. P. Freeman

Introduction

This short chapter explores the place of medieval castles within the historic landscape of Devon and Cornwall and examines their contribution to its evolution and character in the period c. 1050–1500. Its specific aims are twofold: first, to provide a brief overview of the present state of knowledge regarding the landscape settings of medieval castles in the region; and second, to identify some key remaining questions and to highlight some potentially fruitful directions for future research.

Fundamental to any approach to this subject must be the recognition that castles were embedded within the medieval landscape at a variety of levels and scales: as focal points within networks of estates and administrative centres that radiated territorial control; as manorial sites and elite residences that drew on the resources of town and country; as settlements and sometimes catalysts for settlement change; and as icons of lordship whose immediate settings might be manipulated for pleasure, leisure and visual impact (see Creighton 2002). We should also bear in mind that some common preconceptions about the settings of castles within their landscapes do not stand up to close scrutiny. In particular, neither the location of individual sites nor the wider spatial pattern of castle-building show much evidence of a purely military rationale. Indeed, any examination of castles in their wider landscape contexts will by definition draw attention to the social, economic and symbolic as opposed to defensive significance of sites. Thus, in the countryside castles were working manorial centres, while on the urban scene they demonstrate both the intrusion of authority into extant communities, and seigneurial economic ambition through the promotion of boroughs and the growth of nascent settlements. In addition, castles were not always central places in the medieval landscape in a conventional sense. Most did not exist and function as the hubs of discrete hinterlands at all, but can be understood instead as nodes of power in more complex networks of lordship not necessarily manifested in simple physical terms.

The current state of knowledge

At a broad scale Devon's castles have been well studied relative to those of Cornwall, which to date have only been examined as part of a wider synthesis of the county's medieval archaeology (Preston-Jones and Rose 1986; for Devon castles see Higham 1980; 1982; 1987b; 2000a). Work on castles at a national scale, meanwhile, has included the composition of invaluable annotated county listings of sites which provide us with useful starting points for contextual work (e.g. King 1983, 72–80, 114–24; Renn 1968).

Study of the region's castles in their landscape contexts has advanced on several fronts since the late 1970s. Contributions have come from excavation, field survey, documentary and architectural study and, perhaps most pertinently, from projects that have combined and synthesised diverse data sources. Such scholarship has built on a rich heritage of previous fieldwork and archival research, exemplified by the earthwork inventories of the Victoria County History. Through fieldwork in the early years of the twentieth century, these identified and listed many castle sites for the first time (Page 1906a, 451–73; 1906b, 573–630).

Major campaigns of research-led excavation have taken place at the important baronial castles of Launceston and Okehampton and at two castle sites in Lydford. Information from these projects illuminates many aspects of the interaction between sites and their hinterlands. For example, the animal bone reports from Launceston and Okehampton provide exceptionally rich information not only about elite patterns of consumption, but also about the ways in which the castle community drew on the resources of the countryside, with implications for understanding contemporary land management practices. Particularly striking at Okehampton is the evidence from animal bone for the intensification of deer management during the fourteenth century, and the enormous and rich assemblage of fish bones, which shows how the seigneurial site exerted an exceptionally strong 'pull' on this type of food resource (Higham *et al.* 1982, 114–44). At Launceston the sharp decline of fish and bird bones from the sixteenth century onwards helps us chart the site's transformation into an urban tip, and the bone assemblage similarly has implications for how surrounding estates were exploited (Albarella and Davis 1994, 20). At Lydford, meanwhile, excavation of both an early (eleventh- or twelfth-century) ringwork in the angle of the old Saxon *burh* defences and a later stronghouse and stannary prison has clarified the successive chronological relationship between two unusually closely spaced castle sites, which were both intrusive elements within the settlement plan (Wilson and Hurst 1965, 170–1; Saunders 1980).

More modest excavations have taken place at Lundy (Dunmore 1982), Penhallam (Beresford 1974), Bampton (Higham and Hamlin 1990), Barnstaple (Miles 1986), Dane's Castle, Exeter (Nenk *et al.* 1994, 203–4), and Great Torrington (Higham and Goddard 1987). At Barnstaple, for example, three trial trenches on the north side of the bailey revealed an extensive Saxon cemetery under the rampart bank of the early Norman motte and bailey. This work has important implications for our understanding of the castle's impact on the pre-Conquest townscape. At first sight the castle looks like a massive assertion of Norman dominance, aggressively sweeping away the burial ground of the townsfolk. On closer inspection, though, we should note that at least nine of the burials seem to have been exhumed prior to castle-building, presumably for reburial elsewhere (Miles 1986, 68).

Earthwork surveys by the Royal Commission on Historic Monuments for England (RCHME, now the English Heritage Survey Division) have greatly enhanced our understanding of castles at Loddiswell (Wilson-North and Dunn 1990), Bampton (Wilson-North 1991) and Lydford (Newman 2000). Architectural survey and related analyses of masonry remains have also illuminated interrelationships between sites and their settings. At Plympton, for instance, pictorial, topographical, documentary and structural evidence has afforded new insight into the relationships between the castle and the seigneurially planned borough and priory of the Norman period (Higham *et al.* 1985). At the fifteenth-century castle of Berry Pomeroy, detailed fabric analysis has identified the sources of stone used in various phases of the building (Brown 1996). In other cases, studies or surveys of other aspects of the medieval landscape have had a 'spin-off' effect for our understanding of associated castles. Thus at Week St Mary detailed topographical analysis has drawn attention to the borough's intimate relationship with the castle that prompted its growth as a market centre (Preston-Jones and Rose 1992). In addition, a groundbreaking study of Cornwall's deer parks has shown that the emparked settings of castles at Cardinham, Launceston and Restormel were landscapes of exclusion manipulated for aesthetic effect as well as hunting resources (Herring 2003).

Landscapes of castles

The number of castles in the region is at best unknown and at worst unknowable. Estimates have varied considerably. In King's compendium of English and Welsh castles, Devon and Cornwall have 69 sites, including five documented examples whose locations are unknown (King 1983, 72, 114); in the *Historic Atlas of the South-West*, Higham counted 80 castles and fortified houses (2000a). In common with any other type of monument, physical traces of some sites may have vanished entirely and new evidence for others may come to light; in other cases the field evidence is ambiguous. In this context, however, a particular challenge is the difficulty of reaching an adequate definition of what constituted a 'castle'. One part of a workable definition is, of course, a minimum threshold level of defence or defensibility, but it is also important to recognise that medieval society's own view of what constituted a castle was not static, varying through time and within society. Figure 46 presents a map of medieval fortifications that can be considered in some sense as castles, and issues of identification are discussed further below.

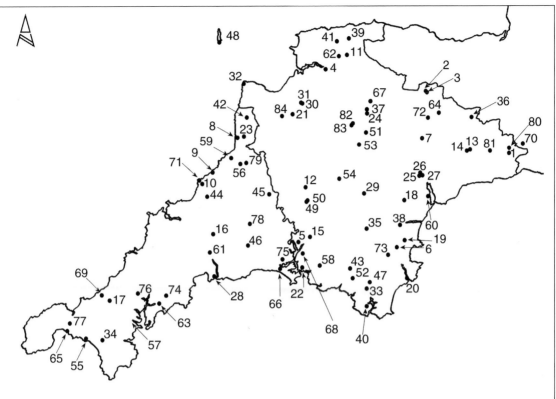

1, Axminster, Vanished; masonry castle?
2, Bampton, Motte and bailey
3, Bampton, Licence to crenellate (1336); vanished
4, Barnstaple, Motte and bailey
5, Bere Ferrers, Licence to crenellate (1337, 1340); strong house
6, Berry Pomeroy, Masonry castle
7, Bickleigh, Masonry castle
8, Binhamy, Licence to crenellate (1335); moated site
9, Boscastle, Ringwork and bailey
10, Bossiney, Ringwork and bailey
11, Bratton Fleming, Motte
12, Bridestowe, Motte and bailey
13, Buckerell, Buckerell Knap, Motte and bailey
14, Buckerell, Bushy Knap, Motte and bailey
15, Buckland Abbey, Licence to crenellate (1337); fortified precinct
16, Cardinham, Motte and bailey
17, Carn Brea, Masonry castle/hunting lodge
18, Chudleigh, Licence to crenellate (1379); fortified bishop's palace
19, Compton, Masonry castle
20, Dartmouth, Masonry castle/artillery fort
21, Durpley, Motte and bailey
22, East Stonehouse, Licence to crenellate (1515); vanished
23, Eastleigh Berrys, Motte and bailey
24, Eggesford, Ringwork and bailey
25, Exeter I, Ringwork within city wall
26, Exeter II, Siege ringwork
27, Exeter, Bishop's palace/close, Licence to crenellate (1290, 1322)
28, Fowey, Masonry castle/artillery fort
29, Gidleigh, Tower house
30, Great Torrington, Vanished; masonry castle?
31, Great Torrington, Licence to crenellate (1328, 1340, 1347)
32, Hartland, Vanished; masonry castle?
33, Hatch, Licence to crenellate (1462); strong house
34, Helston, Vanished; masonry castle?
35, Hembury, Motte and bailey
36, Hemyock, Masonry castle
37, Heywood, Motte and bailey
38, High Week, Motte and bailey
39, Holwell, Motte and bailey
40, Ilton, Vanished; masonry castle
41, Kentisbury, Licence to crenellate (1457); strong house? (vanished)
42, Kilkhampton, Motte and bailey

43, Langford Barton, Motte
44, Lanteglos, Castle Goff, Ringwork and bailey
45, Launceston, Motte and bailey
46, Liskeard, Vanished; masonry castle
47, Loddiswell, Ringwoprk and bailey
48, Lundy, Masonry castle
49, Lydford I, Ringwork
50, Lydford II, Stronghouse/stannary prison
51, Millsome, Coldridge, Ringwork
52, Modbury, Licence to crenellate (1334); masonry castle (vanished)
53, North Tawton, Motte
54, Okehampton, Motte and bailey
55, Pengersick, Tower house
56, Penhallam, Ringwork
57, Penryn, Glasney College, Fortified ecclesiastical site
58, Plympton, Motte and bailey
59, Poundstock, Motte
60, Powderham, Masonry castle
61, Restormel, Ringwork and bailey
62, Roborough, Motte
63, Ruan Lanihorne, Licence to crenellate (1335); masonry castle (vanished)
64, Sampford Peverel, Licence to crenellate (1337, 1339); moated site
65, St Michael's Mount, Fortified monastery
66, Sheviok, Licence to crenellate (1336); strong house
67, Stone Barton, Vanished; motte and bailey?
68, Tamerton, Licence to crenellate (1335); strong house (vanished)
69, Tehidy, Licence to crenellate (1330); strong house (vanished)
70, Thorncombe, Licence to crenellate (1397); strong house
71, Tintagel, Masonry castle
72, Tiverton, Masonry castle
73, Totnes, Motte and bailey
74, Tregony, Motte and bailey
75, Trematon, Motte and bailey
76, Truro, Vanished; masonry castle?
77, Truthwall, Licence to crenellate (1335); strong house (vanished)
78, Upton, Ringwork
79, Week St Mary, Ringwork and bailey
80, Weycroft, Licence to crenellate (1427); strong house
81, Widworthy, Motte
82, Winkleigh I, Motte and bailey
83, Winkleigh II, Ringwork
84, Woodford, Motte and bailey

Most people probably think of castles as major masonry monuments like those preserved at Launceston, Okehampton, Totnes and Tintagel. It is not much appreciated that the majority of Devon and Cornwall's medieval castles were not built of stone, but rather of earth and timber. Their slumped and grassed-over earthworks dot the region's landscape. However, it must also be borne in mind that in some cases such earthworks may also conceal masonry remains, a matter only resolvable through more intensive investigation. In addition, while we might think castles are obvious features of the landscape, new sites continue to be identified, even in counties with long traditions of field archaeology. Thus, a motte with a possible bailey at Poundstock (Cornwall: SX199994) was first identified as such in the 1990s by the RCHME; at Castle Goff (Cornwall: SX082826) a ringwork and bailey previously listed as a prehistoric encampment has been recognised adjacent to a an isolated parish church; and at Bushy Knap and Buckerell Knap (Devon: ST131010 and ST127014) archaeological survey has identified at least one of two enigmatic earthworks as early castles (Figure 47).

This last example forms a notable case study of how landscape analysis can inform castle study and vice versa. The site complex comprises two suites of earthworks. Each is focused on an artificial mound, and they lie little more than 300 m apart at opposite ends of a prominent ridge. The features are undocumented and have variously been identified as barrows, natural features

FIGURE 47
Bushy Knap and Buckerell Knap, based on archaeological earthwork survey (Hawken 2004). The earthworks probably represent two closely spaced motte and bailey castles of the eleventh or twelfth century (source: Hawken 2004).

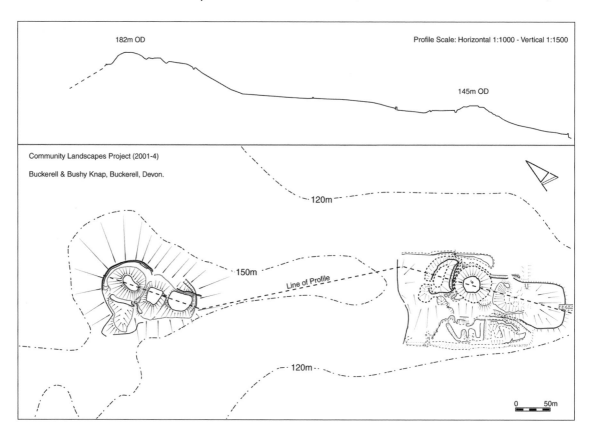

and late prehistoric enclosures, yet the first systematic archaeological survey of the area suggests that at least one, if not both, are motte and bailey castles (Hawken 2004). Whilst the relationship between the two sites remains uncertain, this interpretation is given credibility by reconstruction of the medieval landscape of the area: the ridge formed part of a medieval deer park and in 1086 the area lay within a compact lordship under the Pomeroy family. There are other examples of closely juxtaposed castles at Winkleigh, where two sites may have built under separate lordship and lay in separate manors, and at Exeter, where Dane's Castle was a predatorial work of the twelfth century (see Creighton 2002, 57–9); the relationship between the early castles at Eggesford and Heywood, little more than 600 m apart, remains obscure, though one may again be a 'counter castle'.

There are a number of monuments in the region (as elsewhere) that have been identified and accepted as castles despite a lack of documentary or archaeological evidence confirming their creation or use in the medieval period. Some, like the motte and bailey at Eggesford, have a characteristic appearance that does seem to confirm such an interpretation. Others, particularly ringworks, are much less surely identified as castles on their morphology alone. Some of these monuments, such as Eastleigh Berrys near Bude in Cornwall, are quite large but remain little known and remain to be studied archaeologically. The locations of other castle sites remain obscure: at Axminster and Hartland, for instance, castles (or at least the intention to build them) are documented in the early years of the thirteenth century, yet no physical remains are preserved. Many of these aforementioned examples have in common difficulties in reconciling documentary and archaeological sources: on the one hand, attempting to reconcile a snippet of written information with the physical reality of a field monument; or, on the other, attempting to place what is essentially a 'prehistoric' site into a historical context. Overall, there is much that remains unclear concerning the identification of castles, let alone the understanding of their physical surroundings and wider tenurial contexts.

Deeply ingrained in our preconceptions about castles is their supposed military character. For instance, it is an established tradition to evaluate the defensive value of a site's position when describing its topographical situation. Applying the concepts of modern military thinking to the medieval period – consciously or unconsciously – is fraught with problems, and the distribution map of castles in the South West seems to owe relatively little to any overarching military rationale. Thus, the Norman site of Castle Neroche, perched on a scarp of the Blackdown Hills on the eastern edge of the region, has been described as 'well placed to command the approaches to the south-west peninsula' (Davison 1972, 16). It is questionable whether a castle could itself ever command a route in the way that seems implied, or indeed whether routes of the sort considered significant by modern tacticians ever existed in the medieval period. It may well be that 'commanding positions' are as much about making a statement of power and wealth as military pragmatics. In the case of some castles found close by settlements like Totnes or Boscastle it is easy to imagine that the castles' physical position – looming above the populace on one side, and yet easily accessible from the other – is as much to do with image as it is with military concerns.

If any overarching strategy can be argued for in patterns of castle building, it is at the very beginning and end of the Middle Ages. The systematic construction of Norman castles in the region's four Anglo-Saxon *burhs* during the years immediately after the Conquest was part of a co-ordinated scheme aimed at suppressing not only centres of population and commerce but also the machinery of government (at Barnstaple, Exeter, Lydford and Totnes: see Creighton 2002, 33–7). These castles were intrusive features that precipitated the destruction of parts of earlier settlements in a manner not witnessed in the countryside. At the end of the Middle Ages, the 20 or more fifteenth- and sixteenth-century artillery forts dotted along the region's southern coastline were component parts of what became a system of bulwarks on the borders of an emerging nation-state (for example, fortifications at Dartmouth, Edgcumbe, Fowey, Kingswear and Salcombe: see Saunders 1973; 1989, 15–52). Paradoxically, the resultant 'landscape of defence' did not involve castle-building at all: while the sites of these maritime fortifications were selected for purely military reasons, they were neither private residences nor tied to patterns of landholding. In contrast, the wave of licences to crenellate in the fourteenth and fifteenth centuries relates largely to elite dwellings around the south coast (Figure 46), reflecting private concerns with household security in the face of maritime raids rather than with any military master plan.

Indeed, we should also bear in mind that in the South West castles could be sited with reference to the 'seascape' as much as much to the countryside inland. Estuarine positions were common for castles, as at Powderham, Totnes and Trematon on the south coast and Barnstaple, Binhamy and Boscastle on the north coast. Other sites lay close to harbours or navigable rivers, though the silting-up of waterways means this is no longer obvious at places like Plympton, Restormel and Tregony. Such sites were doubtless selected not only for security but also for ease of communication and sometimes economic potential. The huge dimensions of the moat around the early Norman castle at Barnstaple suggest it may have been a tidal feature, linking the rivers Yeo and Taw. Such a construction arguably demonstrates more of a concern with maritime access than defence; if so, this would have been around two centuries before similar systems were built at Edward I's royal castles in north Wales (Miles 1986, 73). Permission to fortify a site at Hartland was given in 1201, apparently in response to a piratical threat within the Severn, and the royal fortress built on Lundy in the mid thirteenth century can be seen in a similar context (Dunmore 1982). Devon and Cornwall do not, of course, simply represent an outlying province jutting out into an imagined periphery; an essential part of the region's identity in the Middle Ages was derived from its role as a zone of communication for areas linked by the sea. There are close connections, for example, between administrative personnel associated with residences of the social elite on either side of the Bristol Channel (Burls

2003). In this sense Devon and Cornwall represent part of a wider trans-marine region, linked not only to south Wales but also parts of Ireland, and forming a component part of what has been termed the 'Severnside' province (Griffiths 1994).

The physical designs of castles are not generally thought to display a particularly high level of meaningful regional variation. Architectural parallels between elements of castle architecture and parish churches or monastic sites (as at Launceston and Totnes, for instance), emphasise one way in which a link of patronage might be expressed physically. But are other patterns of castle design significant, either within the context of the South West peninsula or in comparison with other regions? The circular shell-keep form is a highly characteristic feature of masonry castle design in the South West, for instance (Toy 1933; Renn 1969), and the distribution actually spans the Bristol Channel. Perhaps emphasising the idea of a Severnside province, circular forms are also common in castles built within Norman lordships in south Wales, such as the donjon at Pembroke and the shell-keep at Wiston, also in Pembrokeshire. Shell-keeps continued to be built relatively late into the medieval period in the South West and they emerge as something of a regional tradition that cuts across trends elsewhere; thus the examples at Launceston and Trematon date to the twelfth century, Restormel to the thirteenth, and Totnes, in almost anachronistic form, to the fourteenth.

The overall sparsity of early castles on the Cornwall distribution map represents the dominant tenurial force of the earldom, present in embryonic form in Robert of Mortain's large Domesday fief of some 277 manors. Here power, wealth and contiguity of lordship actually gave rise to a relatively low density of castles, with sites such as Cardinham, Penhallam and Week St Mary originating as the castles of sub-tenants (Preston-Jones and Rose 1986, 172). Taking a longer-term view, the apparent 'explosion' in the construction of private earth and timber defensive sites in the late eleventh and twelfth centuries could be seen to represent a re-establishment or even continuation of the Iron Age, Roman and post-Roman tradition of 'round' building. We might ask how many ringworks in Cornwall have been mis-identified as rounds, and whether some castles have reused these pre-existing features as castles. Unfortunately, our excavated sample is insufficient to provide a conclusive answer. Nonetheless, it may well be significant that apparently medieval ring-works are predominant in the central-western part of the county while the (larger) mottes are closer to the border with Devon, and many are associated with nucleated settlements (see King and Alcock 1966, 103–5). Rather than the motte distribution representing a low level of Norman penetration into Cornwall (see Pettifer 2002, 17), might the ringworks effectively demonstrate the revival of a characteristically Cornish form of dispersed rural settlement?

Castles and their contexts

The relationship between castles and lordships was complex. The tenurial pattern in the period in question was ever-changing – kaleidoscopic even, given the rise and fall of families in the social order – and the status of castles likewise shifted, removing the *raison d'être* of some and giving others fresh uses. In the late eleventh century, for instance, baronial castles at Okehampton and Totnes were elements within large, scattered estate frameworks incorporating urban and rural properties and a hierarchy of residential and administrative sites. What is clear is that the institution of the castle was flexible, readily adaptable to myriad social and tenurial circumstances; some might be mono-functional, such as the siege castle of Dane's Castle or those built to serve hunting resources, as is likely with the motte at Hembury, Buckfastleigh; the circumstances are so diverse that identification of simple patterns is difficult.

The settlement contexts of castles in the region were and still are distinctive. Sites in relatively isolated though not inaccessible locations were clearly favoured (Higham 1980; 1982; 2000a). Two illustrative sites in this context are the ringwork at Penhallam, Jacobstowe, which enclosed a manor house and estate centre of the Cardinham family from the late twelfth to the early fourteenth century (Beresford 1974), and the ridge-end motte and bailey of Holwell Castle Parracombe (Figure 48) (Higham 2000b); both were manorial centres within parishes whose historic settlement patterns were dispersed. Elsewhere, those sites found in close proximity to parish churches or chapels, such as Bickleigh, Castle Goff, North Tawton, Tiverton and Week St Mary, are a post-Conquest manifestation of the established link between manorial centres and ecclesiastical sites and hold important symbolic connotations as expressions of lordship (Preston-Jones 1994, 80). At Bickleigh, for instance, the Norman chapel almost certainly represents a proprietary foundation related to a manorial focus perpetuated by the later castle.

Where castles are found in association with nucleated settlements these were invariably boroughs. Some prominent examples show hallmarks of seigneurial planning. At Launceston the town plan clearly relates to the castle nucleus, with the radial plan mirroring the castle bailey and the town defences effectively an extension of the seigneurial site. At Plympton the linear street-plan runs parallel to a castle-church nucleus. Rather less obvious, but perhaps more characteristic of the region, are castles by boroughs that remained small or else shrank in the later or post-medieval periods, including places such as Winkleigh and Week St Mary. In dispersed landscapes, castle-lords could also engage actively in borough planning where the towns remained at some distance from the castle, as at Lostwithiel and Okehampton (Figure 49). In some cases, as at Kilkhampton in north Cornwall, field boundary evidence suggests that a change in the structure of the settlement has left a castle in what seems a relatively isolated position.

That the seigneurial grip on market networks was tightening in the immediate post-Conquest decades is clear in the folios of Domesday Book: at

Trematon, Count Robert of Mortain is said to have depleted the Bishop of Exeter's market at St Germans by establishing a rival market, held on the same day, in his castle; at *Dunhevet* (Launceston), the count's actions are more explicit still, having taken away the market under the control of the canons of St Stephens and transplanted it to his castle (Harfield 1991, 375–6). Such markets were presumably held in baileys, highlighting their role as zones of interface between the seigneurial core and wider communities. The motivations are clear: a calculated process of targeting or arrogating rival markets points towards aggressive seigneurial economic policy and a conscious 'Normanisation' of the marketing network. In Cornwall the immediate post-Conquest years certainly saw important baronial castles emerge as new foci for marketing and economic growth; east of the Tamar, by contrast, major castles often perpetuated the economic significance of existing central places. As sources of expenditure rather than taxable assets, however, castles appear only rarely in Domesday Book. In the South West the only other site recorded is Okehampton, where seigneurial economic initiative is again evident in the record of a market in the hands of Baldwin the Sheriff, who held the manor from the king.

Another way in which castles were linked to their surroundings was through obligations of castle-guard, performed by the tenants of outlying estates. At Launceston, Restormel and Trematon, the three principal castles of the Duchy of Cornwall in the fourteenth century, individual fief-holders were responsible for the maintenance of specified stretches of parapet, or the wooden hoardings that surmounted them (Coulson 2003, 57, 279). By this time the duty was largely symbolic rather than motivated by real military need. Nonetheless, it shows one less obvious way in which organisation of the surrounding tenurial landscape was articulated through the physical fabric of the castle itself. Another is highlighted in the arrangement of excavated structures within the bailey of Launceston. Here, a planned arrangement of closely spaced and substantial self-contained stone houses, resembling one planned town within another, is thought to have provided accommodation for the holders of knight's fees on surrounding estates periodically performing castle-guard (Saunders 1977, 129). That such evidence is largely only revealed through excavation does little to reassure us that we understand much about how the majority of castles may have functioned, given that so few sites have received anything beyond minimal archaeological investigation.

We have seen that the name 'castle' was used for a great range of sites having many different roles – from late prehistoric hillforts such as Woodbury Castle, through later medieval 'strong houses' such as Compton, to post-medieval residences like Castle Drogo. The last of these sites – which in no sense meets the definition of a castle from a strictly archaeological or historical point of view – provides an illustrative case in point. A romantic creation of Sir Edward Lutyens for the businessman Julius Drewe and dating to *c.* 1910–30, the dramatic granite-built structure has been described as 'the last castle to be built in England' (see Thompson 1987). Notably, the topographical position of the site was clearly selected to reflect Drewe's perceived ancestral connection to the Norman baron Drogo de Teign, its dramatic setting on a high granite ridge overlooking the Teign marking the presumed centre of the baron's estates. While Lutyens' building project was based on Drewe's immense wealth as a grocery magnate (contrasting with the landed wealth that supported most medieval castle-building), the structure perpetuates a long tradition whereby the castle image was constantly evolving or, more correctly, re-invented, to draw power from the past. An important way in which castle builders achieved this was through the selection of sites and the manipulation of their surrounds. Indeed, the images of medieval castles were themselves reused and manipulated in later centuries as symbols in designed landscapes. The ways that the settings of post-medieval gentry houses drew on medieval imagery, appropriating medieval symbols, for instance to create pseudo-historical deer parks, as at Powderham, is the subject of on-going research (Wainwright 2004).

This type of process can be explored a little further through an example of a castle-building enterprise led by King Henry III's younger brother, Earl Richard of Cornwall, the crusader, international politician, King of the

FIGURE 48
Holwell Castle, Parracombe, showing the exceptionally well preserved earthworks of a motte and bailey.
O.H.CREIGHTON

Romans and contender for the title of Holy Roman Emperor, who held the earldom from 1227 to 1277 (Roche 1966). It is now generally accepted that Tintagel Castle was a creation of Richard in the second quarter of the thirteenth century, shortly after he became Earl of Cornwall (Hartgroves and Walker 1988; Thomas 2002, 85–9). Military factors clearly played no role in the decision to build the castle in this particular place: the remote headland site had little strategic value, and the constraints of the immediate topographical setting ensured an awkwardly planned castle whose inner and outer wards are disjointed. If the castle was not primarily a fortification, then neither was it an estate centre in the manner we might assume most castles were. Documentary sources make it clear that occupation of the castle in the thirteenth century was at a low level and perhaps sporadic, that its administrative functions were negligible, and that its active life was short, being derelict as early as the mid fourteenth century. Fortification of the site seems to have been a primarily symbolic gesture, designed to appropriate and exploit the place's imagined past. Geoffrey of Monmouth's *History of the Kings of Britain*, completed in the late 1130s, saw the place-name '*Tintogel*' celebrated across Europe as the seat of the Cornish ruler Gorlois and the place of the magical conception of Arthur, while the place's romantic connections were further amplified by romances such as Tristan and Isolde, where it was the castle of King Mark (Padel 1988). In a regional context, meanwhile, the folk memories on which Geoffrey of Monmouth embroidered – of Tintagel as an ancient royal centre of the Kingdom of Dumnonia – signifies the appropriation of an icon of Cornishness by a man keen to emphasise such links. Notably, the haphazard design of the castle formed something of a literary landscape in its own right, with features such as the chapel, well and walled garden making conscious reference to contemporary romances (Rose 1994, 177). The long-term perpetuation of myths about this landscape – from Tennyson to Hardy and the modern heritage industry – is therefore part of a very long tradition, of which castle-building was one contributor.

Restormel provides another example of a castle whose medieval surroundings reflect seigneurial planning for display and aesthetic impact. Here a reappraisal of the site, combining structural analysis with broader landscape study, has emphasised that the so-called shell-keep built in the second half of the thirteenth century was not a primarily military structure (Thomas 2000, 28–30; see also Herring 2003). Instead, this innovative keep was designed

FIGURE 50
Restormel Castle, showing the parapet walk of the thirteenth-century shell-keep, which provided views across the surrounding parkland setting.
O.H.CREIGHTON

as an integrated domestic unit as well as a masonry edifice that presented different images to different observers (Figure 50). From the east the day-to-day workings of the bailey were tucked away out of sight. The bailey was never rebuilt in stone, retaining weak and unimpressive earth and timber defences, in contrast to the efforts foisted on the shell-keep, which was set like a jewel in the enveloping deer park. The setting of Restormel also included an isolated chapel and a putative garden enclosure. Together they formed a carefully composed ensemble designed to be visible from the approach roads and the river below. In addition, the seigneurial borough of Lostwithiel lay on the very edge of the castle's park (and at the limit of the view to the south), emphasising further the exclusivity of the seat of lordship. The design of the shell-keep provided ample opportunities for the admiration of this 'landscape of lordship': large windows opened onto parkland views, while the inner hall – representing one of the most private spaces in the design – was provided with direct access to the parapet walk via a stair. In addition, the outer bank of the early ringwork castle was re-landscaped to provide a levelled terrace surrounding the shell-keep, with spoil piled against it to create the illusion that it surmounted a motte (Figure 51). An illuminating parallel can be found at Lydford (Figure 52), where the 'castle', as rebuilt by Richard, Earl of Cornwall in the mid thirteenth century, was similarly contrived to represent a donjon and motte in microcosm. Here the castle was surrounded by ancient structures from the Anglo-Saxon townscape: at least the relict defences of the *burh*, and probably the church of St Petrock too. Excavation has made clear that what seem to be the earliest features – the motte and miniature bailey – were in fact secondary additions that created the image of an old castle (Saunders 1980, 156–64).

Another of Richard's creations in the mid thirteenth century is the shell-keep at Launceston (Figure 53). This feature has traditionally been seen as a military structure, with the separate tiers interpreted as 'fighting platforms' (Renn 1969, 11); in reality, however, the site's famous 'wedding cake' profile seems to have been a largely symbolic creation. It lacked a meaningful residential or domestic function but was furnished with splendid window seats from which the deer park outside could be admired (Herring 2003). Okehampton provides another instructive example of a castle embedded in a parkland landscape. The castle was replanned by the Courtenay family in the early fourteenth century, and the details of the structure related to its environs in an intriguing way (Higham *et al.* 1982, 63–74). To the south, where the site was embraced by a deer park, the window seats in sumptuous domestic lodgings in the donjon and bailey enjoyed spectacular views unimpeded by defences; on the northern side, however, the castle's public face presented a martial façade dominated by an imposing curtain wall to anybody approaching along the old Okehampton Road that led to and from the borough. Thus, while castles in the South West were commonly isolated features, it is clear that surrounding landscapes could be manipulated to form contrived settings. While these did not feature the obvious hallmarks of regular seigneurial planning, there is little doubt that

FIGURE 53
Launceston, showing
the donjon with its
famous triple-tiered
appearance, which
provided views of
surrounding parkland.
O.H.CREIGHTON

they too formed 'landscapes of lordship' (see Liddiard 2000a). Other sites deserving closer scrutiny include Berry Pomeroy (enveloped entirely within a deer park and with water features in the valley below held back by cross-dams) and Ilton and Penhallam (also associated with water features).

Conclusions

While castles might be thought of as dominant features in their landscapes, this chapter has underlined how some quite fundamental questions about them and their impact on town and country remain unanswered. What is certain is that our understanding of the subject will only advance if future researchers come to grips with both the full and diverse range of sources available, and address critically some deeply ingrained and longstanding preconceptions about their functions and significance. It should be underlined that examination of the landscapes of castles must be much more than a scene-setting exercise to provide background information on a significant building. Instead, landscape study can serve both to complement and challenge interpretations based on other sources, and to explore the dynamic relationships between castles, their settings, and the communities that lived both within and beyond their walls.

References

Albarella, U. and Davis, J.M. (1994) 'Mammals and birds from Launceston Castle Cornwall: decline in status and the rise of agriculture', *Circaea* **12.1**, 1–156.

Beresford, G. (1974) 'The medieval manor at Penhallam, Jacobstown, Cornwall', *Medieval Archaeology* **18**, 9–145.

Brown, S. (1996) 'Berry Pomeroy Castle', *Proceedings of the Devon Archaeological Society* **54** (dedicated volume).

Burls, R.L. (2003) 'Medieval "Severnside": Devon and its overseas neighbours before c. 1360', *Report and Transactions of the Devonshire Association* **135**, 71–98.

Coulson, C. (2003) *Castles in Medieval Society. Fortresses in England, France, and Ireland in the Central Middle Ages*, Oxford University Press, Oxford.

Creighton, O.H. (2002) *Castles and Landscapes*, Continuum, London and New York.

Davison, B.K. (1972) 'Castle Neroche: an abandoned Norman fortress in south Somerset', *Transactions of the Somerset Archaeological and Natural History Society* **116**, 16–58.

Dunmore, S. (1982) 'The castle in the Isle of Lundy', *Proceedings of the Devon Archaeological Society* **40**, 153–62.

Everson, P., Brown, G. and Stocker, D. (2000) 'The castle earthworks and landscape context' in *Ludgershall Castle, Wiltshire: a Report on the Excavations by Peter Addyman, 1964–1972*, ed. P. Ellis, Devizes, Wiltshire Archaeological and Natural History Society Monograph No. 2, 97–119.

Griffiths, R.A. (1994) 'Medieval Severnside: the Welsh connection' in *Conquerors and Conquered in Medieval Wales*, ed. R.A. Griffiths, Stroud, 1–18.

Harfield, C.G. (1991) 'A hand-list of castles recorded in the Domesday Book', *English Historical Review* **106**, 371–92.

Hartgroves, S. and Walker, R. (1988) 'Excavations in the Lower Ward, Tintagel Castle, 1986', *Cornish Studies* **16** (First Series), 9–30.

Hawken, S. (2004) *Bushy Knap and Buckerell Knap*, unpublished Report for the Community Landscapes Project, Exeter.

Herring, P. (2003) 'Cornish deer parks' in *The Lie of the Land: Aspects of the History and Archaeology of the Designed Landscape in the South West,* ed. R. Wilson-North, Mint Press, Exeter, 34–50.

Higham, R.A. (1977) 'Excavations at Okehampton Castle, Devon, part one – the motte and keep', *Proceedings of the Devon Archaeological Society* **35**, 3–42.

Higham, R.A. (1980) 'Castles in Devon' in *Archaeology of the Devon Landscape*, ed. S. Timms, Devon County Council, Exeter, 71–80.

Higham, R.A. (1982) 'Early castles in Devon, 1068–1201', *Château Gaillard* **9–10**, 102–15.

Higham, R.A. (1986a) 'Devon castles: an annotated list', *Proceedings of the Devon Archaeological Society* **44**, 142–9.

Higham, R.A. (1987a) 'Great Torrington Castle', *Proceedings of the Devon Archaeological Society* **45**, 97–103.

Higham, R.A. (1987b) 'Public and private defence in the medieval South West: town, castle and fort' in *Security and Defence in South-West England Before 1800*, ed. R.A. Higham, Exeter Studies in History No. 19, Exeter.

Higham, R.A. (1988) 'Was there a castle at Axminster?', *Proceedings of the Devon Archaeological Society* **46**, 182–3.

Higham, R.A. (2000a) 'Castles, fortified houses and fortified towns in the Middle Ages' in *Historic Atlas of the South-West,* eds R. Kain and W. Ravenhill, Exeter University Press, Exeter, 136–43.

Higham, R.A. (2000b) 'Parracombe', *Archaeological Journal* **157**, 445–8.

Higham, R.A. (2001) 'Okehampton Castle, Devon: interpretation, conservation, presentation and restoration from circa 1895 to circa 1995', *Europa Nostra Fédération Pan-Européenne du Patrimoine Bulletin* **55**, 129–52.

Higham, R.A., Allan, J.P. and Blaylock, S.R. (1982) 'Excavations at Okehampton castle, Devon, part two – the bailey', *Proceedings of the Devon Archaeological Society* **40**, 19–151.

Higham, R.A., and Goddard, S. (1987) 'Great Torrington Castle', *Proceedings of the Devon Archaeological Society* **45**, 97–103.

Higham, R.A., Goddard, S. and Rouillard, M. (1985) 'Plympton Castle, Devon', *Proceedings of the Devon Archaeological Society* **43**, 59–75.

Higham, R.A. and Hamlin, A. (1990) 'Bampton Castle, Devon: history and archaeology', *Proceedings of the Devon Archaeological Society* **48**, 101–10.

Higham, R.A. and Rouillard, M. (1989) 'The site of 'Tracey Castle', Bow', *Proceedings of the Devon Archaeological Society* **47**, 122–6.

King, D.J.C. (1983) *Castellarium Anglicanum*, 2 vols, London/New York.

King, D.J.C. and Alcock, L. (1969) 'Ringworks of England and Wales', *Château Gaillard* **3**, 90–127.

Liddiard, R. (2000) *"Landscapes of Lordship": Norman Castles and the Countryside in Medieval Norfolk, 1066–1200*, Oxford.

Miles, T.J. (1986) 'The excavation of a Saxon cemetery and part of the Norman castle at North Walk, Barnstaple', *Devon Archaeology Society Proceedings* **44**, 59–84.

Nenk, B.S. Margeson, S. and Hurley, M. (1994) 'Medieval Britain and Ireland in 1993', *Medieval Archaeology* **38**, 184–293.

Newman, P. (2000) *The Town and Castle Earthworks at Lydford, Devon*, unpublished English Heritage Survey Report.

Padel, O.J. (1988) 'Tintagel in the twelfth and thirteenth centuries', *Cornish Studies* **16** (First Series), 61–6.

Page, W. ed. (1906a) *The Victoria History of the Counties of England, Cornwall*, Volume 1, London.

Page, W. ed. (1906b) *The Victoria History of the Counties of England, Devonshire*, Volume 1, London.

Pettifer, A. (2002) *English Castles. A Guide by Counties*, Woodbridge.

Preston-Jones, A. and Rose, P. (1986) 'Medieval Cornwall', *Cornish Archaeology* **25**, 135–84.

Preston-Jones, A. and Rose, P. (1992) 'Week St Mary, town and castle', *Cornish Archaeology* **31**, 143–53.

Preston-Jones, A. (1994) 'Decoding Cornish churchyards', *Cornish Archaeology* **33**, 71–95.

Renn, D. (1968) *Norman Castles in Britain*, London.

Renn, D.F. (1969) *Three Shell Keeps: Launceston, Restormel, Totnes*, HMSO, London.

Roche, T.W.E. (1966) *The King of Almayne: A Thirteenth-Century Englishman in Europe*, Murray, London.

Rose, P. (1992) 'Bossiney Castle', *Cornish Archaeology* **31**, 138–42.

Rose, P. (1994) 'The medieval garden at Tintagel Castle', *Cornish Archaeology* **33**, 170–82.

Saunders, A.D. (1973) 'The coastal defences of Cornwall', *Archaeological Journal* **130**, 232–6.

Saunders, A.D. (1977) 'Excavations at Launceston Castle 1970–76: interim report', *Cornish Archaeology* **16**, 129–37.

Saunders, A.D. (1980) 'Lydford Castle, Devon', *Medieval Archaeology* **24**, 123–86.

Saunders, A.D. (1989) *Fortress Britain: Artillery Forts in the British Isles and Ireland*, Beaufort, Liphook.

Thomas, C. (2002) 'Cornish Archaeology at the Millennium', *Cornish Studies* (Second Series) **10**, 80–9.

Thomas, N. (2000) *Restormel Castle, a Re-appraisal*, Draft Report, Cornwall Historic Environment Service.

Thompson, M.W. (1987) *The Decline of the Castle*, Cambridge University Press, Cambridge.

Toy, S. (1933) 'The round castles of Cornwall', *Archaeologia* **83**, 203–26.

Wainwright, A. (2004) 'Revision and forgery in the historic landscape', *Society for Landscape Studies Newsletter* (Autumn/Winter Edition), 10–11.

Wilson, D.M. and Hurst, D.G. (1965) 'Medieval Britain in 1964', *Medieval Archaeology* **91**, 170–220.

Wilson-North, W.R. (1991) 'Bampton Castle: an earthwork survey by the Royal Commission on the Historical Monuments of England', *Proceedings of the Devon Archaeological Society* **49**, 115–19.

Wilson-North, W.R. and Dunn, C.J. (1990) '"The Rings", Loddiswell: a new survey by the Royal Commission on the Historic Monuments of England', *Proceedings of the Devon Archaeological Society* **48**, 87–100.

CHAPTER 7

Tinworking and the Landscape of Medieval Devon, *c.*1150–1700

Phil Newman

Introduction

From the mid twelfth to the mid seventeenth century AD, archaeological and historical evidence for the exploitation of metals in Devon is overwhelmingly for tin, and for one short period production even exceeded that of Cornwall. However, unlike Cornwall, where tin mining is deeply rooted in the county's culture, in Devon the importance of the industry is frequently overlooked in regional studies, overshadowed by its ultimately more productive neighbour.

What follows is an examination and summary of the landscape evidence for medieval tinworking in Devon and an attempt to characterise and distinguish the archaeological remains of the medieval period. Tin was an important component of the medieval economy, both locally and for the Crown, who benefited hugely from tin revenue, and the activity of the tinners has had a lasting and dramatic effect on the upland landscape. For the medieval aspects of the tin industry, Devon is in some ways a more fruitful area for study than Cornwall because the field evidence was not subjected to anything like the same scale of disturbance in the eighteenth to twentieth centuries by the reworking of the resource. The focus here will be on tinworking rather than tin mills (where tin was refined and smelted), and on some of the issues surrounding the ways in which this element of the landscape might have developed over approximately 600 years.

The medieval setting

The evidence for tinworking in Devon (Figure 54) is confined mostly to the granite mass of Dartmoor and its immediate borders, although it is known from documentation and field evidence that alluvial tin was also exploited in some lowland areas surrounding the moor, such as Bovey Heathfield.

Today, Dartmoor is frequently misrepresented as a 'wilderness', wrongly suggesting that the hand of man has had only a small part to play in the moulding of this landscape. Archaeological and documentary evidence inform

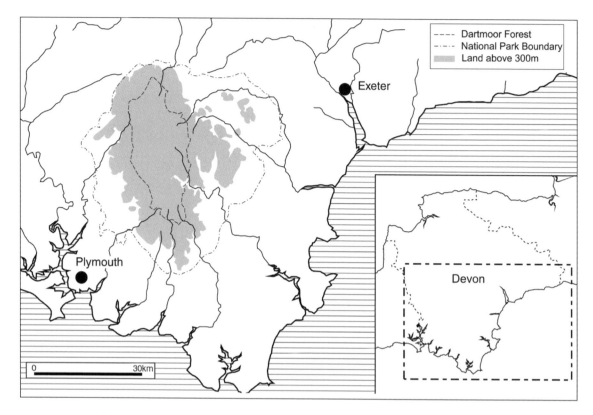

FIGURE 54
Map of south Devon
showing the location
of Dartmoor where the
majority of medieval
tinworking took place.

us unequivocally that quite the opposite is true. The uplands of Dartmoor and its borders have been exploited, settled and farmed by humans for at least 4,000 years, and probably longer. However, because of the altitude and the consequent marginality of the land, the level of settlement on Dartmoor has always fluctuated, dictated by, among other factors, climate and demographic pressures.

The full extent of settlement and agriculture in the centuries preceding the period under consideration is not yet known but it would be unwise to dismiss Dartmoor as unvisited, unsettled and unexploited on the basis of negative evidence and there is clearly much work still to be done on this topic. By 1086, at the time of Domesday, no settlements are recorded on the central uplands though a small but significant number were already established in the sheltered valleys around Widecombe parish, Chagford and some peripheral areas of the moor (Hoskins 1954, 55). After 1240, when the central zone of Dartmoor was disafforested, the group of settlements known as the Ancient Tenements was founded inside the former Forest, many of which remain occupied today. Settlement was also occurring on the higher parts of the moor outside the Forest during the thirteenth century, probably a result of land hunger, and made easier by an improvement in the climate. These pioneer settlers resided in isolated farmsteads, hamlets or small villages; their dwellings usually consisted of stone longhouses with associated stone-walled enclosures and fields. As time went on more settlements were established on the higher ground and in the Forest, while some existing sites were consolidated and continued to expand. However, a significant number were later deserted, particularly those at higher altitudes (over 300 m above OD), their viability being influenced, as noted above, by factors such as worsening climate and, perhaps, demographic changes following the Black Death from 1340 onwards. Analysis of pottery from the excavation of deserted houses at Hound Tor, Okehampton and Hutholes has revealed that such settlements were mostly founded no earlier than 1250 and abandoned by 1450 (Allan 1994, 145). The unenclosed areas, mostly vast tracts of moorland, were still of great importance as common land. They were used for summer grazing by livestock belonging to residents of the settlements on and around the moors. The majority of the former Forest remained unenclosed throughout the medieval period.

Tinworking

The Dartmoor tin industry has been a focus for serious, though sporadic, archaeological study since Robert Burnard's investigation of the Week Ford tin mills in the 1880s (Newman 1993). This work was soon expanded by R. H. Worth between the 1890s and 1930s to include detailed surveys of many more tin mills (Worth 1892–1940). This archaeological activity was preceded and complemented by work on the historical aspects of the industry, by authorities including R. N. Worth (1876), H. P. R. Finberg (1949) and others. The study of the stannary parliament, the legislative body of the tinners, has proved one of the most fruitful avenues for historical research, especially in recent times (Greeves 1987, 2003). Tin mills, where ore was crushed, refined and smelted, remained the traditional focus for archaeological fieldwork, but recently Gerrard has researched tinworks in some depth and published earthwork surveys of individual examples from Devon and Cornwall. This work has provided typologies derived from the analysis of field remains and written accounts, along with a discussion of the associated tinworking techniques (Gerrard 2000). Nevertheless, the collection of accurate field data in Devon is still in its infancy and a great deal of work remains to be done.

There is no documentation or archaeological evidence which is able to provide a date for the beginnings of a tin industry in Devon. Although a recent study examining pollens and river sediments has provided encouraging evidence for early tin streaming, it is somewhat unspecific and only adds weight to what has long been assumed (Thorndycraft *et al.* 2004, 219–36), which is that Dartmoor tin was first exploited at some time in the prehistoric period. This exploitation probably continued throughout the Dark Ages but it is not until the twelfth century that evidence is available. Indeed, Maddicott has proposed a convincing scenario in which the economic success of the city of Exeter and the town of Lydford, an Alfredian burh, could have been built on wealth from the tin trade as early as the tenth century (Maddicott 1989).

Historical evidence for tinworking in Devon is first available from the mid twelfth century, in the pipe roll for 1156 (Finberg 1949). A rapid increase in importance, and probably production, is implied by the increasing organisation of the industry and the operation of the stannaries by 1201. For the second half of the twelfth century tin production in Devon exceeded that of Cornwall, though the situation was reversed sometime in the thirteenth century. After this time, Cornwall remained the major producer. More detailed records of Devon's tin production are available from the early fourteenth century. The statistics show a sharp rise in output from the 1450s to the 1520s, when production reached a peak of 564,288 lbs or 252 tons in 1524 (Spooner and Russell 1967, 286–7), though this figure is still believed to be substantially less than the output of the thirteenth century. A correspondingly steep decline then followed resulting in a negligible output in the years leading up to the civil war in the 1640s, when all production ceased. Production in the later seventeenth to twentieth centuries was completely dwarfed by this medieval zenith of the industry's fortunes.

The field evidence for tinworking

When considering the extent of Dartmoor's medieval tin industry it is important to distinguish between the field evidence which may potentially be associated with that period, and that from the industry's second major episode from the late eighteenth century onwards. The field evidence for the latter period, which continued into the 1930s, is of a different character to that of the medieval period. However, the distinction is sometimes made difficult for the casual observer because the remains from more than one episode of activity may be present at a single location (see Figure 60) which could, therefore, contain several hundred years of chronological depth.

Like copper, silver and lead, tin ore (cassiterite) is found primarily in lodes or veins deposited at various depths beneath the ground surface. The lodes were an important source of ore but, unlike the other metals, tin also has an alluvial form. Lodes that were broken down and eroded by the forces of the weather many millions of years ago, were redeposited in the beds of rivers, streams and valleys. These relatively shallow 'stream' deposits are far richer and more easily exploited than the lodes. Ore from lodes needed to be physically dug from its hard-rock matrix at depth and requires more effort at the processing or 'dressing' stage to produce pure tin. It is not unreasonable to assume that during 800 years of exploitation the first tinners would exploit the easiest source, namely the rich stream deposits. This would be followed by the most accessible shallow lodes, while towards the end of the period, the deep and difficult to reach lode deposits were all that remained to be worked. The later miners, however, benefited from the technological advances of their time, especially in pumping machinery but also explosives and ore 'dressing', enabling them to exploit a resource which was mostly inaccessible to their medieval predecessors.

Streamworks

The Dartmoor tinners of the twelfth century would certainly have exploited the alluvial or stream deposits and it is probably safe to speculate that these continued to be the only sources of tin worked in Devon until at least the fourteenth century. The exploitation of stream deposits continued into the eighteenth century and isolated examples are documented as late as the nineteenth, giving streamworks a potentially very long working life. The remains are highly distinctive and are the most commonly encountered field evidence for tin extraction on Dartmoor. A comprehensive analysis of streamworks has been published by Gerrard (2000), but for the present purpose it is necessary only to note the basic elements which are common to all streamworks.

Exploiting the gravelly alluvial deposits was essentially a matter of separating the small tin stones from the unwanted waste material alongside which they were deposited, such as feldspar, quartz and mica, known collectively as 'gangue'. This process began at the point of extraction by casting the gravels into an artificial stream of water as they were dug from the ground. The greater density of the tin-bearing stones would cause them to sink faster and become separated from much of the lighter waste material which was washed away by the stream. The partially sorted ore could then be taken elsewhere for further refining or 'dressing'. Although each streamwork has a unique set of remains, the varied forms they take are all essentially a result of this basic operation.

Because of the nature of the deposits, streamworks are always located either in river valleys, shallow coombes, or more rarely on hillsides, occupying folds and dips in the ground where the deposits had come to rest. The edge of the working, which forms a perimeter marking the limit of extractive activity, is often defined by a steep scarp cut into the natural contours of the land, and because the interior is at a lower level, the streamwork's appearance offers a marked contrast to the surrounding terrain, being one of uneven and undulating ground. The surviving depth of the perimeter scarps can be up to 5 m, though most are less, the variation reflecting the depth of the deposit; some streamworks are sufficiently shallow as to have no perimeter scarp. The worked area or interior usually consists of linear heaps of stony waste and any water channels that may have survived unburied by the progress of the work. The arrangement of the waste heaps, often in parallel rows, may demonstrate a systematic working method and reveal how the work progressed. Common layouts include sinuous banks following the long axis of the tinwork, shorter heaps at right angles to the axis, or a combination of these two. The unique final appearance of each streamwork was dictated by the nature of the deposit, the local topography, the availability of water and probably the preferences of the individuals who carried out the work. The large streamwork at Beckamoor Combe has been recorded in great detail and demonstrates most of these elements (Figures 55).

The size of streamworks can vary considerably. A large example following the course of the East Okement river on north Dartmoor is 3.13 km in length,

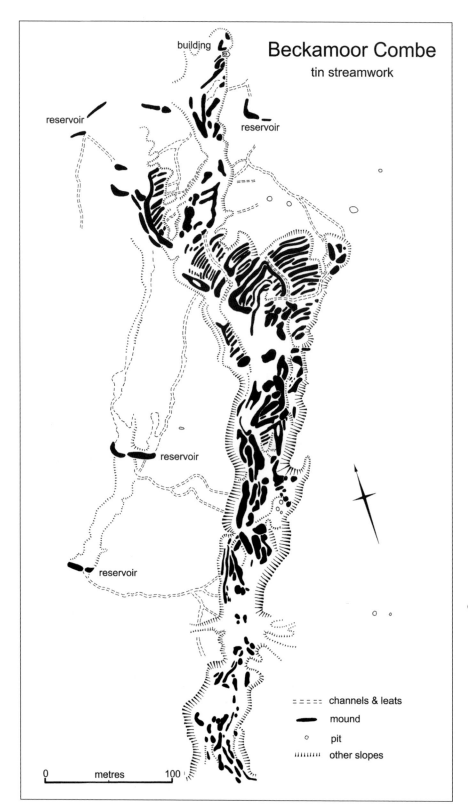

Beckamoor Combe

tin streamwork

building

reservoir

reservoir

reservoir

reservoir

= = = = = channels & leats

━━━ mound

◦ pit

⊔⊔⊔⊔⊔ other slopes

0   metres   100

FIGURE 55
Simplified earthwork
survey of Beckamoor
Combe tin streamwork
(northern section),
showing the steep
scarp marking the
perimeter, internal
dumps of spoil
– some arranged in
parallel – reservoirs
and leats. (Based on
an earthwork survey
by the Dartmoor
Tinworking Research
Group 1991, with
permission.)

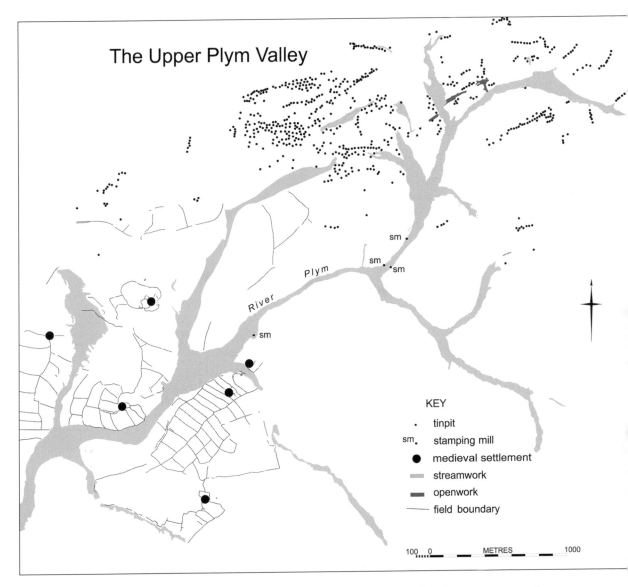

The Upper Plym Valley

Plym

River

sm.

sm
·sm

·sm

KEY

·   tinpit

sm.   stamping mill

●   medieval settlement

   streamwork

   openwork

   field boundary

100 0   METRES   1000

FIGURE 56
Simplified map of the
upper Plym valley
showing the extent
of streamworks and
pitworks within
the watershed. Also
shown are the main
components of
medieval and post-
medieval settlement
and enclosure.

COPYRIGHT ENGLISH
HERITAGE

up to 260 m wide and covers an area in excess of 45 ha. By contrast the very
small streamwork at King's Ford on the River Walkham covers only 1.4 ha.

Streamworks are found on all parts of Dartmoor from the stream valleys
on the high moor, such as the head of the Redaven Brook at 550 m OD on
the slopes of Yes Tor, to the wooded valleys around the peripheries. Gerrard
has compiled a summary map based on air photo sources (Gerrard 2000,
figure 15), which is an important first step. It is nevertheless incomplete
because of the shortcomings of air photography, which cannot reveal areas
covered by trees or other dense vegetation. Terrestrial survey on the uplands
has provided a far more accurate map but as yet this too remains incomplete and the total area of streamworks will not be known until all the
examples on both the upland and around the peripheries of the moors are

included. Additionally, a fair number of streamworks on the high moors have been overwhelmed by peat (e.g. at Foxtor Mires), and the total area of these cannot easily be deduced. Even so, an overview of those parts of the moor where detailed recording has occurred can help establish the scale of these activities.

The moorland section of the Plym valley is famous for its prehistoric ritual landscapes and settlements dating from prehistoric and medieval times. It also contains extensive evidence of streamworks. Approximately 5 km of streamworks within the valley has been archaeologically mapped (Figure 56), as well as the courses of seven tributaries. The perimeters of all the streamworks are interconnecting and continuous and amount to 36 km; the total area covered is a staggering 110 ha. The neighbouring valleys of the Erme, Meavy,

FIGURE 57

Oblique aerial photograph of streamworks along the River Swincombe near Fox Tor showing the steep scarp marking the perimeter of the working and parallel linear dumps. Also visible is the ruined eighteenth-century holding of Fox Tor Farm (centre left), with associated newtake walls, and the nineteenth-century Whiteworks Mine leat.

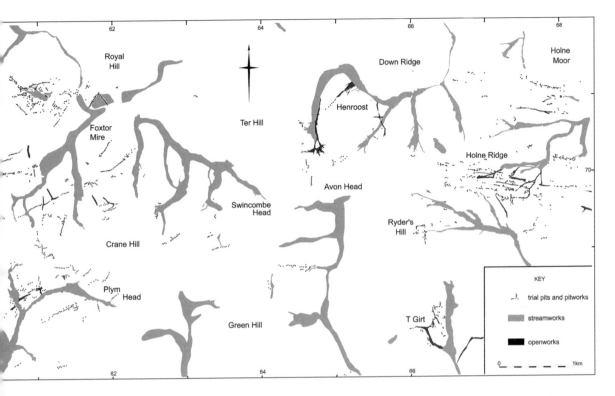

KEY

⌇ trial pits and pitworks

▬ streamworks

■ openworks

0 ___ ___ ___ 1km

FIGURE 58
The central upland of
southern Dartmoor
showing the extent
of tinworking on the
major rivers and their
tributaries.

COPYRIGHT ENGLISH
HERITAGE

Swincombe (Figure 57) and Avon present a similar picture, making the point
that very few river valleys on Dartmoor are unaffected by streamworking.
Figure 58 shows the central uplands of southern Dartmoor, where accurate
mapping has taken place. This shows the scale of working and the visible
impact on the landscape: over 240 ha of streamwork is represented on this
map.

There is a good chance that many more streamworks existed off the moors,
though evidence of them has been disguised by later uses of the land. The
Bovey Heathfield is the most tantalising example of this. Although not
mentioned in contemporary documents, the fact that disused tinworks existed
here was mentioned by Polwhele (1797–1806). Subtle remains of the tinworks,
heavily disguised by later land use and overgrowth of vegetation, can still be
recognised on the heath today.

Lode works
To exploit a tin lode requires more conventional mining techniques, of a type
which might be familiar to silver, lead and copper miners. Lodes occur beneath
the surface of the earth and although Dartmoor possessed some comparatively
shallow lodes, the method was essentially to dig downwards until the ore was
reached. In later centuries this was achieved by sinking deep vertical shafts
linked to horizontal levels or adits, which enabled miners to pursue their prize
underground to great depths. Earlier miners were not equipped with explosives or advanced pumping machinery, and they would have directed their

efforts towards extracting the shallower lodes by digging pits or trenches to attack the back of the lode. This could be carried out until the risk of collapse or flooding became unacceptable. It is impossible to state with certainty when the first attempt at true deep shaft and adit mining occurred on Dartmoor, though the technology was certainly available by the fourteenth century. It is very unlikely that field evidence for 'early' examples of shaft or adits will be identified solely from surface remains.

Prospecting

Locating tin lodes required the ability to recognise their presence through geological indications on the surface. Lodes often occur in the same locality

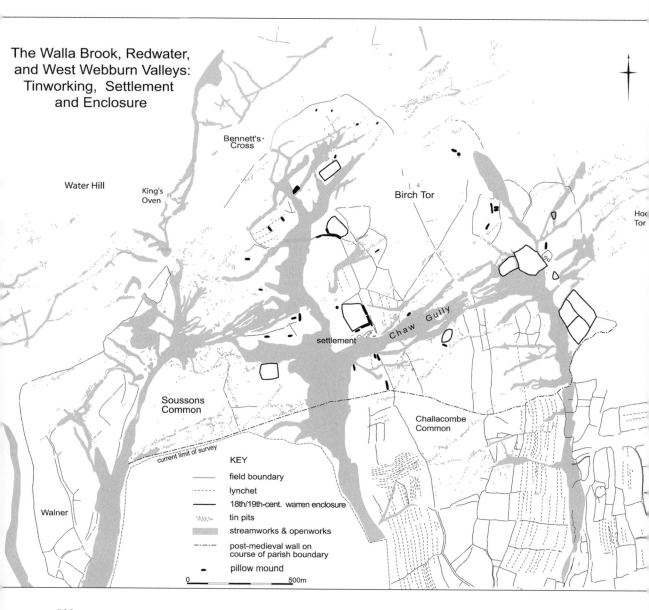

The Walla Brook, Redwater,
and West Webburn Valleys:
Tinworking, Settlement
and Enclosure

Water Hill

Bennett's·
Cross

King's
Oven

Birch Tor

Hoo
Tor

settlement

Chaw Gully

Soussons
Common

Challacombe
Common

current limit of survey

Walner

KEY

	field boundary
	lynchet
	18th/19th-cent. warren enclosure
	tin pits
	streamworks & openworks
	post-medieval wall on course of parish boundary
	pillow mound

0   500m

as stream deposits: this is the case at Birch Tor, where the lodes lay close by the weathered stream tin and may have been evident to tinners working the streamworks in the valley (Figures 59 and 60). Such lodes could have been among the earliest to be exploited. Other more discreet lodes had to be searched for using a range of prospecting techniques. The divining rod was one popular method and considered by commentators such as Pryce (1778) to be highly effective. There is also a documentary description of artificial torrents of water being diverted over valley sides to remove topsoil and reveal lodes beneath (Anon 1670), but field evidence for this method has not yet been identified on Dartmoor. However, several thousands of trial pits or 'essay hatches' provide ample evidence for a technique known as costeaning, where small pits were dug in the vicinity of the suspected course of a lode to search for 'shoad' – detached pieces of tinstone. The more shoad that was unearthed, the nearer the prospectors were to the lode, and additional pits were dug until its precise position was revealed. The pits are usually no bigger than 2–3 m across and are heavily silted, giving a conical profile. Small spoil heaps around the lower side represent the material excavated from their limited depth. They may occur in clusters of three or four or alignments of some considerable length such as that running 500 m west to east across Soussons Common (Figure 59). Invariably trial pits were interspersed with extractive pits (pitworks) as exploitation of the lode developed at the site of successful prospects.

Pitworks or 'lodeback' pits

Pits dug onto the back of known lodes probably represent the earliest form of dedicated lode working. These were not shafts as the term was later used, but alignments of closely-spaced, narrow pits following the axis of the lode. There is no certainty as to the final depth of such pits, or whether they interconnected underground, as this would probably depend on the firmness of the ground. It seems very likely that the risk of collapse and flooding would restrict the depth to which the pits could penetrate. The field evidence consists of alignments of conical impressions, or pits, often closely spaced or conjoined, with heaps of spoil forming collars around the lower side. The pits and their associated spoil heaps are usually larger than trial pits, though not always circular. These tinworks occur most densely, though not exclusively, on the southern portion of Dartmoor, around the tributaries of the River Meavy and at Eylesbarrow, Fox Tor and Birch Tor.

Openworks or beamworks

Many tin lodes were too deep or extensive for simple pitworks and it became necessary to excavate large open trenches to avoid the dangers of working at depth. These openworks or 'beamworks' often developed to massive proportions and are arguably among the most spectacular evidence of human endeavour in the Dartmoor landscape (Figure 61). Openworks are found over much of Dartmoor though, like the pitworks, they are predominantly found on the southern half of the moor, and are far less numerous than streamworks.

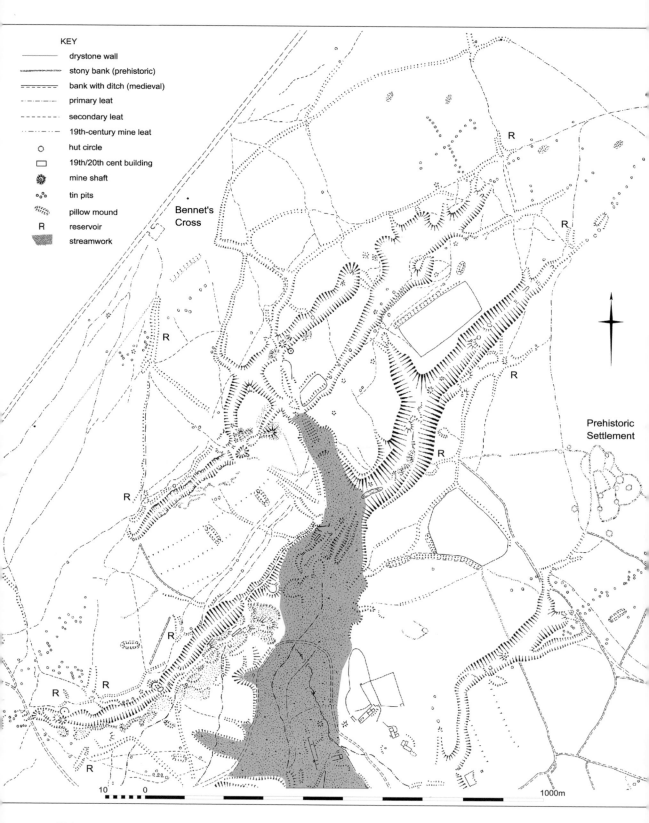

drystone wall
stony bank (prehistoric)
bank with ditch (medieval)
primary leat
secondary leat
19th-century mine leat
○ hut circle
⬭ 19th/20th cent building
mine shaft
tin pits
pillow mound
R reservoir
streamwork

Bennet's
Cross

R

R

R

R

R

R

R

R

R

R

R

Prehistoric
Settlement

10   0   1000m

They may be seen cutting into hillsides or even across the summit of a hill as at Birch Tor (Figure 61). They are usually aligned approximately west to east following the prevailing axis of Dartmoor's tin lodes. Very large examples may be seen at Birch Tor, Henroost and Ringleshuttes. They also occur around the edge of the moor, for example at Bradford Pool near Chagford and Owlacombe at Ashburton, though less frequently.

No contemporary description of techniques used in these openworks is available but it seems likely that material was excavated and sorted by hand, removing the valuable stone containing retrievable ore for dressing while discarding the rest. The method for disposing of this waste, which must have been produced on a massive scale, is something of an enigma. Water supplies, which are always present at this type of working, also present us with certain problems of interpretation; they will be discussed below.

The chronology and development of tin extraction

Precise dates for the various technological developments in tin extraction have not yet been satisfactorily pinned down. This is due mainly to the fact that the understanding of the field remains is entirely dependent on documentation and the random nature of its survival. Little or no documentary evidence alluding to the methods of working tin is available from the first 400 years of the industry's known existence in Devon or Cornwall so there can be no certainty as to precisely how the work was carried out. Archaeological analysis of tinworks so far has progressed no further than a handful of large-scale earthwork surveys; although these can provide very simple relative chronologies for the different elements within individual workings, they cannot provide dates and as yet no typology has emerged which can do so either. Archaeological excavation of these sites is at a very early stage and restricted only to one small area of streamworking (Gerrard 2000, 67–9); archaeologically derived dates for any tinwork are lacking.

FIGURE 60
Part of the RCHME/
EH 1:2500 earthwork
survey of Birch
Tor showing the
complexity of the
site. Included in the
plan are streamworks,
openworks, pits, leats
and reservoirs from
the medieval period as
well as pillow mounds
from the eighteenth-
century Headland
Warren, shafts, adits,
leats and buildings
from nineteenth- and
twentieth-century tin
mining.

The dating of streamworks poses a particular problem. It is known that working of Dartmoor tin had commenced by AD 1156 and was occurring on a large scale by 1200 (Finberg 1949, 155). However, reference to individual tinworks is vague for this period, with no mention of named tinworks. The first reference to a recognizable streamwork is to 'la Dryworke' (today known as Dry Lake) on the boundary of the Forest of Dartmoor in 1240 (Rowe 1896, 290). Documentation becomes more common between the fifteenth and eighteenth centuries, when a good number of streamworks were recorded by name; the location of these can be identified in the field if the name survives in use today. Unfortunately there is also field evidence for many other streamworks which lack known documentation. Additionally, a mention in a document is rarely any help in establishing the origins of a streamwork, which could have existed long before its first known reference. The total working life of a streamwork before final exhaustion could add up to several centuries and the earthworks generally represent only the last

phase of activity. There can be few examples of medieval or post-medieval earthworks in Britain which are so difficult to date with confidence, even within four or five centuries. The fact is that a streamwork surviving in the field could have origins as early as the twelfth or as late as the eighteenth century and the earlier it was first worked the more likely it is to have been reworked at a later date.

Several contemporary descriptions of streamworking survive, though the earliest is of the seventeenth century and all are from Cornwall (Carew 1602; Pryce 1778). It seems very likely that these writers were describing a process which would also have been used in Devon and, because of its simplicity, may have changed very little since its beginnings 500 years or so earlier. But there is no certainty that the earliest tinners were using identical techniques or working as efficiently as their later counterparts, whose skills and knowledge accumulated over several centuries.

The date at which the tinners began to turn their attention to tin lodes is also far from certain. This development was not recorded by any medieval writer and it has always seemed a safe assumption that as long as tinners of the twelfth to fifteenth centuries had a plentiful supply of stream tin then the working of lodes, which required far greater expenditure of labour in both extraction and dressing, would not have been a priority. The documentary evidence would appear to validate this notion because references to known lode works are only available from the fifteenth century onwards; thereafter references to so-called 'beamworks' become common until the eighteenth century (Greeves 1981). But as references to all types of tinwork are rare in the period before 1450, and the categories of workings are scarcely mentioned in such early documents, this may be a distortion of the data. Tin, however, was sufficiently valuable that the earliest tinners may have extracted ore from any source they could find, restrained only by the technology available to them rather than the economic merits of individual types of tinworks.

One source of evidence which supports a later origin for the working of lodes is provided by the apparent late introduction of stamping mills. These were water-powered mechanical devices contained within small buildings, used for crushing tinstone. The mills have been described in detail elsewhere (Newman 1998; Gerrard 2000) and there is archaeological evidence for at least 60 stamping mills on Dartmoor. Although the technology is thought to have been available earlier, stamping mills do not enter the documentary record until 1402 in Cornwall and 1504 in Devon (Gerrard 2000). One possible reason for the development of these mills could have been an increased demand for processing caused by greater quantities of lode tin, which required more crushing than stream tin. This does not explain the existence of all stamping mills, however, as many were sited some distance from lode workings; in the Plym valley at least four mills are located in an area dominated by stream-works (Figure 56).

The earliest date for working lodes underground is also uncertain. Miners were working the silver mines of the Bere Alston peninsula as early as 1303 (Hamilton Jenkin 1972, 84), so the knowledge was available if not widely practised by this time. Greeves has concluded from various documentary sources that shafts probably were in use at Dartmoor tin mines by the fifteenth century (Greeves 1981). In that period, before adequate pumping technology was available, underground mines needed to be 'free draining' i.e. sited on hillsides or in sufficiently steep valleys to allow water to drain out via horizontal adits. This technique was certainly used by the Dartmoor tinners, but a date for its inception has not been established and field evidence for early examples is yet to be recognized. In 1599 the historian John Hooker described Devon tinners as spending their time '... like a mole or earth-worm underground mining in deep vaults ...' (Hoskins 1954), so underground mining must have been well established by this date.

Water supplies

Archaeological evidence for water supplies is associated with openworks and streamworks. Water was also important for the dressing and smelting processes which took place in water-powered mills. Extensive field evidence survives in the form of artificial water courses (known as leats) and small earthwork reservoirs.

All the contemporary accounts of streamworking mention the use of water but for openworks no such descriptions survive and there is uncertainty as to precisely what the water was used for. It is possible that a supply was needed for washing the ore as part of the sorting process or for sluicing out areas of the working to expose the lode prior to digging. Another possibility is that the upper strata of some lodes may have been sufficiently weathered and broken down that they could be worked by methods similar to that of a streamwork before the underlying material was exploited by excavating an openwork. The remains of a water supply might therefore be the only surviving element of the earlier phase.

Water was mostly diverted to the tinworks from existing streams via leats. When the tinwork was higher than any nearby streams, rainwater run-off was collected in channels dug across hillsides, or boggy areas were tapped and diverted. In all three cases the water was frequently retained in small earthwork reservoirs near the tinwork. These were simply created by digging a hollow on sloping ground and using the material removed to create a dam on the downslope side. Many fine examples exist but the Birch Tor area, where 40 have been recorded (Figure 60), contains the most representative selection.

The leats consist of shallow ditches, mostly no deeper than 0.5 m, which usually follow a level course along the contours of the hillsides. The water was often diverted over a considerable distance; the central section of the East Okement streamwork, mentioned above, was supplied by a leat which had its source near the headwaters of the River Taw and conveyed the water over 3 km, traversing the saddle of Oke Tor Ridge in its progress.

In areas where many tinworks exist, the systems of leats may be highly complex. This is well illustrated by Figures 60 and 61, which show part of the Birch Tor area. Primary leats brought water from the supply to the tinwork location or the reservoir while smaller secondary leats diverted it over shorter distances to the required part of the tinwork.

The effect of tinworking on the inhabitants of Dartmoor and elsewhere

The effect of large-scale tinworking on the inhabitants of Dartmoor was on occasion profound. The depletion and pollution of water supplies, together with the disturbance of farm and grazing land already in use must have been one important issue, but the usefulness of the land after being worked for tin would also be affected. In 1314 the 'poor men of Devon' complained that the tinners were destroying good farm land as well as houses (Finberg 1949, 161).

The relationship between medieval tinners, their environment and the other occupants of Dartmoor is yet to be the subject of focused research, and a study which brings together historical and archaeological evidence for medieval settlement and tenure alongside that from the tin industry is long overdue. In the meantime, archaeological evidence and some documentation gives a little insight into some of the issues.

It has been demonstrated elsewhere (Newman 1994, 233) that tinworking in the moorland section of the River Meavy and its tributaries was carried out during a documented period from the fifteenth to the seventeenth century in an area of established farmland. Although this apparently had a drastic effect on the land of some farm holdings, it probably did not cause the tenants lasting upheaval. This part of south-west Dartmoor was once among the most intensively exploited tin districts and although it was never possible for land that had been so deeply scarred by streamworks, openworks and pits to be fully reclaimed, the tenants of these farms managed to work around the problem. Field boundaries were repaired and the integrity of many fields was re-established. This may have been because many of the tenants during this

FIGURE 62
Map of part of Whitchurch Common showing Barn Hill and the southern half of Beckamoor Combe streamwork (i.e. south of the B3357) and the fragmentary remains of medieval settlement and enclosures affected by the spread of the tinwork.

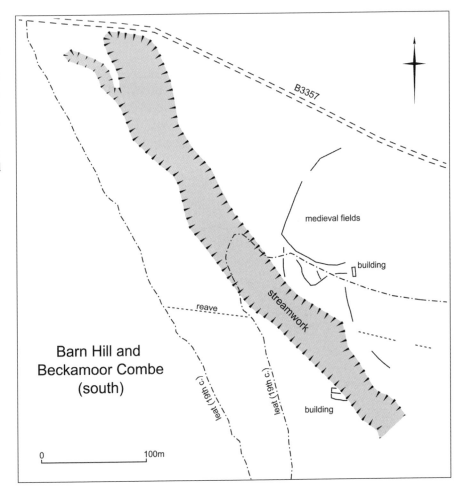

Barn Hill and Beckamoor Combe (south)

period were involved in the tin industry themselves and would have little problem tolerating the inconvenience caused. Of 13 farms studied, all but two had at some time during this period been occupied by at least one tenant who had links with the tin industry, usually as shareholders in named tinworks, which in some cases proved to be in the vicinity of the farms. Glimpses into the documentation from the thirteenth to early fourteenth centuries revealed the possibility of a similar picture at that time too.

The farms in the Meavy study were, with few exceptions, products of a period of settlement expansion on Dartmoor which took place from the mid twelfth century. These holdings were clearly successful enough to survive into later centuries, despite the activities of the tinners. In other places a different story emerges: to the east of Barn Hill on Whitchurch Common is a gently-sloping, south facing piece of land on which elements of a deserted medieval settlement are evident, comprising the earthwork and stone remains of two small rectangular houses and traces of an undeveloped field system (Figure 62). Bisecting the field system is the huge streamwork known as Beckamoor Combe. One of Dartmoor's larger streamworks, it extends approximately 2 km north–south from the slopes of Cox Tor down to the River Walkham, and cut one of the deserted houses in half as work progressed. Regrettably, the origins of this massive tinwork are undocumented and though the sequence of events here is quite clear, we can only guess at the issues and precise chronology that lay behind them. Settlements elsewhere on Dartmoor are known to have been abandoned as late as 1450 (cf. Allan 1994, 48) but if earlier, this site may well have been deserted before tin working commenced. Alternatively, perhaps tinworking on a limited scale took place while the houses were still occupied, desertion occuring when living amongst such massive upheaval became intolerable, illustrating only too well the grievances of the 'poor men of Devon' outlined above. A final possibility is that the residents of these farms were tinners themselves, like those of the Meavy valley.

A similar example can be found at Birch Tor, east of Postbridge (Newman 2002). This is the single most intensively tinworked area of Dartmoor. Streamworks occupy the beds of the Redwater Brook, Walla Brook and West Webburn River and the hillsides between the river valleys are gashed by some of Dartmoor's largest openworks. There is also a complex system of leats and reservoirs (Figures 60 and 61). It is quite clear, however, that long before tinworking reached its final extent, the land had been settled and farmed. On the slopes of Birch Tor and in the Redwater valley are subtle traces of a once extensive field system at the centre of which lies the partial remains of a settlement (Figure 59). Vestiges of two longhouses, survive though it is likely that the settlement was once larger; as at the Barn Hill settlement, a large tinwork has sliced through the courtyard only metres from one of the houses. It is intriguing that this settlement is adjacent to Challacombe, a village thought likely to have been founded in the thirteenth or fourteenth century, which still survives as a single farm. Challacombe is remarkable for its strip lynchets which documentation shows were still in use as part of a communal system of agriculture until the end of the eighteenth century (Pattison 1999, 68). The fortunes of Challacombe and its deserted neighbour just north of the parish boundary at Birch Tor were very different. The latter, whose field system appears to be an extension of the Challacombe system at higher altitude (and therefore established later), was clearly abandoned a very long time ago, its fields obliterated by tinworking. Although the struggle to continue conventional farming was lost several hundred years ago at this place, a rabbit warren was established on the slopes of Birch Tor in the eighteenth century; an agricultural activity for which the condition of the land was perhaps less important (Newman 2002).

Disposal of waste

Waste produced by tinworks and the means of its disposal had implications far beyond the immediate locality. Discarded topsoil and gangue from the streaming and dressing of tin found its way unavoidably into the streams and rivers. This would not only have polluted the water supplies of those living downstream but it also contributed to the silting of estuaries and harbours.

Complaints about silting from the havens of Dartmouth and Plymouth were heard by the stannary court who, in 1532, passed a statute whereby tin waste had to be disposed of in disused works rather than washed into rivers (Radford 1930, 239). One hundred years later, in 1638, tinworking is implicated in the silting of Catwater harbour in Plymouth when the tinwork of Clasiewell was mentioned by name. Very large, openworks such as Clasiewell and others in the Birch Tor and Holne area confirm that a truly massive quantity of material was dug out of the ground, yet associated spoil heaps are almost universally absent. It is possible that the tinners were following the orders of the stannary parliament and disposing of waste responsibly in old tinworks but evidence for this has not readily come to light.

Conclusion

Tinworking was a fundamental component of Dartmoor's medieval landscape. The effect on the land was massive and the field remains make up the majority of Dartmoor's archaeological evidence from the period 1150–1700. Although archaeologists now have a more intimate understanding of the variety of remains than ever before, we are still far from understanding crucial details of chronology. We can, however, suggest how individual components fit approximately into the known sequence.

Streamworks are by far the most numerous and widespread remains of medieval tin extraction on Dartmoor. We can state with confidence that stream deposits were the first to be exploited in the twelfth century and continued to be a major source of tin up to at least the 1640s and probably beyond. As yet there is no suggestion that any of the streamworks surviving today provide evidence of the earliest recorded period of activity in the twelfth century. It may be that all streamworks with clear remains date from the fifteenth to the eighteenth centuries, whether first worked in that period or reworked from earlier times but it seems improbable that not a single streamwork from the twelfth century even partially survives. The identification of an 'early' streamwork through archaeological or scientific methods is a priority for the future.

It is probably safe to suggest that the great majority of lode workings date from the fifteenth century onwards, though their earliest origins are less certain. The beginning of underground mining on Dartmoor is particularly obscure; our best guess would place this in the fifteenth century but all such methods were probably introduced gradually.

Future archaeological and historical research will hopefully examine links between tinworking and other medieval activities more closely. Only then will the complexities of this landscape be better understood. In the meantime we can be confident that the extraction of tin pervaded the lives of medieval people on all areas of Dartmoor. They may have been tinners themselves or the owners of tinworks, or just residents whose day to day existence was affected by metal extraction. But on present data it is impossible to know what impact the tin industry was having on the upland landscape, either in terms of active tinworks and their attendant problems of pollution and destruction of land, or the quantity of redundant tinworks, in any one period. The extent of the landscape evidence appears massive to us in the twenty-first century, but the activity responsible for these remains was spread over 900 years. Profound alterations to the landscape are likely to have been localised and slow to occur.

National grid references of tinworks etc. referred to in the text

Beckamoor Combe, Walkham	SX 5350 7500
Birch Tor	SX 6800 8100 (centred)
Bovey Heathfield	SX 8217 7682
Bradford Pool	SX 7000 9100
Clasiewell (Crazywell Pool)	SX 5820 7048
Dry Lake	SX 6607 7059
East Okement	SX 6060 9000
Eylesbarrow Mine	SX 7580 6820
Foxtor Mires	SX 6161 7043
Henroost	SX 6520 7120
King's Ford, Walkham	SX 5567 7770
Meavy Valley	SX 5700 7000
Owlacombe Beam	SX 7660 7330
Plym Valley	SX 6056 7730 (centred)
Red a ven Brook	SX 5856 8989
Ringleshuttes	SX 6750 7000
Sousson's Common	SX 6799 8143

NB: public access to sites mentioned in text should not be assumed.

References

Allan, J. (1994) 'Medieval pottery and the dating of deserted settlements on Dartmoor', *Devon Archaeological Society Proceedings* **52**, 141–8.

Anon (1670) 'An account of some mineral observations touching the mines of Cornwall and Devon; etc', *Philosophical Transactions of the Royal Society of London* **5**, 2096–113.

Carew, R. (1602) *The Survey of Cornwall,* ed. F. Halliday (1953), Melrose, London.

Finberg, H. P. R. (1949) 'The Stannary of Tavistock', *Transactions of the Devonshire Association* **81**, 155–84.

Gerrard, S. (2000) *The Early British Tin Industry*, Tempus, Stroud.

Greeves, T. A. P. (1981) *The Devon tin industry, 1450–1750: an archaeological and historical survey*, unpublished PhD thesis, University of Exeter.

Greeves, T. A. P. (1987) 'The Great Courts or Parliaments of the Devon tinners 1484–1786', *Transactions of the Devonshire Association* **119**, 145–67.

Greeves, T. A. P. (2003) 'Devon's earliest tin coinage roll 1302–3', *Transactions of the Devonshire Association* **135**, 9–30.

Hamilton Jenkin, A. K. (1927) *The Cornish Miner*, Allen & Unwin, London.

Hoskins, W. G. (1954) *Devon*, Collins, London.

Maddicott, J. R. (1989) 'Trade, industry and the wealth of King Alfred', *Past and Present* **123**, 3–51.

Newman, P. (1993) 'Week Ford Tin Mills', *Devon Archaeological Society Proceedings* **51**, 185–97.

Newman, P. (1994) 'Tinners and tenants on South-West Dartmoor: a case study in landscape history', *Transactions of the Devonshire Association* **126**, 199–238.

Newman, P. (1998) *The Dartmoor Tin Industry: A Field Guide*, Chercombe Press, Newton Abbot.

Newman, P. (2002) 'Headland Warren and the Birch Tor and Vitifer Mines', English Heritage Archaeological Investigation report (AI/34/2002), Swindon.

Pattison, P. (1999) 'Challacombe Revisited' in *Patterns of the Past: Essays in Landscape Archaeology for Christopher Taylor*, eds P. Pattison, D. Field and S. Ainsworth, Oxbow, Oxford.

Polwhele, R. (1797–1806) *The History of Devonshire*, Cadell, Dilly & Murray, London.

Pryce, W. (1778) *Mineralogia Cornubiensis* (reprinted 1972), Bradford Barton, Truro.

Radford, Lady (1930) 'Notes on the tinners of Devon and their laws', *Transactions of the Devonshire Association* **62**, 225–47.

Rowe, J. B. (1896) *A Perambulation of Dartmoor* (reprinted 1985), Devon Books, Exeter.

Spooner, G. M. and Russell, F. R. S. eds (1967) *Worth's Dartmoor*, David & Charles, Newton Abbot.

Thorndycraft, V. R., Pirrie, D. and Brown, A. T. (2004) 'Alluvial records of medieval and prehistoric tin mining on Dartmoor, south-west England', *Geoarchaeology* **19.3**, 219–36.

Worth, R. H. (1892–1940) Various articles on tin mills published in *Transactions of the Devonshire Association* (summarised in Spooner and Russell 1967).

Worth, R. N. (1876) 'The ancient stannary of Ashburton', *Transactions of the Devonshire Association* **8**, 311–22.

CHAPTER 8

Imagined Landscapes: Archaeology, Perception and Folklore in the Study of Medieval Devon

Lucy Franklin

When he came to himself again, for a moment he could recall nothing except a sense of dread. Then suddenly he knew he was imprisoned, caught hopelessly; he was in a barrow. A Barrow-wight had taken him …
(Tolkien 1954, 137)

Introduction

Within medieval archaeology little consideration has been given to the ways in which people visualised and understood their environment and those of others. Conventional landscape studies focusing on the post-Roman periods are generally concerned with 'material' landscapes – that is, the physical traces of people's lives and occupations. The notion of 'mental' landscapes, relating to the 'superstructures of meanings and values' attached to these material remains, are not explored, although commonplace in prehistoric studies (Bradley 2000, 2; Altenberg 2003, 3). In this chapter I will discuss methods that can help to create a more textured image of Devon in the medieval period. My examples are drawn mostly from that county, but I will also refer to other sites throughout the United Kingdom.

By combining historical sources, archaeology and psychology Brian Bates has gained a clearer insight into the period formerly known as the 'Dark Ages', and discussed the way Anglo-Saxon landscapes were full of meaning (Bates 2002, 44). Natural places such as forests were not only areas that were depended upon for fuel and materials for shelter and weapons, but were also places where a more intimate relationship arose between the Anglo-Saxon communities and their environment – a place of magic and power which had near-religious significance.

The medieval landscape of south-west Britain has been approached from a geographer's perspective, addressing territoriality and the role of hagio-graphical legends in Cornwall (Harvey 2000). David Harvey has argued that in medieval Cornwall the 'hero-saints' were exploited not only to legitimise elite authority and prestige, but were also used by communities as part of their identity; a form of 'early Cornish "patriotism"' (Harvey 2000, 205, 208). Another study of south-western moorlands in the medieval period has examined the ways landscapes and the local superstitions, rituals, and folklore that resulted were perceived by different groups including the Church, secular land owners, and peasant farmers (Altenberg 2001; 2003).

Focusing on the more recent past, the power of landscapes has been highlighted by the archaeologist Andrew Fleming through his work on Hirta, the main island of the St Kilda archipelago, and at Great Blasket in the Blasket Isles off the Dingle Peninsula (Fleming 2001). He has argued that relationships between landscape/seascape, magic, ritual, and fate on these islands were intrinsically intertwined (Fleming 2001, 4). Studying relatively modern societies like these allows archaeologists to see landscapes imbued with folkloric meaning, particularly when visible prehistoric remains have survived (Fleming 2001, 18–19).

Despite this recent work the general trend in medieval studies still addresses the physical aspects of landscapes. By removing people and their beliefs from the landscape historians and archaeologists have tended to see the past as 'another country', a place where they cannot see or understand human relationships and emotions (Tonkin 1992, 1).

It is crucial to understand that past landscapes were full of changing meanings, and it is crucial that we do not continue to regard them as merely academic resources, fit only for the study of agriculture, trade or craft production. Landscapes are socially constructed entities. Although natural forces shape them, they rely on what has been called the 'mechanics of the mind' to give them meaning and structure, and this varies depending upon the individual or group (Children and Nash 1997, 1). Following this argument we can argue that *how* people saw and perceived the world around them depended on their experiences, either for good or ill. Such perceptions could be altered through time, crucially by ideas associated with particular places. As people bond with the landscapes they dwell within, they make places culturally alive (Taçon 1994, 135). Places become vested with identities through physical and social experiences like crop failure, war, plague, religious ritual and supernatural belief. As a result areas come to be considered good or bad, sacred or profane, focal or marginal (Ucko 1994, xviii).

The creation of alternative landscapes

Within landscapes, stories and legends help create histories which eventually come to be accepted as truths (Children and Nash 1997, 1). This is especially the case when they become stable elements for a number of generations. J. R. R. Tolkien's academic work on Anglo-Saxon texts in the 1930s and 40s raised many issues relating to history and myth, not only for the Middle Ages but also for later periods. Tolkien suggested that myths and history drew from the same sources in reality and contained elements that were more powerful than simple abstract folk-tales (1936/1983, 15; 1947/1983, 127). His view was that myths are a 'soup pot' which 'is always boiling, and to it have continually been added new bits ...' drawing from other sources and historical narratives over time (Tolkien 1947/1983, 110).

An important factor in the creation of mythical landscapes is that stories and myths can become strongly attached to particular landscape features. These tend to be highly visible or prominent in the landscape, such as hills, rock outcrops and cliffs, but also include the places we think of now as archaeological sites. This use of recognisable places within stories provides vital links to the perception of particular areas in the landscape. The links between folklore and reality situates fictitious myth in the flow of people's day to day lives (Propp 1984, 49), and we can seen how particular places, perhaps unusual sites – especially in rural areas – could develop their own alternative histories. Oral historians describe this as 'linguistically appropriating the landscape' (Green 2000, 26): people using stories and metaphors to make sense of the world around them (Lévi-Strauss 1966; Gosden 1999, 113).

Stories were associated with archaeological features in an attempt to explain their existence and origin when, as we see it, the true nature of their origins was unknown. Monuments like burial mounds became the graves of giants and kings, or the homes of dragons; the Cornish 'Rounds' and Irish 'Raths' became the dwellings of fairies and pixies, and standing stones became petrified people. These visual archaeological features served as powerful mnemonics, and their stories helped to give an area a strong spatial identity, ordering the landscape on a human level, serving to create a recognisable and understandable world. This can be clearly seen in the early medieval period.

The use of prehistoric monuments such as barrows and standing stones in Anglo-Saxon charters reflects their prominence in early medieval landscapes. These sites were often given a distinctive name that suggests their importance in a particular landscape was well known and part of contemporary history or folklore (Reynolds 2002, 181). Many of the barrows and cairns found on Dartmoor and Exmoor were thought to contain treasure but people believed they were protected by supernatural creatures like the Phantom horses at Broken Barrow, or dragons as at Chapman Barrow on Exmoor (Grinsell 1976, 94). Prehistoric burial mounds are a particular focus for folklore owing to their association with fairies, pixies and other supernatural entities. A Barrow-wight, for example, dwelt not only in Tolkien's fictional Middle Earth, but also in a barrow in Somerset (Briggs 1967, 67).

Dragons were especially significant in the medieval period (Tolkien 1936/1983, 16). Semple suggests that they were seen as 'evil' and 'wasters of people', and that they were feared as terrible barrow-dwellers (Semple 1998, 110). This indicates how barrows were regarded as landscape features, and that they were not places where ordinary people went. Semple notes a number of other early place-names for barrows which indicate similar beliefs about supernatural creatures (Semple 1998, 112). Shucklow in Buckinghamshire was *scuccan hlæwe* or 'Goblin Barrow' in early medieval accounts, and Adam's Grave in Wiltshire was known in the chronicles as *Wodnes-beorh* ('Woden's Barrow') (Grinsell 1937, 252). Such names emphasise the demonic associations of these places. In later centuries barrows and other prehistoric monuments were used as cemeteries for executed criminals, showing the stigma attached to such sites (see below).

Special significance is also attributed to wildernesses such as moors or commons, particularly as the haunting grounds of ghosts, demons and other spirits. Gallagher argues that medieval people regarded Europe's untamed wildernesses as living symbols of chaos and danger that teemed with demons and monsters (Gallagher 1993, 221). Many supernatural encounters occur either late at night or as the mist comes in; and the potency of these stories must have been reinforced by the bleakness of winter on the moors.

Crucial to many of these stories, particularly those based on the moors, is the night. It served an important role, being in temporal terms both real yet indistinct; known, but containing unknowns (Young and Harris 2003, 138). To medieval communities the night became home to unexplainable, imagined horrors (Young and Harris 2003, 135).

A fear of wilderness could also be derived from more everyday concerns. Early medieval law codes indicate the danger of leaving the road for fear of being ambushed by outlaws, or being mistaken for one. The Kentish laws of Wihtred, dating to around 690, state that 'If a man from afar, or a stranger, quits the road, and neither shouts, nor blows a horn, he shall be assumed to be a thief, [and as such] may be slain or put to ransom' (Attenborough 1922, 31). In the Blackdown Hills on the Devon/Somerset border (discussed in more detail below), many late and post-medieval bandits and thieves traded on this superstition and fear in order to move through the landscape unchallenged (Coxhead 1954, 147–8). The organisation of the landscape, and the fear of those who dwelt beyond the 'civilised' boundaries of the settlements and tracks, helped to reinforce this perception.

The otherworldliness of these areas of wilderness had particular resonance in the medieval period. Such places could be seen as hostile or foreboding due to their very nature – being prone to sudden changes in weather and often isolated – so it is perhaps no surprise that the stories are frequently based around sounds and phenomena that occur in such climatic conditions. In Yorkshire, Essex, and on Dartmoor – all of which have barren areas of marsh or moor – spirits are supposed to pipe and wail on the wind (Baring-Gould 1913, 91)

Particular kinds of landscapes and archaeological sites have, therefore, long had magical and symbolic meaning. The material culture associated with these sites was also linked to multi-layered stories through the ages. In England, Neolithic stone axes have been found in Roman temples, and in later periods medieval scholars carried on the classical tradition of ascribing mineralogical, medicinal, and supernatural properties to prehistoric flints and axes (Carelli 1997, 398–9).

Carelli has discussed the widespread association of prehistoric stone tools with thunderbolts (in particular stone axes; Carelli 1997, 399). In excavations at Lund in Sweden during the early 1990s, for example, a number of prehistoric stone artefacts were found in purely medieval contexts. The tradition that these artefacts were intrinsically magical and gave protection continued into the 1930s in Lund (Carelli 1997, 414–15).

Worked flints were frequently known as Elf-stones, and when found in a field's ploughsoil were thought to indicate a pixie presence. This was especially the case when associated with ploughed-out ring-ditches, commonly known as fairy rings (Grinsell 1976, 80). Although these flints were sometimes used as amulets, particularly in Scotland (Davidson 1956, 154), they commonly had negative mythological associations. Pixies, for example, were believed to use flints to injure cattle (Figure 63). It is clear that the presence of fairies in the landscape was something to be treated with reverence and some caution, and this belief in 'little people' is not restricted to one region. Wales, Ireland, Scotland, France and Scandinavia also have such special connections, and many of the stories told are interchangeable between these regions. The occurrence of prehistoric flints as Elf-stones is a reaction not only in Britain but also across Scandinavia, France, and the rest of western Europe where they are known as elf-darts, elf-shots, or fairy arrows (Grinsell 1937, 248).

FIGURE 63
'The Pixies' Revenge'
by K. Hablot Browne
(from Bray 1853, 153).

Just as the archaeological record provides the impetus for folkloric traditions, myths can point to 'unknown' archaeological sites which had been destroyed or remained buried. At Broughshane in County Antrim (Northern Ireland) the farmer would not work in one of his fields for fifty years, believing that it was inhabited by fairies. It was only with a change of ownership in the 1990s that a souterrain was discovered buried under this field, a favourite haunt for fairies in Ireland (Franklin 2001, 14) (Figure 64). This is interesting as souterrains in Northern Ireland are thought to date to the early medieval period; in Northern Irish myths fairies are often linked with the Danish, who were believed in many cases to have constructed these underground chambers.

*Imagined
Landscapes:
Archaeology,
Perception and
Folklore in the
Study of Medieval
Devon*

Field archaeology and folklore: a suggested methodology

In Devon and Cornwall (and indeed elsewhere), it can therefore be suggested that folklore concerning fairies and pixies is most commonly linked to archaeological features. Pixies were thought to roam the countryside here well into the post-war period of the twentieth century. The occurrence of pixies and fairies was used to explain a range of everyday experiences, from the souring of milk to the presence of earthworks. Stories tell that fairies and pixies inhabit archaeological features, which appear as ruins to human eyes, but in their world are substantial standing settlements and castles (Gray 1996, 23).

Access to such information through archaeological investigation is difficult but by no means impossible. Past research has treated folklore as a form of historical science, and attempted to recreate the mythical past though organised and regimented analysis, particularly in its immediate social context (Krappe 1930, xv; Phythian-Adams 1975, 6–7). However, as mentioned above, the importance and potential of medieval folktales within landscape studies has not been appreciated fully. This is a period whose written record is largely restricted to legal or religious documents, but in some ways we can regard folktales as the 'literature' of the rural communities – communities with a rich repertoire of symbols and meanings for all parts of life, and practices that had not changed for decades or even centuries (Yeats 1888, xii). Local myths, superstition and folklore can be accessed with care through documentary sources, place- and field-name studies, and oral history. Folklore can be a significant source for the mythical structures that overlay medieval landscapes.

Current work on the prehistoric complex at Avebury in Wiltshire provides an example. We know that the megaliths of the Avebury henge became a particular focus for ritual deposits in the third millennium BC (Gillings and Pollard 1999, 184). However, the site was not important only in prehistory. During the late medieval period a number of the sarsen stones were deliberately concealed in cut 'graves' (Gillings and Pollard 2004, 94–5). The mid-nineteenth-century inhabitants of Avebury believed that the sarsens grew out of the ground, which hints that burial may have been an attempt at returning the stones to the earth or 'killing' them (Gillings and Pollard 2004, 94–5). It is perhaps significant that the sarsens that were buried the deepest were the stones that are unusual or physically marked in some way, suggesting these were singled out as the most likely to attract folkloric attention (Gillings *et al.* 2000, 7; Gillings and Pollard 2004, 95).

Roymans' work on the late prehistoric urnfields of the Meuse/Demer/Scheldt region of the Netherlands provides another example of how landscape archaeology and folkloric evidence from sources such as sagas can be combined (Roymans 1995). Dwarves, gnomes, and giants were all related to these burials in the sagas (which were first recorded in the nineteenth century), and are also found in associated place-names such as *alvenberg* or *kabouterberg*, meaning 'dwarf mound' (Roymans 1995, 13). The high Middle Ages saw large-scale destruction of these funerary monuments and the subsequent

location of gallows close to them. This was combined with the process of *diabolisation* (see below) where original saga creatures were transformed into 'new' characters such as the devil and witches (Roymans 1995, 12–15). This 'reordering' of the landscape fundamentally changed the way it was seen by contemporary societies.

As can be seen from these examples, documentary sources for landscapes are varied, providing a number of different avenues to investigate. In particular, post-medieval documentary evidence is very important for undertaking any such research, as it can provide the 'voice' of the communities which are being discussed, and can reflect earlier communities.

Perhaps the most straightforward but useful of these sources are Tithe Surveys and Apportionments. Although they date to the nineteenth century they provide an image of a pre-industrial countryside, and using the explanation of the land holdings it is possible to 'regress' the landscape backwards towards the medieval period (Rippon 1997, 24). Field-name and descriptions listed within the Tithe Apportionment can indicate associations with fairies, ghosts and spirits (see Field 1993, 248–9). Evidence of folklore influencing the naming of places can be seen clearly on Exmoor. This area has a number

*Imagined
Landscapes:
Archaeology,
Perception and
Folklore in the
Study of Medieval
Devon*

pixie stories (and there is even reference to the creatures in Blackmore's *Lorna Doone*). The place-name evidence reflects this – Pixie Copse, near Bury, Pixie Meadow in Selworthy, Pixie Lane in Minehead, and Pixie Rocks in Challacombe (Hurley 1973, 32).

By combining traditional archaeological research, oral history, and folklore we can begin to develop a more textured understanding of the past. The rest of this chapter will assess whether these techniques can help us better understand the medieval and later landscapes of Devon.

Imagined landscapes – some south-western examples

Grinsell (1976) has drawn attention to the relationship between folklore and prehistoric sites in Devon and Cornwall. At one level this shows the attitudes more modern communities held about existing monuments. However, I intend to argue that it may also indicate more about medieval attitudes than previously thought.

The South West is steeped in folklore and myths which manifest themselves in a range of landscapes. There is some evidence to suggest that belief in the supernatural was not considered occult or pagan. In many cases priests called on local people to remove spells and curses and, interestingly, archaeological evidence hints at a degree of syncretism between Christianity and other beliefs. Christian artefacts, such as the Norman font at Luppitt (Figure 65), include a number of folkloric elements, such as centaurs, dragons, and other mythical beings. The Luppitt font was found in the hedge of the churchyard by the vicar towards the end of the nineteenth century (Sage 1992), and the removal of this object may reflect an uneasiness with its conflicting imagery.

As noted above, the stories we can draw upon frequently relate to areas which are seen as isolated or remote by external communities. The special features of Devon's topography – the maze of steep hills and long valleys – may have acted as a barrier with the rest of England and helped to create the external view of a 'secretive, half-tamed countryside' (Whitlock 1977, 13). Similar forces probably acted within the region so that stories are common-place in Devon for remote parts of Dartmoor, Exmoor, the Blackdown Hills, and the North Devon coast; and in Cornwall on Bodmin Moor, the Isles of Scilly, and the western and Penwith coasts. The following section will deal in greater detail with just four of these areas, namely Dartmoor, the south and north Devon coast, and the Blackdown hills in east Devon.

Dartmoor

Dartmoor is perhaps the area of Devon with the highest concentration of supernatural beings recorded in medieval and post-medieval sources. This is surely related to the survival of archaeological remains, many of which are prehistoric and lie upon uncultivated moorland. Many of the standing stones and cists have stories attached to them – not only about their origin (like the Nine Maidens), but also their purpose – from sacred circles to hide-aways for the devil and pixies.

Many stories concerning these stone monuments involve the petrifaction of individuals for wrong doing, mainly for dancing on the Sabbath, and this has been observed as being particularly common in Devon and Cornwall (Grinsell 1937, 254). Frequently these stones are thought to be able to move, independently and at will; 'Greywethers' is thought to turn around at sunrise, and 'Eight Rocks' in Cosdon is supposed to dance when the bells of South Tawton church are rung (Grinsell 1976, 56). Grinsell (1937, 255) puts an early origin to the myths which contained the element of church bells or cocks crowing, as these, he suggests, are associated with pre-clock communities.

The place-name Greywethers itself may help indicate why the Dartmoor stones were thought to move. The name refers to young rams, and is commonly used in reference to sheep, which have long been numerous upon Dartmoor. From a distance, sheep share a likeness to granite boulders; in some stories the monuments were thought to represent petrified sheep turned to stone with their heartbroken shepherd (Skinner 1939, 41).

Several important myths with possible medieval origins refer to the devil. It is possible that these ideas were cultivated during the medieval period by the church in order to 'paganise' sites that were associated with pre-Christian mate-rial culture. The abundance of prehistoric monuments surviving on Dartmoor became the focus for this *diabolisation*, the transformation process in which more and more devilish traits are attributed to non-Christian sites (Roymans 1995, 15). This reorganisation of the landscape is generally considered to be a product of the later medieval period, and is spatially significant as the newly reinterpreted myths are linked tightly to particular, predominantly prehistoric, sites (Roymans 1995, 16, 21). The idea of diabolisation is a key issue when

*Imagined
Landscapes:
Archaeology,
Perception and
Folklore in the
Study of Medieval
Devon*

considering the medieval landscape in this way. Prominent monuments were consciously chosen by religious leaders to promote Christian ideals, serving as visual reminders of the fate of those who err from the true path, rather like the stained glass windows in churches.

It has been suggested that most people living on Dartmoor stopped believing in spirits and pixies centuries ago, and the belief was kept alive through strangers from 'up-country' (St Leger-Gordon 1965, 17). There may be an element of truth in this. Nevertheless, Ellen Mem, who grew up on the edge of Dartmoor in the 1930s, remembers that as a child her parents worried about her riding on Dartmoor as there was a 'presence on the moor that would lead you astray'. Apparently many farmers' wives would not go out at certain times of the year for fear of being pixie-led (being enchanted and not being able to find your way on known routes) (SRA, 1988, tape 12, side 1:4). Further, villagers of Leusdon believed that Canon Hall, their new minister, had control of the 'piskies' as a pair of gates taken by the wind had swung open in front of him. This was a belief which Canon Hall himself accepted as 'it was the environment' in which he lived (SRA, n.d, tape 297, side 1).

South Devon coast
Many similar stories relate to coastal areas, and a whole chapter could be given over to sea-borne myths, such as mermaids, in areas that were intrinsically linked to the fishing industries. Coastal areas also bear similarities to Devon's marginal uplands.

In the coastal parish of Thurlestone during the medieval and post-medieval periods there was a strong belief in pixies. The villagers here believed that the pixies moved the foundations of their new parish church overnight to its present position further inland as the construction was located on pixie dwellings (Coupe 1920, 84–5). This is also said to have occurred at West Gifford Church in Devon, and Grinsell (1937, 254) suggested that this phenomenon commonly indicates the presence of barrows on an intended church site. Along the coastal area of Thurlestone parish, where the church was said to have been originally sited, there are numerous archaeological sites, which may support Grinsell's idea. For example, Bantham Ham is the site of a significant earthwork with associated kitchen middens and hearths and occupation dating to Iron Age, Romano-British and sub-Roman periods. There are also flint scatters dating to the Mesolithic along the coast, and evidence of four bowl barrows (SMR SX64SE/10; /114; /98; /110). A landscape of this type, filled with the remains of hearths, evidence of food preparation, and flints associated with barrows, would allow stories of non-human groups living along the coast to grow.

In the South Hams these beliefs may be due in part to the area's proximity to Dartmoor. There was transhumance between the moors and the fertile fields of the South Hams, with cattle brought down to graze in the winter (SRA, n.d, tape 297, side 1), and it is generally assumed that the late medieval accounts of stock movement to and from the uplands reflect more ancient

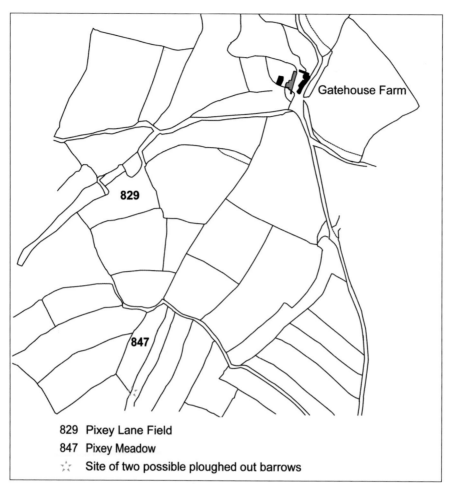

829 Pixey Lane Field
847 Pixey Meadow
☆ Site of two possible ploughed out barrows

customs (Austin 1985, 73). These links could have encouraged the spread of folklore between communities.

Gatehouse Farm, on the east Devon coast, provides a good example of how beliefs were manifested in place-names. The Tithe Survey for Dawlish lists the field-names Pixey Lane Field (TA 829) and Pixey Meadow (TA 847) (Figure 66). The settlement at Gatehouse dates to at least the fourteenth century, and the main elements of the fields which surround it are thought to be contemporary. Significantly there is evidence of two possible ploughed-out barrows in and around Pixey Meadow (SMR SX97NE/14) which may suggest the origin of the names. As discussed, these structures were often thought to be the homes of fairies and spirits, and the naming of fields in this way reinforces how strong the belief in pixies was in rural areas, remaining even though the barrows had long since been destroyed. These pixies were beings to be respected, and it is important to highlight that such myths were intrinsically bound up in the landscapes of medieval and post-medieval farming communities. Placating the pixies meant that animals would remain well, and crops would be threshed overnight.

North Devon coast

It is often suggested that fairies and pixies are simply regional names for the same beings. However, Mrs. Bray (Bray 1853, 11–12) argues that in the South West they are two very different kinds of creatures. Indeed, she notes that the fairies wanted to establish themselves in Devon but the Devonian pixies objected, so war subsequently ensued and finally ended with a defeat for the fairies (Bray 1853, 11). Perhaps coincidently the story states that the battle of the Devon fairies and pixies left Oberon* with an incurable wound to his leg, a fate which is said to have befallen Gereint, a tribal leader in the Arthurian stories associated with Clovelly Dykes on Devon's north coast (Lauder and Williams 1982, 17). Such myths indicate how stories were changed and manipulated to fit the landscapes in which they were set.

The medieval myths of the Arthurian legends associated with Tintagel in Cornwall and Clovelly Dykes on the North Devon coast (thought by some to be Camelot) are confirmation enough of the association with past kings. The Arthurian associations are undoubtedly later, but perhaps build upon earlier

---

* The name of a demon that was said to be conjured frequently by fifteenth- and sixteenth-century wizards and later Shakespeare's King of the fairies in *Midsummer Night's Dream* (Thomas 1971, 727-728; Kittredge 1929, 110, 208, 210).

myths used to explain the presence of large-scale earthworks like those at Clovelly and Tintagel. Hartland Point, to the west of Clovelly Dykes, might provide a link to these earlier myths. *Hercvlis*, or Hercules Promontory, is one of only three named Roman sites within Devon (as listed by the Ordnance Survey Historical Map of Roman Britain). In 1789 the antiquarian Camden stated that the name arose from Hercules coming to Britain to fight giants, and suggests an origin of Phoenician sailors trading with Devon (cited in Pearce Chope 1940, 6). This is an origin which Polwhele (1797, vol. 1, 136) also suggests. Although the Phoenician origin is doubtful, the occurrence of the giants on Hartland Point, which is the site of a cliff-castle, is an interesting one, and reinforces the general trend for such creatures to be associated with these monuments. It is easy to see how myths of Hercules could be updated to Arthur and moved six miles inland – a clear example of Tolkien's 'soup bowl' in action.

The Blackdown Hills

As has been discussed, external perceptions of so-called marginal areas have played a key part in the formation of myths in Devon landscapes. For the Blackdown Hills this is particularly the case. Straddling the border between Devon and Somerset, they are considered an isolated place, and associated with things wild and sinister (Figure 67). As a result, the area is blanketed in myths and superstition. Many of the roads within the Blackdowns had sinister reputations in the past (Tongue 1965, 97); for example, the stretch of the Hemyock road between Broad Street (Clayhidon) and Cityford (Churchinford) was supposed to be haunted (Tongue 1965, 97). This road runs along the former common of Ridgewood, and large tracts of heathland (many of which remain unenclosed) were a focus for many of the myths attached to the Blackdown Hills.

Within the Blackdowns, the hills were supposed to be haunted by Spunkies or Will-o'-the-Wisps – thought throughout Devon to be the souls of unbaptised children – and care was taken to keep out of their path (Webber 1976, 177). The idea of the souls of unbaptised children wandering the earth is common throughout European folklore, and can be traced back into the medieval period. Anglo-Saxon law codes show that non-baptism of children within thirty days of birth was a fineable offence of 30 shillings 'compensation'. However, if the child died and was still unbaptised, then the laws warned that the infant 'shall pay as compensation all he possesses' (Attenborough 1922, 37).

Further references to lost souls wandering the Blackdown Hills are attributed to the Monmouth Rebellion of 1685, as it is known that men from the local communities joined the rebel army and camped on Luppitt Common. Local stories state that many of these men were executed on Black Down Common (Coxhead 1954, 144, 147). Further, as mentioned above, fear of these spirits also allowed human aggressors to roam freely through the area. One example of this was recorded in the *Western Circuit* on 2 October 1690, detailing the 'Bewitching' of Mr. Jacob Seley by the ghosts of 'Monmouth's

*Imagined
Landscapes:
Archaeology,
Perception and
Folklore in the
Study of Medieval
Devon*

Men … hang'd on the sign post' and the stealing of his horse after an evening at a public house *en route* to Taunton (Coxhead 1954, 145–6).

The stories associated with the Blackdowns are mostly based upon broad areas – generally the uplands – rather than specific archaeological sites. However, an exception to this is Simon's Barrow in the parish of Hemyock, on the Devon/Somerset border. This monument has two stories attached to it. In the first, the barrow, which was destroyed in the nineteenth century, was thought to have been the burial site of Simond or Symmond, the overlord of Exmoor and leader of the Blackdowns, who was killed in a battle near to the location of his supposed grave (Webber 1976, 14). The second myth attached to the site refers to it as the Devil's Lapful, believing that the devil wanted to stop the construction of nearby Wellington church, so he carried the building stones off in his apron. However, the strings of the apron broke, leaving the stones in five mounds (Dudridge 1984, 8; Grinsell 1976, 97). The site of the barrow is thought to be protected by the devil, who is also hiding gold there. As such, he returns the boulders to their original location if removed (Palmer 1976, 28). This mix of supernatural and legend to describe the formation of this site perhaps epitomises the nature of these mythical constructs of landscape. The idea of the Devil's Lapful explains the occurrence of a barrow cemetery when all that is visible is the capping stones, and perhaps is an earlier myth than that of Symmond. The barrow was only opened when it was removed by a road contractor in the 1870s. As Palmer (1976, 28) notes, the devil obviously did not do his job of guarding the stones very successfully!

Conclusion

The aim of this chapter is to provide an alternative view of medieval and post-medieval landscapes where places are invested with meaning. What I have tried to demonstrate is how such information can be accessed, and what it indicates about the environments in which these places are found. It is clear that more work needs to be carried out – by combining documentary, archaeological and folkloric evidence – than this short chapter can allow, but from these examples it is hoped that the potential of such a holistic methodology to create a more layered narrative of the past can be seen.

The use of supernatural explanations for earlier monuments allows the construction of mental landscape maps. Social groups create habitable worlds that are full of significance and value, but which provide a sense of security and order and the ability to cope with everyday life (Gillis 1996, 61).

The occurrence of the 'devil' place-names on Dartmoor and Exmoor confirms a re-ordering of the medieval landscape in order to conform to the Christian mindset, removing 'pagan' elements, and emphasising the control of the Church in this period. Further, the custom of setting out food for pixies and fairies was common during the Middle Ages and into the post-medieval period, but was (some say inevitably) condemned by church leaders as propitiation of other deities and fell out of practice (Thomas 1971, 728).

Small-scale rituals provide an insight into this medieval world. The act of apple wassailing, traditionally carried out during the winter months in order to bring fertility and good fortune for the coming year, can be traced back to the 1630s in Devon, but is possibly even older (Hutton 1994, 13–14) and shows syncretism between Christianity and older beliefs. This act, and its longevity, shows that daily routines were filled with the importance of small-scale rituals. Much folklore has been passed through the generations, providing an insight into rural communities which cannot be gained through traditional documents alone. Caunce (1994, 13) argues that on their own, documents can only record a thin slice of life; but combined with archaeological research, folk beliefs and myths, a more comprehensive view can be achieved.

St Leger-Gordon (1965, 11) suggests that 'sticklers for the truth and scientific accuracy should ignore the subject of folklore … for folklore by its very nature is compound of inaccuracies'. This may be so, but through this statement she is missing the point about the nature of the subject. Folktales may be wild and contradictory, but they are a product of the landscapes in which they were (and are) told and retold, and therefore provide an insight into the communities of which they are part. Myths and stories reveal not facts about the past, but show instead its significance (Gazin-Schwartz and Holtolf 1999, 13), and the information acquired from folklore, and also more conventional landscape tools such as place- and field-name studies, can provide a link to the environments of past communities.

The mythical landscape that is being discussed here is superimposed over the visible economic and social landscape that surrounds us. It is not the grand large-scale rituals of prehistory that we see in the medieval and post-medieval rural communities, but small personal beliefs. It is these understandings of the world that are fundamental in discussing how landscapes were formed and operated in the past – 'ideational' landscapes that are places where meaning can be personified through the imagination and emotions (Knapp and Ashmore 1999, 12).

Landscape archaeology relies on a number of interconnecting quantitative and qualitative approaches (Children and Nash 1997, 2). When approaching the medieval landscape, the type of enquiry outlined here can usefully be added to our repertoire of methodologies.

Acknowledgements

The research on which part of this chapter is based was prepared as part of the author's PhD thesis in the Department of Archaeology, University of Exeter. Thanks to Phil Hull and Steve Clark for access to the Sam Richards Archive, and Mark Gillings and Howard Williams for their helpful comments.

Abbreviations

SMR   Sites and Monuments Record, Devon County Council.

SRA   Sam Richards Archive. University of Plymouth, Rolle Campus, Exmouth

TA   Tithe Apportionment Dawlish 1839.

References

Altenberg, K. (2001) 'Marginal life: experiencing a medieval landscape in the Periphery', *Current Swedish Archaeology* **9**, 93–113.

Altenberg, K. (2003) *Experiencing Landscape: A Study of Space and Identity in Three Marginal Areas of Medieval Britain and Scandinavia*, Almqvist and Wiksell, Stockholm.

Attenborough, F.L. ed. and trans. (1922) *The Laws of the Earliest English Kings*, Cambridge University Press, Cambridge.

Austin, D. (1985) 'Dartmoor and the upland village of the South-West of England' in *Medieval Villages: a Review of Current Work*, ed. D. Hooke, Oxford University Committee for Archaeology, Oxford, 71–7.

Baring-Gould, S. (1913) *A Book of Folklore*, Praxis Books, Pulborough.

Bates, B. (2002) *The Real Middle Earth Magic Mystery and the Dark Ages*, Sidgwick and Jackson, London.

Bradley, R. (2000) 'Mental and material landscapes in prehistoric Britain' in *Landscape: the Richest Historical Record*, ed. D. Hooke, Society of Landscape Studies Supplementary Series 1, Birmingham, 1–11.

Bray, A.E. (1853) *A Peep at the Pixies; or Legends of the West*, Grant and Griffith, London.

Briggs, K.M. (1967) *Fairies in Tradition and Literature*, Routledge, London.

Carelli, P. (1997) 'Thunder and lightning, magical miracles on the popular myth of thunderbolts and the presence of stone age artefacts in medieval deposits' in *Visions of the Past: Trends and Traditions in Swedish Medieval Archaeology*, eds H. Andersson, P. Carelli, and L. Ersgård, Lund Studies in Medieval Archaeology 19, Central Board of National Antiquities, Lund, 393–417.

Caunce, S. (1994) *Oral History and the Local Historian*, Longman, London and New York.

Children, G. and Nash, G. (1997) 'Establishing a discourse, the language of landscape' in *Semiotics of Landscape, Archaeology of Mind*, ed. G. Nash, BAR International Series 611, Oxford, 1–4.

Coupe, F.E. (1920) *Thurlestone Church and Parish*, Kingsbridge.

Coxhead, J.R.W. (1954) *Legends of Devon*, The Western Press, Westwood Ho!

Davidson, T. (1956) 'Elf-shot cattle', *Antiquity* xxx, 149–55.

Dudridge, M. (1984) *Superstition and Folklore of the West Country Dorset, Devon and Somerset*, Nigel J. Clarke Publications, Lyme Regis.

Field, J. (1993) *A History of English Field-Names*, Longman, London.

Fleming, A. (2001) 'Dangerous islands: fate, faith and cosmology', *Landscapes* **2(1)**, 4–21.

Franklin, L. (2001) *Study of the physical and mythical landscapes of an early Christian souterrain in County Antrim Northern Ireland*, unpublished MA dissertation, University of Wales, Lampeter.

Gallagher, W. (1993) *The Power of Place. How our Surroundings Shape our Thoughts, Emotions, and Actions*, HarperCollins Publishers, New York.

Gazin-Schwartz, A. and Holtolf, C. (1999) '"As long as I've known it … " on folklore and archaeology' in *Archaeology and Folklore*, eds A. Gazin-Schwartz and C. Holtolf, Routledge, London, 1–25.

Gillings, M. and Pollard, J. (1999) 'Non-portable stone artefacts and contexts of meaning, the tale of Grey Wether (www.museums.ncl.ac.uk/Avebury/stone4.htm)', *World Archaeology* **31(2)**, 179–93.

Gillings, M., Pollard, J. and Wheatley, D. (2000) 'The Beckhampton avenue and a 'new' Neolithic enclosure near Avebury, an interim report on the 1999 excavations', *Wiltshire Archaeological and Natural History Magazine* **93**, 1–8.

Gillings, M. and Pollard, J. (2004) *Avebury*, Duckworth, London.

Gillis, J. R. (1996) *A World of their own Making. Myth, Ritual, and the Quest for Family Values*, Harvard University Press, Cambridge MA.

Gosden, C. (1999) *Anthropology and Archaeology. A Changing Relationship*, Routledge, London.

Gray, T. (1996) *Saint Patrick's People. A New Look at the Irish*, Warner Books, London.

Green, A. (2000) 'Coffee and bun, Sergeant Bonnington and the tornado, myth and place in Frankton Junction', *Oral History* **28**(2), 26–34.

Grinsell, L. V. (1937) 'Some aspects of the folklore of prehistoric monuments', *Folklore* **48**, 245–59.

Grinsell, L. V. (1976) *Folklore of Prehistoric Sites in Britain*, David and Charles, Newton Abbot.

Harvey, D. C. (2000) 'Landscape organisation, identity and change: territoriality and hagiography in medieval west Cornwall', *Landscape Research* **25**(2), 201–12.

Hurley, J. (1973) *Legends of Exmoor*, The Exmoor Press, Dulverton.

Hutton, R. (1994) *The Rise and Fall of Merry England. The Ritual Year 1400–1700*, Oxford University Press, Oxford.

Kittredge, L. K. (1929) *Witchcraft in Old and New England*, London.

Knapp, A. B. and Ashmore, W. (1999) 'Archaeological landscapes, constructed, conceptualized, ideational' in *Archaeologies of Landscape Contemporary Perspectives*, eds W. Ashmore and A. B. Knapp, Blackwell, Oxford, 1–30.

Krappe, A. H. (1930) *The Science of Folklore*, Methuen, London.

Lauder, R. A. and Williams, W. (1982) *Strange Stories from Devon*, Bossiney Books, St Teath.

Levi-Strauss, C. (1966) *The Savage Mind*, University of Chicago Press, Chicago.

Palmer, K. (1976) *The Folklore of Somerset*, BT Batsford, London.

Pearce Chope, R. (1940) *The Book of Hartland*, The Devonshire Press, Torquay.

Phythian-Adams, C. (1975) *Local History and Folklore, A New Framework*, Bedford Square Press, London.

Polwhele, R. (1797) *The History of Devonshire in Three Volumes, Volumes 1*, Trewman & Son, Exeter.

Propp, V. (1984) *Theory and History of Folklore* (trans. A. Y. Martin and R. P. Martin), Theory and History of Literature, vol. 5, Manchester University Press, Manchester.

Reynolds, A. (2002) 'Burials, boundaries and charters in Anglo-Saxon England: a reassessment' in *Burial in Early Medieval England and Wales,* eds S. Lucy and A. Reynolds, Society for Medieval Archaeology, London, 171–94.

Rippon, S. (1997) *The Severn Estuary Landscape Evolution and Wetland Reclamation*, Leicester University Press, London.

Roymans, N. (1995) 'The cultural biography of urnfields and the long-term history of a mythical landscape', *Archaeological Dialogues* **2**(1), 2–24.

Sage, J. (1992) *St Mary's Church Luppitt, Devon*, unpublished pamphlet.

Semple, S. (1998) 'A fear of the past: the place of the prehistoric burial mound in the ideology of middle and later Anglo-Saxon England', *World Archaeology* (**30**)1, 109–26.

Skinner, A. G. (1939) *Tales of the Tors*, The Epworth Press, London.

St Leger-Gordon, R. (1965) *The Witchcraft and Folklore of Dartmoor*, Peninsula Press, Newton Abbot.

Taçon, P. S. C. (1994) 'Socialising landscapes, the long-term implications of signs, symbols and marks on the land', in 'Social Landscapes', eds L. Head, C. Gosden and J. P. White, *Archaeology in Oceania* **29**.3, 117–29.

Thomas, K. (1971) *Religion and the Decline of Magic*, Penguin Books, London.

Thomson, E. P. (1991) *Customs in Common*, Merlin Press, London.

*Imagined
Landscapes:
Archaeology,
Perception and
Folklore in the
Study of Medieval
Devon*

Tolkien, J. R. R. (1936/1983) 'Beowulf: The monster and the critics' in *The Monsters and the Critics and other Essays*, ed. C. Tolkien, Allen and Unwin, London, 5–48.

Tolkien, J. R. R. (1947/1983) 'On Fairy-Stories' in *The Monsters and the Critics and other Essays*, ed. C. Tolkien, Allen and Unwin, London, 109–16.

Tolkien, J. R. R. (1954) *Lord of the Rings: the Fellowship of the Ring*, Harper Collins, London.

Tongue, R. L. (1965) *Somerset Folklore*, The Folklore Society, London.

Tonkin, E. (1992) *Narrating our Pasts. The Social Constructions of Oral History*, Cambridge University Press, Cambridge.

Ucko, P. J. (1994) 'Foreword', in *Sacred Sites, Sacred Places*, eds D. L. Carmichael, J. Hubert, B. Reeves, and A. Schanche, Routledge, London, xiii–xxiii.

Webber, R. (1976) *The Devon and Somerset Blackdowns*, Robert Hale and Company, London.

Whitlock, R. (1977) *The Folklore of Devon*, BT Batsford, London.

Yeats, W. B. (1888) *Fairy and Folk Tales of the Irish Peasantry*, Walter Scott, London.

Young, D. and Harris, S. (2003) 'Demonizing the night in medieval Europe: a temporal monstrosity?' in *The Monstrous Middle Ages*, eds B. Bildhauer and R. Mills, University of Wales Press, Cardiff, 134–54.

Index

....

Entries in **bold** refer to pages with figures

Contributors

Oliver Creighton is Senior Lecturer in Archaeology at the Department of Archaeology, University of Exeter.

Harold Fox is Professor of Social and Landscape History at the Centre for English Local History, University of Leicester.

Lucy Franklin has recently concluded her PhD thesis on the medieval landscape of Devon at the Department of Archaeology, University of Exeter.

J. P. Freeman is an independent archaeologist working in south-west England.

Ralph Fyfe is Lecturer in Geographical Information Systems at the School of Geography, University of Plymouth.

Peter Herring is Principal Archaeologist at the Historic Environment Service, Cornwall County Council.

Phil Newman is an Investigator with the English Heritage Archaeological Survey and Investigation Team based at Exeter.

Sam Turner is Lecturer in Archaeology at the School of Historical Studies, Newcastle University.

Also available from Windgather Press ...

Landscapes of Britain

Britain has an extraordinarily rich mix of historic landscapes. This major series explores this diversity, through accessible and attractive books that draw on the latest archaeological and historical research. Places in Britain have a great depth of historical connections. These books show how much there is to be discovered.

To purchase these titles go to **www.windgather.co.uk**.

Also available from
Windgather Press

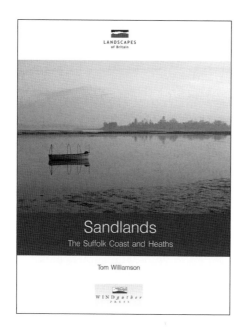

Sandlands
The Suffolk Coast and Heaths
Tom Williamson

'... captures in words and images 'the peculiar character of the area',
concentrating on components such as heaths, marshes, forests, hedges,
fields, settlements and coast. Williamson stresses the fragile and
changing nature of the landscape and the impact of humans.' *Antiquity*

'Williamson's choice of subjects to illustrate and elucidate is masterly ...
Here in *Sandlands*, history is making decisive contributions to the
understanding and conservation of one of our most vulnerable and
sensitive areas, varied and sublimely beautiful.' *The Local Historian*

Published with the support of Suffolk County Council.

180 pp; illus: 30 col., 40 b/w;
ISBN 10 1-905119-02-X; ISBN 13 978-1-905119-02-8;
Paperback; 2005.

Also available from
Windgather Press

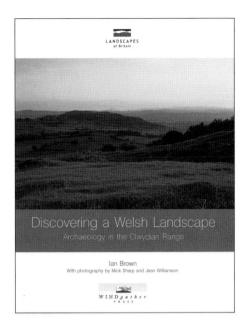

Discovering a Welsh Landscape
Archaeology in the Clwydian Range
Ian Brown
with photography by Mick Sharp and Jean Williamson

'An attractive work, well-produced and superbly illustrated.'
Heritage in Wales

'A richly illustrated book that tells the history of this landscape: a history of Wales in microcosm. The Clwydian Range has a very rich archaeology; it is a crossroads where outside influences have always been profound.'
Cheshire Life

Published with the support of Denbighshire County Council.

160 pp; illus: 32 col., 75 b/w;
ISBN 10 0-9545575-7-3; ISBN 13 978-0-9545575-7-7;
Paperback; 2004.

The Humber Wetlands

The Archaeology of a Dynamic Landscape
Robert Van de Noort

'… a formidable contribution to the excellent Windgather Press series …
Enjoy the dark, brooding and atmospheric cover photograph of the
Derwent in flood, then turn to page 1 to begin a thoroughly compelling
and enlightening journey.' *Landscape History*

The lowlands of the Humber Basin form one of Britain's most extensive
wetland areas. This book reveals for the first time the buried ancient landscapes which lie under the peat. It is the result of a ten-year English Heritage
funded project, which aimed to identify and explore this archaeology before it
was damaged by peat extraction, development and drainage.

Robert Van de Noort explores people's experience of the Humber Wetlands
over the last 10,000 years. He reveals how prehistoric peoples settled the
wetlands at places such as Holderness, and how they used natural resources, for
spiritual as well as economic reasons. The discovery of unparalleled prehistoric
boats in the area has transformed our understanding of prehistoric maritime
history. Roman, Vikings, and climate change have also left their mark on
today's landscape.

Published in association with English Heritage.

208 pp; illus: 6 col., 75 b/w;
ISBN 10 0-954-5575-4-9; ISBN 13 978-0-9545575-4-6;
Paperback; 2004.

Also available from
Windgather Press

The Peak District
Landscapes though Time
John Barnatt and Ken Smith

> 'Authoritative and well-illustrated … can confidently be read by those
> wishing to be introduced to the area.' *British Archaeology*

The Peak District – Britain's first National Park – has some of Britain's richest archaeological landscapes. This new edition of the indispensable introduction and guide to the area's landscape draws on the extensive archaeological research that has taken place in the Peak since 1997. With new maps and interpretations, it tells the story of a famous landscape's evolution.

Prehistoric barrows, stone circles, Romano-British settlements, medieval fields, ancient drove-ways, nineteenth-century lead mines: all are prominent in this extraordinary area. The authors in particular explore the Peak's prehistoric sacred landscapes, such as the great henge at Arbor Low; the dramatic impact of farmers on the land in medieval and post-medieval times; and the industrial archaeology. The book also features a gazetteer of sites and a comprehensive bibliography.

160 pp; illus: 14 col., 74 b/w;
ISBN 10 0-9545575-5-7; ISBN 13 978-0-9545575-5-3;
Paperback; 2004.

A Frontier Landscape
The North West in the Middle Ages
N. J. Higham

'Higham modestly describes his book as a brief introduction to the landscape history of the North West. It is more than that. He succinctly merges his own extensive researches with those of other archaeologists, geographers, local and landscape historians, and place-name specialists ... It should become essential reading for anyone interested in this diverse, evocative and tantalizing region.' *The Local Historian*

'An important book, which makes a major contribution to our understanding of a region whose landscapes have been sadly neglected in most national surveys of the subject.' *Cheshire History*

260 pp; illus: 12 col., 75 b/w;
ISBN 10 0-9545575-6-5; ISBN 13 978-0-9545575-6-0;
Paperback; 2004.